The Logic of Moral Discourse

Paul Edwards

The Logic

of

Moral Discourse

With an Introduction by Sidney Hook

THE FREE PRESS, *New York*

COLLIER-MACMILLAN LIMITED, *London*

To Ernest Nagel

"The search after the unit is the delusion."

(A. B. Johnson)

"All argument is not deduction, and giving reasons in support of a judgment or statement is not necessarily, or even generally, giving logically conclusive reasons."

(Stuart Hampshire)

Contents

Preface

The Logic of Moral Discourse was originally written during the academic year of 1950/51. Doubts about the soundness of my theory made me refrain from any attempts at publication at that time. After an interval of four years, however, my views are the same and I have been urged by several persons whose judgment I highly respect to publish my book with some small changes and additions. For the reader's convenience I have brought the bibliography up to date, but in the body of the work there is no reference to literature which has appeared after 1950.

In the last two chapters I am taking to task some of the critics of the so-called emotive theory who, I am sure, would be equally opposed to my views. I regret to note the recent death of Dr. C. E. M. Joad at whom some of my most sustained attacks are directed. I should like to make it clear that my hostility to Dr. Joad is of a purely philosophical character and that I never had any hard personal feelings towards him. This comment is superfluous as far as professional philosophers are concerned. But the emotive theory has been widely discussed in non-professional circles and I wish to make sure that my attitude will not be misunderstood anywhere.

I am indebted to my friend, Mr. Albert Hofstadter, of Columbia University, for countless major and minor ideas, as well as for constant encouragement while I was writing this book. I also wish to thank Mr. Charles Frankel, of Columbia University, with whom I had many stimulating conversations. I believe that these conversations led to several significant improvements in my book.

I have done my best to present my discussions not only lucidly, but also with some liveliness. This will explain the somewhat unusual nature of many of my illustrations.

PAUL EDWARDS

New York City, March 1955

Introduction

IT IS NOT OFTEN that a book in philosophy is a contribution of the first importance to fundamental theoretical questions, is argued with skill, incisiveness and erudition, has wider bearings of concern to all reflective persons and not merely professional philosophers, and is written with a delightful and piquant vivacity. Mr. Paul Edwards' *The Logic of Moral Discourse* is such a book.

I wish briefly to say something about all four of these points.

The Logic of Moral Discourse is an important contribution to ethical theory because it is the soundest and most systematic fusion, in the study of metaethics, of the emotive and objective naturalistic points of view. Mr. Edwards restates the central contentions of the emotive theory persuasively and at the same time shows that it does not imply the paradoxical conclusion that moral judgments are never true or false. His analysis establishes that moral judgments do indeed express attitudes, chiefly those of approval and disapproval, but they are at the same time assertions about the *objects* of these attitudes. Moral judgments are thus seen to possess objective meaning and Mr. Edwards develops in considerable detail the ways in which this objective meaning tends to vary from situation to situation. In consequence, such a theory enables one to admit that moral expressions are indefinable without having to concede either that they are descriptively meaningless or that they designate some mysterious "non-natural" qualities.

Mr. Edwards takes as his point of departure distinctions that are commonly recognized whenever human beings seriously discuss what actions should be done or left undone insofar as they affect others. Then by introducing a set of his own distinctions, useful in describing or talking about ethical judgments, he shows how many of the perplexities, bewilderments and violent paradoxes which

[13]

have always dogged ethical theories may be avoided. The result is more than a triumphant vindication of common sense attitudes toward the descriptive meaningfulness of ethical assertions. It is an illuminating clarification of the viewpoint of common sense, and proof that common sense is rather more sophisticated than philosophers from Plato to G. E. Moore had assumed. Because of the importance of these distinctions, it is strongly recommended that the chapters be read in the order in which they are published.

Another way of putting the main point is that Mr. Edwards has shown that knowledge makes a relevant difference to the moral judgments we utter and especially to those we believe true or false, and that a scientific approach to the resolution of moral conflict is therefore intelligible and likely to be fruitful. Although arrived at independently and from a different methodological approach, Mr. Edwards' position is close to that taken by John Dewey. The chief difference between them, so far as I can see, is that Mr. Edwards exempts what he calls "fundamental moral judgments" from his claim that all moral judgments have a descriptive meaning as well as an emotive one, and therefore in principle can be confirmed or disconfirmed. If I understand Dewey, he would be prepared to show that whenever such moral views are introduced in relation to a concrete problem, they have "referents" which may or may not sustain their claim to validity. At any rate, I would be so prepared to show. Thus, when I say, to use some illustrations suggested by Mr. Edwards' own discussion, "We should go down fighting rather than live under the regime of a Hitler or Stalin," or "An innocent man should never be punished," "It is better to be kind than cruel," I am, to be sure, expressing something about my own attitude or choice, but I am also prepared in the concrete situation in which I utter these judgments to give reasons and grounds which, if shown invalid or false, would seem to me to affect the truth of my judgments. If such sentences are considered expressions of nonfundamental moral judgments, it would seem that "fundamental moral judgments" are not only very rare but hardly justify characterization of them as "moral."*

---

* For a further discussion of this point see my "The Emotive and Desirable" in *John Dewey: Philosopher of Science and Freedom.*

The second meritorious feature of Mr. Edward's work is its analytic keenness. This is not achieved by ignoring other views or difficulties in his own position. His is the first comprehensive reply to all of the best-known objectons to the naturalistic and/or emotive theory which have been urged by critics. And he considers them in their strongest form, scrupulously recognizing the empirical facts about ethical language and moral behavior to which they call attention. Particularly noteworthy in this connection is his discussion of the alleged "naturalistic fallacy," a hurdle which must be cleared by everyone who wishes to undertake serious analysis of ethical issues without departing from the framework of naturalistic empiricism; and his demonstration that there is a perfectly clear sense in which "ought"-judgments may follow from statements of fact, so that the latter become as relevant to the truth or falsity of the former as they do to hypotheses in other fields. This outflanks the absolute separation which Kant makes between categorical and hypothetical imperatives.

This is a book not merely for philosophers but everyone concerned about understanding the nature of moral disagreement. And what feature of our modern world is more conspicuous than the facts of moral disagreement? They are not the sole or even always the most important cause of violent conflict between nations and classes and individuals but they are almost always a contributory factor.

Most men philosophize more naturally about the meaning of "good" and "bad" than about other themes which engross professional philosophers. Now from the *theory* that moral disputes or conflicts cannot in principle be capable of mutually satisfactory resolution by investigations of the grounds and reasons on which our moral judgments of approval are based, together with an envisagement of the probable consequences of the actions proposed to give effect to our judgment, it does not follow *as a matter of fact* that we must settle conflicts by counting noses or bashing in heads. It is possible to apply one sense of the maxim *de gustibus non disputandum est* to all things including moral approvals and, if our taste does not run to violence or propaganda, live peacefully with each other, tolerating each other's quaint conceits and appetites. Nor, on the other hand, if a belief like Mr. Edwards' is true and therefore moral disputes and conflicts *are* capable of resolution by discovering the truths which bear on conflicting claims, does it necessarily follow that human beings actually will resolve the conflict of claims by scientific inquiry. For men may not love the truth or seek to find it. If men, however, can be educated to seek the truth, to become more reasonable—and in some fields they already manifest such a disposition—then the belief that it is possible to resolve moral disagreement by discovery of the relevant facts will undoubtedly contribute to strengthening the habits of inquiry and investigation as methods of fixing moral belief and resolving moral disputes. Whether the theory of moral intuitionism is accepted or rejected, I do not believe it would make the slightest difference to human behavior, for nothing is indicated as to any procedure which must be followed in setting about to resolve disagreements by the discovery of the relevant truths—no matter what our will to do so. On the type of emotive, naturalistic theory developed by Mr. Edwards, the indications as to how one should proceed are quite plain—*if* we have the will to do so. If we believe that the truth *can* be found, we may look for it. If we believe there is no truth to be found, we certainly won't look for it.

Finally, I wish to comment on Mr. Edwards' refreshing style, apt illustrations, and autobiographical references. These are the only elements he has in common with some Existentialist writers who use them in a spirit utterly different from Mr. Edwards' passion for clarity. They should not be left to those who make a cult of obscurity. Here and there an illustration or a joke may appear odd or out of place but nothing in Mr. Edwards' argument depends upon it. That in the main they lighten and brighten his pages the reader will discover for himself. So much of philosophical writing in the past has made for dreary reading that we ought to welcome the new mode established by Mr. Edwards. The reader will find that without being less serious in substance than duller written books, this work in philosophy is also fun.

SIDNEY HOOK

CONTENTS

Chapter I

Preliminary
Clarifications

1. The Subject-Matter
of this Study

THE LANGUAGE by whose means we communicate to each other
and state for ourselves our moral convictions and doubts is very
manifold. However, there are certain words which occur in such
contexts with great frequency—especially the words "good" and
"evil," "desirable" and "undesirable," "right" and "wrong," "duty,"
"ought," and "obligation." According to a widespread practice
among philosophers these terms are referred to as "ethical" or
"moral" predicates.

In the present study I hope to be able to throw some light on
the functions which these ethical predicates fulfill in human discourse. There are three interconnected questions with which I
shall be concerned:

(1) What do people mean, if they mean anything, when they
apply an ethical predicate to something—when they say such things
as that mercy-killing is always wrong, that lying for one's country
is right, or that Shelley was a good man whereas Byron was an evil
person?

(2) When people apply opposing ethical predicates to the same

thing, what kind of disagreement is there between them and is it in principle possible to show that one side is in the right while the other is in the wrong?

(3) Can a statement which contains an ethical predicate ever be validly inferred from a statement or a set of statements which do not contain any such predicates?

The ethical predicates, as has often been noted, occur not only in sentences by whose means we express our moral views. Thus we may say of a man that he is a good tailor but a bad man and only the second of these sentences would express a moral belief. Or again a doctor might say to a patient, "You ought to use more powerful glasses," and to his son, on catching him in the act of stealing, he might say, "You ought to be ashamed of yourself— my son of all people!" Here, too, only the second sentence expresses a moral view. When the ethical predicates occur in sentences which express moral views, many philosophers say that they are used in a "characteristically ethical sense." I do not wish to deny that there is such a "characteristically ethical sense." But I believe that our inquiry will be more fruitful and proceed more smoothly if, in its earlier stages at any rate, we pay no attention to this characteristically ethical sense. Accordingly, I propose to mean for the time being by the term "moral judgment" any sentence in which an ethical predicate is used,[1] whether it is employed in a characteristically ethical sense or not. By "moral disagreement" I shall mean any situation in which two or more people make moral judgments, in the sense just defined, about the same subject which are or imply formal contradictories. When somebody infers a moral judgment from other statements, whether these other statements are themselves moral judgments or not, I shall say that he has engaged or put forward a "moral argument."

Using this terminology, I can rephrase the three questions which form the basic subject matter of my inquiry as follows:

(1) What is the meaning, more broadly: what is the function of moral judgments?

(2) What kind of disagreement is moral disagreement?

---

1. Cf. Section 8 of this chapter for a discussion of the difference between using and mentioning a word.

(3) Are moral arguments whose premises do not include any moral judgment ever valid?

2. Three Senses of "Meaning"

BEFORE GOING ANY FURTHER it is imperative to distinguish between three of the senses in which sentences or phrases are said to have meaning. Let us begin by considering the following simple case: my alarm clock is out of order and I ask a friend to call me at 8 o'clock the next morning, so as to make sure that I shall not be late for school. In the course of the conversation he asks me what time my first class begins to which I answer, "it starts at 10 o'clock." Let us refer to this utterance, in the circumstances described, as "s." Now, it is easy, and as we shall soon see, very important to distinguish three things here:

(i) The facts whose existence I assert in uttering s—the facts whose existence would make s true and whose non-existence would render it false,

(ii) what I intend to achieve by uttering s, and

(iii) anything concerning myself which, in virtue of what is generally known about the psychology of human beings, could be inferred from my utterance of s—in this case *my belief* that the first class the next day would start at 10 o'clock.

It will be helpful to generalize this distinction and to introduce three technical terms at this stage: the fact whose existence would make a sentence true and whose non-existence would make it false we shall call "the referent" of the sentence; to what the user of a sentence intends to achieve by means of it we shall refer as "the Objective" of the sentence (using a capital "O" to distinguish this sense of the word from others which we shall meet later); and anything which it is possible to infer concerning the author of the sentence on the basis of his utterance we shall call, following Meinong and Ross,[2] "what the sentence expresses."

Under "utterance" we are including here the tone of voice in which a sentence is spoken and any gestures or grimaces which may accompany it. We mean the *concrete* utterance as it is deliv-

---

2. Cf. Ross, *The Foundations of Ethics*, pp. 254-5.

ered.[3] In the case of written sentences we would include such signs as quotation or exclamation marks, as e.g., in the sentence, "that great 'authority' in the field of genetics, Joseph Stalin." It is worth observing that not only what a sentence expresses but equally its referent may be determined by the manner in which it is uttered as well as by the words it contains. Thus if one man says, "the *Saturday Review* is a truly weighty organ of opinion" in tones of awe and another pronounces the same words with a special sneer as he comes to the word "weighty," the sentence in the former context both expresses a different attitude from what it does in the other and it also has a different referent: the first man asserts that the *Saturday Review* is influential while the second man asserts that it is not. An interesting example showing how the Objective may vary with the emphasis is found in the *Logics* of Whately, De Morgan and Jevons: the sentence, "thou shalt not bear false witness against thy neighbour" obviously demands something very different according to where the emphasis is placed.

Something further must here be said about our use of "express" in the phrase, "what an utterance expresses." This word, more especially as referring to actions and gestures, is used in two somewhat different senses which require to be distinguished. When, for instance, we see one man, A, shaking his fist at another man, B, we say that A's shaking of his fist is an expression of his anger. And by this we may either mean (1) that in view of what is known concerning the close correlation between a man's shaking his fist and a feeling of anger in his mind, it is very probable, other things being equal, that A is feeling angry at B, or (2) that A's shaking his fist at B is part of a complex whole of which A's introspectible feeling of anger is another part. If "expressing his anger" is used in the first sense, the sentence, "A's shaking his fist at B expresses his anger at B, but really he feels no anger" is not a contradiction. On the other hand, if "expresses his anger" is used in the second sense, that sentence is a contradiction. In this study we shall use "express" in the first sense exclusively. In this sense my statement, in the circumstances described above, "my first class tomorrow

---

3. Cf. J. E. Ledden, "On the Logical Status of Value," *Philosophical Review*, 1950, p. 357.

starts at ten" would express my belief that my first class starts at ten even if I had no such belief.

"Express," as used in this sense, is exactly synonymous with "imply" as this term is used by G. E. Moore in the famous passage in which he mentions his semi-conversion to the emotive theory of moral judgments. He there speaks of the sense of "imply" in which,

when a man asserts anything which might be true or false, he *implies* that he himself at the time of speaking, believes or knows the thing in question—a sense in which he *implies* this, even if he is lying. If, for instance, I assert, on a particular day, that I went to the pictures the preceding Tuesday, I imply by asserting this, that, at the time of speaking, I believe or know that I did, though I do not *say* that I believe or know it. But in this case, it is quite clear that this, which I *imply*, is no part of what I *assert;* since, if it were, then in order to discover whether I did go to the pictures that Tuesday, a man would need to discover whether, when I said I did, I believed or knew that I did, which is clearly not the case. And it is also clear that from what I assert, namely that I went to the pictures that Tuesday, it does not *follow* that I believe or know that I did, when I say so: for it might have been the case that I did go, and yet that I did not, when I spoke, either believe or know that I did.[4]

There seems to me to be nothing mysterious about this sense of "imply." . . . (It is seen not to be mysterious as soon as one remembers) the fact, which we all learn by experience, that in the immense majority of cases a man who makes such an assertion as this does believe or know what he asserts: lying, though common enough, is vastly exceptional. And this is why to say such a thing as "I went to the pictures last Tuesday, but I don't believe that I did" is a perfectly absurd thing to say, although what is asserted is something which is perfectly possible logically.[5]

Now, very commonly when we say about a sentence that it has a certain meaning we are talking about its referent. Thus, to take a very trivial example, when we say that "Jones is a father" does not mean the same as "Jones is an old man," we mean that the sentences have different referents. On the other hand when we say

---

4. "A Reply to My Critics," in *The Philosophy of G. E. Moore* (ed. Schilpp) p. 541.

5. *Ibid.,* pp. 542-3. Cf. also *Ethics*, p. 78. There Moore makes a distinction between "expressing" and "implying" a state of mind, using "express" in what I earlier called the second sense and "imply" in the same sense as in the passages cited in the text.

that the imperative, "Drive me to East 42nd Street!" has a different meaning from "Drive me to West 56th Street!", we are referring to the different Objectives of the two sentences. Again, in most cases one encounters, "alas!" means something different from "how wonderful!" and at least part of what we mean by saying that these expressions have a different meaning is that they *express* different states of mind.

For a proper understanding of the logic of moral discourse it is vital to realize that utterances may mean the same in one of the senses of "meaning," just distinguished, without meaning the same in one or both of the other two senses. To take a few examples: I am the host at a party and it is already very late. I am anxious that my guests should leave, but they show no signs of intending to do so soon. So I announce, "I have a nine o'clock class tomorrow." Here the Objective of my utterance is the breaking up of the party and I express not only my belief that I have a nine o'clock class the next morning but also my desire that my guests leave very soon. Supposing, however, I had said, "I have a nine o'clock class tomorrow" in reply to a question by somebody who is offering to drive me to school at a party which, by previous arrangement, is to last till eight in the morning. In that case my utterance, though having the same referent, would have a totally different Objective, namely, supplying of the necessary information to the person who asked the question. In this case, too, my utterance would *not* express a desire that my guests should leave very soon. To take another example: a person whom I have no desire to outrage or annoy asks me, "Do you care for any contemporary American composers?" I truthfully answer, "I admire Richard Rodgers and Sigmund Romberg." Here the sole Objective of my answer is to give the questioner the information about my taste which he is seeking. If, however, this question had been put to me by X.X., an impossible snob whose mere presence gives me a pain, I would have given the same answer, even if it were not true; and in that case my Objective would have been to annoy my questioner. To take one final case: I might utter the verbally identical curse "Hell!" simply for the purpose of relieving my soul, to intimidate somebody in my surroundings, or to inform a person of my displeasure.

3. Proving a Theory and Getting It Accepted

THERE ARE MANY foolish people in the world who, misinterpreting the data of cultural anthropology, make pronouncements such as, "There is no such thing as objective truth—even 'two plus two equals four' is not necessarily true in other cultures." Partly under the influence of such views, but also from other causes, more and more people are confounding the *truth* of a theory with its *acceptance* and the disproof of a theory with its rejection.

Supposing there is a lunatic who maintains that Harry Truman is a German spy, that his real name is "Wahrhaftig," and that he was born in Deckendorf near Munich, in Bavaria, and not in Independence, Missouri. By careful investigation of all the birth certificates in Deckendorf and Independence, by interviewing Harry Truman's mother and the doctor delivering her children, by interviewing his friends and his enemies, by consulting newspaper files of several decades we could, if we felt so inclined, produce enormous evidence for the view that Truman is not a German spy who was born in Deckendorf; but that he is an American, who comes from Independence, Missouri. In other words, we could *prove* or render very highly probable the view that Truman was born in America and we could *disprove* the view that he was born in Deckendorf.

Somebody might retort to this: "You can't prove it *to* the lunatic. He will say that all your documents are forged, that all your witnesses are liars, and that you yourself are another German spy, from Zwickau near Reichenbach in Saxonia, engaged with Wahrhaftig in a plot to overthrow the American system of government." The reply to this is that if you really prove a statement, you do not prove it for A and for B but not for C. You prove it, period; or you do not. If a statement is true then it is true, period; it is not true for A and false for B. If it is really raining now then it is true that it is raining, whatever a recluse shut up in his lonely apartment may think.

"But you can't prove it to the lunatic" is really just a somewhat misleading way of saying, "the lunatic *will not accept* your state-

ment even after you have presented your evidence." You succeed
in proving a statement or in at least rendering it probable if you
produce certain evidence, whether you succeeded in convincing
others or not. And conversely, convincing others in itself in no
way proves that what you say is true. If a man simply makes an
assertion without producing any evidence for it, then it is perfectly proper to say to him, "That's just your opinion." But if he
presents careful and extensive evidence for his claim then it is
absurd to say, "That's just your opinion."

Actually, of course, there are plenty of instances of theories
which have been proven although not everybody accepts them,
e.g., that the earth is not flat but approximately round, that the
Nazis maltreated countless people, especially Jews, in their extermination camps, or that Trotzky was not guilty of the acts with
which he was charged by Stalin and his agents in the trials of
the 1930's. Conversely, everybody knows of plenty of instances
of statements which are widely or commonly accepted although
no evidence has been produced on their behalf. Thus, if at a party
a man says about some well-known figure, preferably a musician
or a playwright, "You know, So-and-So is a homosexual," everybody believes it instantly, whether any evidence is given or not.
The people who hear this not only believe it without demanding
evidence; if they happen to see Such-and-Such in So-and-So's
company one day, they will say with complete confidence at the
next party that Such-and-Such is a homosexual.

In other words, if a theory has been proven this does not imply
that it is generally or even widely accepted; and conversely, if a
theory is widely or even generally accepted, this does not imply
that it has been proven.

It might be thought that I have been laboring an all too obvious
point. But the truth is that in their treatment of many topics
philosophers have ignored this seemingly so obvious distinction.
This, as we shall see in Chapter VIII, is especially true of ethics.
But it is also true in other cases. Thus it is widely held that
solipsism, however incredible, cannot be "logically refuted." In
support of this it is said that no matter what object you show
to a solipsist, no matter how many other human beings you pre-

sent to him, he will always reply, "Further contents of my mind." However, this only shows that the solipsist *will not accept* a "common sense refutation" like the presentation of other human beings. It in no way shows that such a presentation does not *disprove* solipsism. Unless the solipsist is using language in a strange way, the presentation of other human beings shows beyond a shadow of a doubt that solipsism is false, that the solipsist is not the only object in the universe. Solipsism is so incredible for precisely this reason: that it is so plainly false and so easy to *disprove*.

If we adopted the linguistic recommendation implicit in statements like "But you would not have *proved it* to the lunatic" and used the word "prove" only where we succeeded in convincing the other party, we would require a new term to do the work which "prove" does now. We would need some word to distinguish those cases of "failure to prove" where we did not convince the other side and actually had insufficient evidence from those cases where we failed to convince our opponents although we had perfectly adequate evidence.

It would be equally pointless to adopt the recommendation implicit in other statements occasionally made by "cultural relativists"; e.g., "a tiger who lives in the jungle and whom you never perceived does not really *exist for you*." It is absurd to say that things exist for A and B but not for C and D. They *exist* or they do not, though A and B and not C and D may be the organisms who perceive the things in question. If we started applying "exist" to physical objects only when they are perceived, then we would need another name to help us distinguish between "non-existing things" which would be perceived if we fulfilled certain conditions—e.g., brains in our heads, animals in the jungle, the books in my briefcase when it is closed—from "non-existing things" which would *not* be perceived even if we fulfilled these conditions—e.g., apples in our heads, griffins in the jungle, gold in the average person's briefcase.

If we are clear about the difference between proving a theory and getting it accepted, it will be easy for us to distinguish between two very different senses in which such phrases as "settling a dispute" or "resolving an issue" are commonly used. In one sense—

to be called sense (1) from here on—a dispute is settled if one party has been shown to be in the right, if he has *proven* his case and the other party has been shown to be wrong. In another sense—to be called sense (2) from here on—a dispute is settled simply if both parties *have come to hold the same view*, whether that view has been proven or not.[6]

From our previous observations in this section it should be plain that the settlement of a dispute in sense (1) does not imply that it is settled in sense (2). Equally the fact that a dispute has been settled in sense (2) does not imply that it is settled in sense (1). It equally follows that considerations which are relevant to the settlement in sense (1) are not necessarily relevant to its settlement in sense (2) and vice versa. It will become apparent in later chapters that this is a very important point.

4. Types of Disagreement

ANOTHER DISTINCTION which is of great importance for some of our subsequent discussions is the distinction between "disagreement in belief" and "disagreement in attitude." Let us first explain how we are going to use the term "attitude." "It is characteristic for living mind," says Perry, "to be *for* some things and *against* others . . . this duality appears in many forms, such as liking and disliking, desire and aversion, will and refusal, or seeking and avoiding."[7] To any such state, act or disposition, Perry gives the name of "interest" and many contemporary writers, especially Stevenson, use the word "attitude" to mean the same thing.[8] Following Barnes, however, I wish to use it in a somewhat narrower sense. I wish to use the term in such a way that liking or willing or seeking do not *by themselves* constitute an attitude. To quote Barnes:

What distinguishes an attitude, *pro* or *contra*, from, say liking or disliking, is that these latter are *not* directed to a *kind* of action. I may like

---

6. The two senses of "settling a dispute" here distinguished are not the only ones. A third sense will be discussed in Section 6 of this chapter.

7. *General Theory of Value*, p. 115.

8. *Ethics and Language*, pp. 3 ff.

helping people in trouble and yet dislike you or any one else helping such people. If I have a favourable attitude toward helping people in trouble, I help them myself, encourage you and others to do likewise, and am pleased if you do so. More formally: if there is a kind of action which a man has a disposition to do himself, to encourage others to do, and to feel pleased at, when done by others, then he has a pro-attitude to that kind of action. An anti-attitude can be defined similarly.[9]

An attitude in this sense, then, has three components: (i) a feeling and tendency to act in a certain way towards a certain class of objects, (ii) a disposition to encourage others to feel and act the same way, and (iii) a tendency to be pleased if others do feel and act likewise. It is necessary to insert the "tendency" provision in view of a possible conflict of attitudes in any given case.

Following Stevenson, we shall say that two people "disagree in belief" if they make mutually incompatible statements about the same subject, where by "mutually incompatible statements" we mean a pair of statements which cannot both be true. Thus if one man says, "Napoleon was born in 1764" and another says, "Napoleon was born in 1762" and if both are referring to the same man, they are disagreeing in belief.

We shall say that two people disagree in attitude if they have opposing attitudes towards the same thing. Thus, if one man likes boogie-woogie, encourages others to like it and is pleased when other people share his liking, and another man dislikes boogie-woogie, wants others to dislike it and is pleased when he finds them disliking it, they disagree in their attitude towards boogie-woogie.

5. The Meanings of "Objective" and "Subjective"

THERE ARE MANY PEOPLE who maintain that no moral judgment ever has "objective validity" and there are many other people who heatedly contradict this. This dispute is a special case of the more general dispute between the so-called believers in the "subjectivity

---

9. "Ethics Without Propositions," *Aristotelian Society*, Suppl. Vol. XXII, p. 19.

of values" and the believers in the "objectivity of values." Unfortunately the terms "objective" and "subjective," especially when they are applied to sentences, are highly ambiguous. It will help many of our subsequent discussions if we now pause to distinguish some of the senses of these terms.

Perhaps the most familiar use of "objective" and "subjective" is in connection with events or things and not in connection with sentences. Thus we commonly contrast a chair or a mountain as something "objective" with visual images of mountains or with feelings of anger, referring to the latter as "subjective." In this sense, a thing or an event is "objective" if it exists outside anybody's mind and it is "subjective" if it is or is part of somebody's state of mind. This account is somewhat indefinite in view of the vagueness of such phrases as "outside anybody's mind." But for our purpose it is, I think, sufficient.

Several philosophers have come to use "objective" and "subjective" in connection with sentences in a sense which roughly corresponds to the sense in which these terms are applied to things and events. A statement is an objective statement or claim in this sense if its *subject matter* is something other than a mental event in somebody's mind. A statement is a subjective statement or claim if it asserts the existence or describes the features of a mental event. Thus if I say, "the sun is ninety million miles away from the earth" or, "London is east of New York" I am making objective statements in this sense. If I say, "I feel sleepy" or "Truman is very angry now," I am making subjective claims. We shall from now on refer to the sense of "objective" and "subjective" just explained as sense (1) of these terms.

Some philosophers have also used these terms in the following sense which we shall call sense (2): a statement is an objective statement or an objective claim if its subject matter is something other than an event *in the mind of the author of the statement*. It is a subjective statement if it asserts the existence or describes the features of an event in the author's mind. Thus if *I* say, "The sun is ninety million miles from the earth" or "Acheson is the fourth Secretary of State to serve under Truman" I am making objective claims in the sense just defined since the subject matter of my statement is not a state of my own mind. On the other hand if I say, "I feel angry" or "I once liked H. G. Wells but now I don't any more" I am making subjective claims. If I say, "Truman is angry now" or "H. G. Wells envied Bertrand Russell for his intellectual gifts" I am making *objective* claims although I am talking about mental events. My statements are objective since the mental events are not events which are asserted to exist in *my* mind.

It will be seen that any statement which is objective in sense (1) is ipso facto objective in sense (2), while any statement which is subjective in sense (2) is ipso facto subjective in sense (1). The converse holds in neither case.

There is a third sense in which philosophers and many ordinary people use "objective" and "subjective." We shall refer to it as sense (3). To say that a statement is objective in this sense implies nothing about its subject matter but does imply something about the author's background. A statement is objective in this sense if it is not or not greatly colored by the author's emotions. It is subjective if it *is* greatly colored by the author's emotions. Thus a man who earns a hundred thousand dollars a year and hates anybody whom he suspects of being a socialist is not making an objective statement in this sense when he says, "Socialism would lead to the ruin of civilization." But, in any normal circumstances, a teacher who tells his class that there are more inhabitants in London than in Paris or that the sun is further away from the earth than the moon is making objective statements in this third sense.

Now, practically all philosophers who believe in the "objectivity of values" have, I think, wished to maintain: (a) that moral judgments are in general objective statements in sense (1) and therefore, of course, also in sense (2); (b) that some of them at least are also objective in sense (3); and (c) that some of them, furthermore, are known to be true. Among the believers in the "subjectivity of values," some, Russell for instance, have undoubtedly maintained that all moral judgments are subjective in sense (2), while some, like Perry for instance, have asserted the milder view that moral judgments are subjective in sense (1).

It should be noted that a great many statements are objective in sense (2) although they are exceedingly subjective in sense (3).

Thus a man suffering from a persecution complex may assert, on the basis of no evidence whatsoever, "my wife is planning to kill me" or "the Jews are plotting to overthrow the United States Government." These statements, being entirely based on their author's diseased emotions, are subjective in sense (3); but, being *about* something other than his state of mind, they are objective and not subjective in sense (2).

It is interesting to observe that if we define "autobiographical statement" to mean "statement asserting something concerning the author of the statement," then while all statements which are subjective in sense (2) are ipso facto autobiographical, the converse does not hold. Thus if I say, "my height is five foot eight inches" this is autobiographical but not a subjective statement. Although it is about me, it is not about an event in my mind. On the other hand, "I feel fine," is both autobiographical and subjective.

We shall soon find that in the dispute between objectivists and the subjectivists about the nature of moral judgments, the most interesting question is the question as to whether or not they are objective in sense (2). Till the end of Chapter VI, when a further sense of "objective" will be introduced, I shall use "objective" and "subjective" exclusively in this sense.

Subjective statements ought to be carefully distinguished from statements which have the same verbal appearance but which are quite clearly objective. Supposing a certain political analyst, named Gassner, is giving a lecture on the international situation on January 1st, 1951. After giving detailed evidence concerning the aggressive intentions of the Communist leaders and the military superiority of the Communist-dominated nations he ends with the sentence, "It is therefore my considered belief that war will break out between Russia and the United States within six months." Let us call "s_1" this concluding statement of Gassner's lecture, as made in the circumstances described. Let us also suppose that Gassner is at about the same time beginning psychiatric treatment and that his doctor asks him one day to enumerate all the considered beliefs he has concerning his own future and the future of the human race. In these circumstances he again says, among other things, "It is my considered belief that war will break out between Russia and the United States within six months." "s_2" will be short for this statement, as made in reply to the psychiatrist's question.

Now, supposing war does not break out between Russia and the United States in the first half of 1951. Suppose also that when he spoke to the psychiatrist, Gassner really believed, however wrongly, that war was going to break out within six months. In that case s_1 would be false but s_2 would be true. Supposing on the other hand war does break out in the first half of 1951, but that Gassner was lying to the psychiatrist, i.e., that he did not really believe that war would break out within six months. In that case although s_1 would have been shown true, s_2 would be a falsehood.

The difference in what s_1 and s_2 refer to can also be brought out in the following way:

s_1 means *there is going to be a war within six months* (I believe).

s_2 means *in me there exists a belief* that there is going to be a war within six months.

s_1 refers to the future course of the world, of Russia and the United States, while s_2 refers to a belief in Gassner's mind at the time. If this belief really *exists* in Gassner at that time, s_2 is true, however false the belief turns out to be. s_2 is a subjective claim while s_1, although consisting of the very same words, is an objective claim.

To state this point in general terms: phrases such as "It is my conviction that," "In my opinion," "I believe," "It seems to me," are employed for two entirely different purposes. On the one hand, as in s_1, their function is to indicate how confidently or unconfidently the speaker is making his assertion. On the other hand, they have the totally different function, as in s_2, of locating the subject matter of the statement. In the first type of case the statement asserted by the speaker may be and usually is an objective statement. Hence the mere presence in a sentence of phrases like "I think" is no evidence that the statement is subjective. In Chapter II we shall see how important it is to keep this distinction in mind.

This is perhaps the place to mention a confusion of which many writers, from Berkeley to Jeans, have been guilty. The confusion is that of supposing that because a statement is what has sometimes, very loosely, been referred to as "relative," because its predicate is what the older logic-books called a "relative term," it is therefore subjective. This is a complete mistake. When I say that Jesse Owens was a fast runner, that he could move very quickly, I of course mean that he could move very quickly as compared with other human beings. I do not mean that he could move quickly as compared with dogs or horses or airplanes. But there is nothing subjective about my statement. It is not a statement about my state of mind but about Jesse Owens: it is verifiable by reference to observations made on Jesse Owens and human beings in general and not by investigating my mind. The same of course applies to explicit comparisons. John Laird has stated this point with admirable clarity:

Comparison implies a related series, but there is nothing in the least subjective about this circumstance. For example, the statement that a league is longer than a mile, although comparative, is as thoroughly objective as any statement could be. The same is true of superlatives. To speak of the oldest rabbit in Australia, or to say that the motion of light is the fastest in the physical universe is to express what is completely objective.[10]

Before bringing this section to a close, I should like to say something about the difference between the claim that moral judgments are objective and the claim that they refer to what are called "non-natural" qualities or relations. As "non-natural" is usually employed by philosophers, it follows from the fact that a statement refers to a non-natural quality or relation that it is an objective claim, while from the fact that a statement is an objective claim it does not follow that it refers to a non-natural quality or a non-natural relation.

A "non-natural" quality or relation may, for our purposes, be defined as one which is or can be *directly* apprehended not either by sense-perception or by introspection,[11] but through a special faculty. According to Moore—and I fully agree with him in this—

10. *The Idea of Value*, p. 241.
11. For an interesting discussion of this topic, cf. Broad, "Certain Features of Moore's Ethical Doctrines," in *The Philosophy of G. E. Moore*, pp. 57-67. Cf. also Chapter IV of the present work.

what is really the basic disagreement among moral philosophers is not whether moral judgments are subjective or objective claims but rather whether or not they refer to something non-natural. He writes:

Let us suppose it to be held that what is meant by saying that one type of human being A is "better" than another type B, is merely that the course of evolution tends to increase the numbers of type A and to decrease those of type B. Such a view has, in fact, been often suggested, even if it has not been held in this exact form; it amounts merely to the familiar suggestion that "better" means "better fitted to survive." Obviously, "better," on this interpretation of its meaning, is in no sense a "subjective" conception; the conception of belonging to a type which tends to be favored by the struggle for existence more than another is as "objective" as any conception can be. But yet, if I am not mistaken, all those who object to a subjective view of "goodness," and insist upon its "objectivity," would object just as strongly to this interpretation of its meaning as to any "subjective" interpretation. Obviously, therefore, what they are really anxious to contend for is not merely that "goodness" is "objective," since they are here objecting to a theory which is "objective"; but something else . . . ,[12]

namely, that it is non-natural. Furthermore,

Many of those who hold strongly (as many do) that *all* kinds of value are "subjective" certainly object to the so-called "objective" view, not so much because it is *objective*, as because it is not *naturalistic* or *positivistic*. To a view which is at the same time both "naturalistic" or "positivistic" and also "objective," such as the Evolutionary view which I sketched just now, they do not feel at all the same kind or degree of objection as to any so-called "objective" view. With regard to so-called "objective" views they are apt to feel not only that they are false, but that they involve a particularly poisonous kind of falsehood—the erecting into a "metaphysical" entity of what is really susceptible of a simple naturalistic explanation. They feel that to hold such a view is not merely to make a mistake, but to make a superstitious mistake. They feel the same kind of contempt for those who hold it, which we are apt to feel towards those whom we regard as grossly superstitious, and which is felt by certain persons for what they call "metaphysics." Obviously, therefore, what they really object to is not simply the view that these predicates are "objective," but something else . . . ,[13]

namely, that they designate non-natural properties.

---

12. *Philosophical Studies*, pp. 255-256.
13. *Ibid.*, pp. 258-259.

Particularly among British philosophers it is almost taken for granted nowadays that anybody who claims that moral judgments are objective is committing himself to the view that they refer to something non-natural. It is important for us to keep these notions apart, since I shall be advocating a theory which is, in large measure, a form of objectivism. But at the same time my theory is an attempt to do without non-natural qualities or relations.

6. Ambiguities of the "Evidence-Words"

ONE MIGHT GROUP together the words "proof," "evidence," "follows," "imply," "reason," "justification," and several others under some such title as "evidence-words." All these words are highly ambiguous and lack of attention to their various meanings has led to many confusions, especially in discussions of induction and ethics. In this section, I shall say something about certain ambiguities of some of these expressions. This will help us, I believe, to avoid widespread errors concerning the nature of moral judgments and moral arguments.

First of all, it is necessary to point out that we commonly defend or support statements having an autobiographical referent by means of objective claims. Let me take a very simple example. My name is Fabian and I am a famous conductor. I am pacing up and down in my office, obviously very agitated. My secretary asks me, "What is the matter today, Mr. Fabian?" "I am awfully mad at Steiner." "Why on earth at Steiner?" "Well, wouldn't you be—he has snatched away my first violinist, he has stolen my best baton and he is circulating rumors that I have murdered my three late wives." Fabian's statement, "I am mad at Steiner" is an autobiographical statement: if Fabian is not really mad at Steiner at the time at which he makes the statement then the statement is false; if he is mad at Steiner at that time then his statement is true. Nevertheless he supports his statement not with evidence concerning the existence of his violent anger, but with statements concerning the *object* of his anger, namely Steiner.

Before going any further it should be noted that we often say about certain states of mind that they are "justified" or "rational" or "appropriate," meaning more or less the same thing by these words. When we say that a state of mind is justified what we mean, in the sense of referent, is that *its object has certain features.*[14] In the case of different states of mind we refer to different features of the object and even with the same state of mind different people and especially different cultural groups tend to refer to somewhat different features.

Thus supposing X is a man who gave me a job when I needed one badly and who has ever since helped me out financially when my state was low, without making any demands upon me. Supposing, furthermore, that I feel grateful to X for what he has done. Most people, in our society, anyway, would think that my feeling of gratitude is justified or appropriate, meaning thereby simply that X helped me and never made any demands upon me. Supposing that in the example of Fabian, the conductor, Steiner, the man at whom Fabian was angry, really snatched his first violinist, stole his best baton, and spread the story that Fabian had murdered his three dead wives and that this story is altogether false. In that case, too, most people would say that Fabian's anger at Steiner was wholly justified. In using the word "justified" in these two cases we may be expressing the same feeling or attitude. However, the features of the two situations are quite different.

Autobiographical statements, quite generally, may be supported by reasons in two very different senses of the word. In one sense, a statement is a reason for an autobiographical statement if it tends to show that the autobiographical statement is true. Thus if somebody doubted whether Fabian was really mad at Steiner, Fabian might point to the speed of his pulse and heartbeat, to his record of never lying about his own feelings, etc. But there is another sense in which a statement may be a reason for an autobiographical statement. In this other sense, it is a reason if it tends to *justify* the autobiographical statement, if it tends to show that the object of the

---

14. These and some of the subsequent remarks were in part suggested to me by J. N. Findlay's article "Morality by Convention," *Mind*, 1944, especially pp. 196-198. However, I am not sure that Findlay would agree with my points.

state of mind whose existence is asserted by the autobiographical statement, has the feature or features to which we refer when we say that the state of mind is justified. That we use the word "reason" (and other evidence-words) in this second sense, is clearly shown by the following consideration: supposing Fabian's secretary in the above illustration were to reply to his denunciation of Steiner: "You are all wrong. It's Beecham who snatched away the violinist, and it is Krauss who stole your baton, and it is Schlussnuss who started the rumors about your murdering your wives." Supposing she produces conclusive evidence for these statements. Fabian might then admit, "I was all wrong." By "I was all wrong," he obviously would not mean, "I did not really feel angry at Steiner." He would mean, "My anger was unjustified." He would mean "I had no good reason for being angry at *Steiner.*" He would mean "The statements with which I supported my autobiographical statement are false."

I am now in a position to draw attention to an interesting ambiguity in our usage of the word "imply." To begin with, there is a sense which has received more than adequate attention from philosophers. In this sense a person, in asserting p, implies q if q is a *logical consequence* of p, that is, if "p and not q" is a self-contradiction. Let us call this sense of "imply" sense (1). A person who asserts that all politicians are corrupt implies in this sense that some politicians are corrupt. Equally in saying that Björling is a Swede, one implies in this sense that he is a Scandinavian.

There are also several other senses in which "imply" is frequently used. In one of these other senses—which we shall call sense (2)—a person implies q, in asserting p, if he would give q as a reason for p, where "reason" may mean deductive reason or inductive reason or reason in the sense in which "X gave me a job and money when I was down and out," is a reason for "I feel grateful towards X." In this second sense p may imply q although "p and not q" is not a self-contradiction. "I am mad at Steiner although he did not spread any vicious rumors about me, did not steal my best baton and did not snatch my first violinist," is not a self-contradiction. Nor indeed is "I am mad at Steiner—he always helped me when I needed help and never did me any harm" a self-contradiction.

There is also a further sense of "imply" which, in some contexts at least, ought to be carefully distinguished from sense (2). In this sense, a man, in asserting p, implies q, if q would be considered by all or most members of the group to which the man belongs as a good reason for p. The group may of course be different in different situations, but most frequently it is the society or culture to which the man belongs. Thus if I say, in any normal circumstances, "I am mad at Steiner," I imply "Steiner has done something or other —something having the features which are regarded in our society as justifying anger." Let us refer to this sense as sense (3) of "imply." Supposing I am a lunatic who feels violent anger towards Steiner, and give as my reason the statement, "His name reminds me of a certain Scheiner who once stole my baton." In that case, "I feel mad at Steiner" would imply, in sense (2) of the word but not in sense (3), "He reminds me of a certain Scheiner who once stole my baton." We shall see in later chapters how important these distinctions can become.

At this stage something must be said about a sense of "meaning" additional to the three senses distinguished in Section 2 of this chapter. We sometimes talk about the meaning of a sentence when referring neither to the referent of the sentence nor to its Objective nor to what it expresses. Thus a man might say, "Gangle says Steiner is kind. What he means is that Steiner gave him a job when he needed one badly. Really Steiner is not kind. . . ." Or a man might say: "I admire Erna Berger as a singer—I mean to say that her tones are securely emitted, that she has a perfectly equalized scale, a natural legato style and that she has the ability to color her cool, instrumental-like voice however she wishes." Or again somebody might say, "Gangle disapproves of Acheson's foreign policy—he means that Acheson's softness towards the Chinese Communists is responsible for the present war in Korea." In all these and similar cases the meaning of the statement is not its referent but the fact which is or would be brought up as the reason for the statement—either in the sense of inductive reason or in the sense of which "X helped me when I was down and out" is a reason for "I feel gratitude towards X." We shall from now on refer to this sense of "meaning" as sense (4) of the word.[15]

In Section 3 of this chapter we distinguished between two senses in which a dispute may be capable of settlement and between two corresponding senses of "relevant." We must now point out a third sense in which these expressions may be used. Let us consider the following case. Horn and Riker regard much the same features in a human being as reasons for admiring him. They both tend to admire a man if he is genuinely kind, gentle, and if he does not lie and if he keeps his promises. Horn and Riker also consider much the same features as reasons for detesting a man: they both tend to detest a man if he is full of ambition, envy and malice. They are talking about Gangle. Horn says: "I admire this man." Riker says: "That surprises me for I absolutely detest him." Horn proceeds as follows: "I admire Gangle because he is very kind and gentle, especially with children, and because he always keeps his promises." Riker counters this by saying, "I cannot understand you. Gangle is a very cruel man. He really hates children and animals whatever he may pretend in your presence. He keeps his promises to people he needs and wants to impress. When he deals with a person he no longer needs he has not the least compunction about breaking his promises. He is full of crazy ambitions. To further his end he will stop at nothing."

Let us suppose that subsequent investigation shows Riker's supporting statements to be entirely correct. It shows that Gangle is really a cruel man who, among other things, hates children and animals. It shows that he keeps his promises only when keeping them seems to advance his personal ambitions. It is found that in front of Horn he has simply been putting on a clever act. In that case Riker would be shown to be in the right and Horn in the wrong. The dispute would have been settled in Riker's favor. This simply means that the statements which Riker's "I detest Gangle" imply, in sense (3) of the word, turned out to be true, whereas the statements which Horn's "I admire Gangle" implied in the same

---

15. Cf. Stuart Hampshire, "The Fallacies of Moral Philosophy," *Mind*, 1949, p. 477.

sense turned out to be false. It does not mean that Horn's "I admire Gangle" was a false statement when he made it. Nor does it mean that Horn has come to feel about Gangle the same way as Riker—even if Horn died before the truth about Gangle came out, Riker would have been shown to be in the right provided the statements which his "I detest Gangle" implied turned out to be true. We have here, in other words, a sense of "settling a dispute" which is distinct from both in the senses we met before. We shall from now on refer to it as sense (3) of that phrase.

Similarly, we have to distinguish a third sense of "relevant." In this sense a consideration is relevant to a statement simply if it tends to show that the *reason* for the statement is true. "Gangle begins to maltreat his pussy cat the moment he thinks nobody is around to see or hear him," is in this sense relevant to Riker's "I detest Gangle" although it has not the least tendency to show that "I detest Gangle" is a true statement.

7. Public Definitions, Verbal Stipulations and Descriptions of Usage

To AVOID MISUNDERSTANDINGS, not uncommon among writers on ethics, it is necessary to distinguish between definitions which attempt to give information concerning the way or ways in which a term is *actually used* by a given group of people or a "linguistic community" and a person's *proposal* to use a term in a certain way. Any definition which attempts the former I shall call a "public definition." Any proposal of the latter kind I propose to call a "verbal stipulation." All dictionary definitions are instances of public definitions. The first introduction of a technical term is an instance of a verbal stipulation.

It should be observed that verbal stipulations may be rational or irrational, sensible or senseless, but they can never be true or false. Public definitions, on the other hand, can be true or false and their truth or falsehood is determined by the observation of the linguistic habits of the members of whatever group is in question. " 'Father' means 'male parent' " is a true public definition because people who speak English mean the same by these two expressions.

" 'Father' means 'sick old man' " is a false public definition because
the two terms are not used synonymously in English. All this, by
the way, applies just as much to what, following Russell and
Whitehead,[16] are called "definitions in use" as it does to straight
genus-differentia definitions. And it also applies both to what W. E.
Johnson called "ostensive" and to what he called "extensive definitions."[17]

It has often been pointed out in recent years that genus-differentia definitions are not the only and very often not the best way
of giving information concerning the meaning of a word. In the
case of some words like "red" or "hard" or "angry" it is obvious
that only ostensive definitions are possible. But to this it should be
added that there is quite a different class of words for which *public*
genus-differentia definitions are also impossible. I mean words
which tend to have different referents on different occasions of
their employment while yet *expressing* the same state of mind each
time. The word "nice," as applied to food, is an example,[18] and there
are many others. In the case of such words no genus-differentia
definition can by itself give anything like a complete account of
the word's meaning or meanings. The best one can do—and it is
often perfectly sufficient—is to give a description of the *types* of
features to which the word refers and the types of situations in
which it is used. I shall refer to this procedure as "*description* of a
word's use" to distinguish it from definitions in the usual sense.[19]

The distinction between what we decided to call a public definition and what we decided to call a verbal stipulation is so obvious
that my remarks may be thought redundant. I should like to point
out, however, that again and again philosophers confuse the one
with the other. The confusion occurs even in general discussions concerning the nature of definitions. Thus Russell, in the
Introduction to *Principia Mathematica*, makes the following blanket
statement:

---

16. *Principia Mathematica*, (2nd ed.; Cambridge: Cambridge University
Press, 1925) Introduction, Ch. III.
17. *Logic*, Vol. 1., pp. 104 ff.
18. Cf. Chapter V.
19. On this point cf. Hampshire, *op. cit.*, pp. 480-481.

A definition is a declaration that a certain newly introduced symbol or combination of symbols is to mean the same as a certain other combination of symbols of which the meaning is already known. . . . it is not true or false, being the expression of a volition, not of a proposition.[19a]

There is certainly nothing arbitrary about public definitions. Even verbal stipulations are usually not arbitrary in the sense that there is very commonly a reason why a certain phenomenon is given a name. What is, to some extent at least, arbitrary is the selection of this word rather than that to symbolize a given phenomenon. Thus there is a perfectly good reason why we have a special word, namely the word "dog," to refer to animals which are four-legged, domesticated, carnivorous, and which bark, while we have no special word to refer to animals which are carnivorous, domesticated, have sixteen noses, seven eyes and sing "Il Mio Tesoro" twice a day.[20] Presumably arbitrary was our selection of the word "dog" rather than of some other word, e.g., the word "bog" or "rog," to designate animals of the former kind.

8. Moral Judgments and Metaethical Theories

LOGICIANS, since Russell, have come to distinguish carefully between what they call *"using* a word" and what they call *"mentioning* a word." When a word is employed in order to refer to something beyond itself, it is said to be used, but if something is said about a word, if the word itself is the *subject matter* of discussion, the word is said to be mentioned.

Let us consider the following pair of sentences:

s_1—Truman is a courageous man.

s_2—"Truman" has six letters.

Now, in s_1 the word "Truman" is used since what we are talking about is the man, Truman. In s_2, on the other hand, the same word which was used in s_1 is now the subject matter of discussion and is therefore mentioned. Our customary convention for show-

---

19a. Volume I, p. 11.

20. Cf. Cohen and Nagel, *An Introduction to Logic and Scientific Method* (New York: Harcourt, Brace and Co., 1934), p. 246.

ing this is to put the word inside quotation marks. When a word is used, it is not put inside quotation marks; when it is mentioned it is put inside quotation marks, though sometimes the context makes adherence to the latter convention unnecessary. It should be noted that while the word without quotation marks is mentioned in s₂, the *whole* symbol with the quotation marks is used—it is used to refer to the word without quotation marks. If we wanted to talk about or mention the grammatical subject of s₂ we would have to use double quotations or some other name of the symbol.

This distinction, although simple and obvious, is still frequently ignored. Thus, in a well-known textbook of logic there is the following passage:

Certain words, such as nouns and adjectives, may function as terms in a proposition; other words, such as verbs, adverbs, prepositions, and conjunctions, usually do not. And the same is true of word-combinations such as phrases and clauses. For example, in the proposition 'all normal men are rational,' the phrase 'all normal men' is the subject term, while the adjective 'rational' is the predicate. In exceptional cases, however, words and combinations of words, not usually employed as such, may become subject or predicate terms, as, for example, in the preposition, 'of is a preposition.'[21]

"Of is a preposition" is nonsense. To make sense of it we must substitute " 'of' is a preposition." But here the subject-word is the word with the quotation marks, which is quite a different symbol, as far as its function, though not as far as its physical appearance is concerned. It is, to all intents and purposes, a noun. It is not a preposition.

It will be recalled that we defined a moral judgment as any sentence in which an ethical predicate is *used.* Now, statements *about moral judgments* may but need not themselves be moral judgments. Thus the statement, "anybody who says 'Byron was a good man' must himself be an evil man" is a statement about a moral judgment and at the same time it is itself a moral judgment. In it the word "good" is mentioned while the word "evil" is used. On the other

---

21. Creighton, *An Introduction to Logic,* 5th ed., revised by H. R. Smart; New York: Macmillan Co. (1932), p. 59.

hand the statement, "Keats thought that Shelly was a good man" is a statement about a moral judgment but is not itself a moral judgment. Here the word "good" is mentioned and there is no ethical predicate that is used.

All relevant answers to the basic questions of this study are statements about moral judgments without being moral judgments themselves. They are theories which attempt to define ethical predicates, or more broadly, they all attempt to describe the function of moral judgments in human discourse. To distinguish these theories from moral judgments it will be helpful to have a special term at our disposal. Following some recent writers I shall appropriate the term "metaethical theory" or simply "metaethic" for this purpose, A metaethic, then, will be any theory which attempts to define or else to describe the way or ways in which moral judgments are *actually* used by human beings.

9. Types of Metaethical Theories

METAETHICAL THEORIES may be conveniently divided into four types:[22]

(1) Firstly, there are the theories according to which moral judgments are objective claims, referring to non-natural qualities or relations. These theories could very aptly be called "objective non-naturalism." Most commonly they are referred to as "intuitionism."

(2) Secondly, there are the theories according to which moral judgments are objective claims referring to *natural* qualities or relations. Utilitarianism, interpreted not as a moral judgment but as a metaethic, analyzing ethical predicates in terms of happiness, is an example of such a theory. Dewey's theory also falls, I think, under this heading. We shall refer to theories of the second type as "objective naturalism."

(3) Thirdly, we must mention the theories according to which moral judgments *assert* the existence of a feeling or an attitude in

---

22. This division was suggested to me by a passage in Sidney Hook's review of C. I. Lewis' *Analysis of Knowledge and Valuation,* in the *New York Times Book Review,* January, 1948.

the speaker's mind. We shall call theories of this type "naive sub-jectivism."

(4) Finally, there are the theories which maintain that moral judgments have "emotive meaning" only. They possess no referent but are either expressions of attitudes or imperatives prescribing how to act, or both. Following customary usage, we shall call theories of this fourth type "emotive theories."

In this list I omitted mention of several theories which resemble theory (3) in varying degrees and which may, in a broad sense, be called forms of "subjectivism." Among these are (a) the theory, sometimes called "public subjectivism," according to which moral judgments assert the existence of a feeling or attitude in all or the majority of a certain group of people; (b) the view which one might call "causal subjectivism" and according to which moral judgments assert that a certain object is producing or did produce a certain feeling or attitude in the person making the judgment;[23] and (c) the view which I will call "the error theory," according to which moral judgments refer to something outside the speaker's mind but are always false since all that the speaker has a right to say is that he has a certain feeling or attitude. When people talk of "moral scepticism" they mean, I think, any theory according to which no moral judgment is both an objective statement and true. By this test both naive subjectivism and the error theory would be forms of moral scepticism. To keep the error theory distinct from theories (1) and (2) we shall amend our definitions of the latter to include in both cases, "and some moral judgments are known to be true."

It is interesting to observe that all famous supporters of naive subjectivism have also at the same time, knowingly or unknow-ingly, held one or more other theories. Thus Russell, in addition to being a naive subjectivist, also advocates an emotive theory.[24] Westermarck, in addition to advocating naive subjectivism, also makes some statements which imply an emotive theory, other state-

---

23. Cf. James Ward Smith, "Senses of Subjectivism in Value Theory," *Journal of Philosophy*, 1948, pp. 383 ff.
24. Especially in his "A Reply to My Critics," in *The Philosophy of Bertrand Russell* (ed. Schilpp), pp. 721-722.

ments which imply the error theory, and still others which imply causal subjectivism.[25] Hume, finally, advances an emotive theory as well as public and causal subjectivism in addition to naive subjectivism.[26]

I think the reader has a right to know from the outset where I stand. I have provided the above survey mainly because it enables me to indicate my own position with some clearness even at this early stage. My own view, rejecting intuitionism and all forms of subjectivism, combines features of objective naturalism with features of emotive theories. However, as I shall explain at length in Chapter VII, insofar as it falls under objective naturalism, it differs greatly from all classical forms of that theory.

In the next three chapters I shall engage in a critical discussion of three of the theories which I reject: naive subjectivism, the error theory, and intuitionism. Then, after some further and crucial clarifications of a general nature, I shall state and defend my own metaethic. As far as Chapters II to IV are concerned, I should like to emphasize that the discussions are *not* undertaken primarily in a polemic spirit. My desire in each case is to learn as much as possible from the discussions so as to provide a theory which will be free from the difficulties of those I reject.

---

25. The passage in which Westermarck commits himself to Public Subjectivism is found in his *Origin and Development of Moral Ideas,* p. 105. Passages in which he implies the other theories are quoted or referred to in Chapter II.

26. On Hume's several doctrines cf. Raphael, *The Moral Sense,* pp. 75 ff., and Prior, *Logic and the Basis of Ethics,* pp. 60 ff. Hume also holds a still further theory which closely resembles my own. On this cf. Chapter VII below.

CONTENTS

Chapter II

Naive Subjectivism

1. Correct and Misleading Formulations of Subjectivism

NAIVE SUBJECTIVISM has already been defined in Chapter I: it is the theory that moral judgments are subjective—they are statements to the effect that the person who makes the judgment has or tends to have a certain feeling or attitude towards a certain object.

Naive subjectivists have differed among themselves as to what attitude or feeling moral judgments refer to. Westermarck and Hume claimed that the feelings were mainly those of approval and disapproval while Russell for the most part holds that moral judgments refer to the speaker's desire, frequently his desire for other people to have certain desires. There is no reason why a naive subjectivist should not hold a combination of these theories, i.e., that some moral judgments, e.g., those involving the words "good" and "evil," refer to approval and disapproval, while others, e.g., those involving "ought," refer to the speaker's desires.

It is worth observing[1] that, according to naive subjectivism, ethical predicates cannot be defined "in isolation," meaning by this, that no phrase can be substituted for any of them, without changes being made in other parts of the sentence. They can only be given what is called a definition in use. "Good" or any of the other ethical predicates is *not* synonymous on this view with "approved" or

1. Cf. Prior, *op. cit.*, p. 59.

"desired," but sentences containing the former phrase are analyz-
able into sentences containing the latter. If a man, A, says, "cruelty
is evil" this, on Westermarck's view for instance, does not mean
"cruelty is disapproved." It means, rather, "I, A, have a tendency
to disapprove of cruelty." Not only has the word "good" been
eliminated, but the subject of the sentence too has changed. Naive
subjectivism has often been misrepresented by philosophers who
paid no attention to this point.

According to naive subjectivism, moral judgments *refer* to and
do not merely *express* feelings or attitudes on the part of the
person who makes the moral judgment. According to it, therefore,
moral judgments *are* true or false. It follows from naive subjectivism that if a person really has the attitude whose existence he is
asserting by means of the moral judgment, then the moral judgment is true, while if he does not really have that attitude, his
judgment is false. Westermarck, unlike some other supporters of
naive subjectivism, is quite content to admit this consequence:

. . . it may be true or not that we have a certain emotion, it may be
true or not that a given mode of conduct has a tendency to evoke in us
moral indignation or moral approval. Hence a moral judgment is true
or false according as its subject has or has not that tendency which the
predicate attributes to it. If I say that it is wrong to resist evil, and
yet resistance to evil has no tendency whatever to call forth in me an
emotion of moral disapproval, then my judgment is false.[2]
. . . if I am right in my assertion that the moral concepts intrinsically
express a tendency to feel a moral emotion of either approval or disapproval, it is obvious that a judgment which contains such a concept may
be said to be true if the person who pronounces it actually has a tendency to feel the emotion in question with reference to the subject of
judgment. . . . If "good" expresses a tendency to feel moral approval,
the proposition in question is, as already said, true if there really is such
a tendency with regard to that of which goodness is predicated, and
false if there is no such tendency—people are often hypocrites in their
moral judgments.[3]

Russell is not prepared to admit this consequence. " 'I ought to do
so,' " he says in one place, "primarily means, 'this is the act towards

2. *Origin and Development of Moral Ideas*, Vol. I, pp. 17-18.
3. *Ethical Relativity*, pp. 141-142.

which I feel the emotion of approval.' "[4] But he also says: "I see no property analogous to truth that belongs or does not belong to an ethical judgment."[5]

In Chapter I, Section 9, I took pains to distinguish naive subjectivism from other theories which may be regarded as forms of subjectivism. I should now like to distinguish it from yet another theory which I shall call "rational subjectivism." By this I mean the view that moral judgments are statements asserting the existence of the speaker's feeling or attitude, where the feeling or attitude is *based on reasons* in a sense we shall fully discuss in a later chapter. According to rational subjectivism when one man says, "X is good" and another says, "X is evil" they may both be speaking the truth at the same time. But one of them may be more *rational* than the other. I do not know of anybody who ever held exactly this theory, but I mention it because it seems to me far more plausible than naive subjectivism. Many of the objections which are valid against naive subjectivism are not valid against rational subjectivism.

Before going any further, something should be said about a very misleading formulation of naive subjectivism, which is frequently found in popular critics of the theory, but occasionally also in the writings of subjectivists themselves. Thus Hume says that moral and esthetic taste "has a productive faculty and gilding and staining all natural objects with the colors borrowed from internal sentiment, raises in a manner a new creation."[6] "It is . . . our desires," in Russell's words, "which confer values."[7]

Let us compare this last sentence with another one in which the word "confer" is used, e.g., "President Butler conferred an honorary degree upon Richard Rodgers." Here we have three distinct entities: (i) President Butler, the man who confers the degree; (ii) Richard Rodgers, the man upon whom the degree is conferred; and (iii) the degree which is conferred. Similarly, Russell's formulation suggests that according to his view there are three entities, namely, (i) the human beings who have certain desires, (ii) the

---

4. *Outline of Philosophy*, p. 234.
5. *The Philosophy of Bertrand Russell*, p. 723.
6. *An Enquiry Concerning the Principles of Morals* (ed. Selby-Bigge), p. 294.
7. *What I Believe*, p. 25.

objects which they desire, and (iii) the values which their desires "confer" on the objects. What would distinguish subjectivism from objectivism, according to this formulation, is the "original location" of the values, not the existence of a separate type of entity over and above human desires and their objects. What the objectivists would not accept is that the values came into being as a result of the activities of desires.

I am sure this is not what Russell or any other defender of naive subjectivism intended. What he really meant to say is that there are *not* three types of entities in the "moral situation," but only *two*: (i) people having certain desires, and (ii) the objects which they desire. Talking about the value of objects is another way of talking about human desires for the objects.

There is an interestingly similar confusion or ambivalence in Hume's attack on the Rationalist view of causation. In one set of passages, especially in the *Treatise*, Hume says quite definitely that there is no such thing as a logical "must," a "logical tie" linking the cause with the effect. But in other passages, especially in some sections of the *Inquiry*, he seems to hold the following view: there is a "logical tie" linking cause and effect, but nobody can ever know it. All we can know are invariant concommitances. I.e., he says both that the Rationalists were wrong in believing in the existence of a logically necessary connection between cause and effect and also that they were wrong, not in believing in its existence, but in believing that human beings can know it. Similarly, Russell says on the one hand that the objectivists are mistaken in thinking that in the moral situation there is something besides human desires and the object desired and on the other hand that they are not mistaken in *this*, but in the "location" of this further entity. In both cases it is, I think, the former theory which is mainly intended and which is by far the more plausible. In the sequel I shall concern myself with naive subjectivism only in the former sense.

2. The Arguments for Naive Subjectivism

ACCORDING TO MOORE, "nothing whatever" can be said for naive subjectivism, "except that so many philosophers have been absolutely convinced that it is true. None of them seem to me to have succeeded in bringing forward a single argument in favor of their view."[8] This suggests that the writings of naive subjectivists are full of nothing but dogmatic pronouncements. This is far from being the case. Several arguments are commonly advanced by them and I now wish to consider those I believe to be the most important.

(i) First, there is the argument from the widespread differences of opinion on moral questions. This argument is more commonly advanced in support of public subjectivism. But it has also been used to back naive subjectivism. The argument, briefly, is this: We find enormously widespread differences on practically all moral questions. In one culture polygamy is considered right and natural, in another it is considered highly immoral; in one society burning widows is considered a duty while in another it is believed to be utterly wrong. Moreover, even within the same culture or society there are frequently very widespread differences of opinion on moral questions. Thus many people in our society regard the segregation of Negroes as shameful while others consider equality of treatment reprehensible. Some think that cruelty to animals is justified in the interests of science while others do not. Countless other instances could be cited. All this, it is said, shows that moral judgments are merely "subjective."[9]

This argument, by itself, proves absolutely nothing. For it rests on a major premise which is quite certainly false. The major premise is this: on *any* topic on which there is widespread difference of opinion the statements of both parties are only about their own attitudes or states of mind. This is simply not so. There are very widespread differences of opinion as to whether there are slave

8. *Philosophical Studies*, p. 331.
9. Cf., e.g., Russell, *Religion and Science*, p. 238.

labor camps in the Soviet Union, but the *subject matter* of both of the sentences, "there is plenty of slave labor in the Soviet Union" and "there is no slave labor in the Soviet Union" are not attitudes or feelings on the part of the speakers. Again, there is very widespread disagreement on the cause of neurosis and phychosis and on the efficacy of different types of treatment. But statements like "the cause of neurosis is the patient's emotional isolation" are quite plainly objective in the only relevant sense.

(ii) It is very commonly maintained by subjectivists that moral judgments must be merely subjective since moral disputes are undecidable in the sense that nothing can be done to prove the views of one side and disprove those of the other. If moral judgments were objective claims this would not be so. Russell has urged this argument in several passages:

Let us consider two theories as to the good. One says, like Christianity, Kant and democracy: whatever the good may be, any one man's enjoyment of it has the same value as any other man's. The other says: there is a certain sub-class of mankind—white men, Germans, gentiles, or what-not—whose good or evil alone counts in an estimation of ends; other men are only to be considered as means. I shall suppose that A takes the first view, and B the second. What can either say to convict the other of error? I can only imagine arguments that would be strictly irrelevant. A might say: If you ignore the interests of a large part of mankind, they will rebel and murder you. B might say: that portion of mankind that I favor is so much superior to the rest in skill and courage that it is sure to rule in any case, so why not frankly acknowledge the true state of affairs? Each of these is an argument as to means, not as to ends. When such arguments are swept away, there remains so far as I can see, nothing to be said except for each party to express moral disapproval of the other.[10]

Again he writes:

Bentham's creed that pleasure is the Good roused furious opposition, and was said to be a pig's philosophy. Neither he nor his opponents could advance any argument. In a scientific question, evidence can be adduced on both sides, and in the end one side is seen to have the better case—or, if this does not happen, the question is left undecided. But in a question as to whether this or that is the ultimate Good, there is no evidence either way; each disputant can only appeal to his own

---

10. *The Philosophy of Bertrand Russell*, p. 721.

emotions, and employ such rhetorical devices as shall rouse similar emotions in others. We have here a sharp disagreement of great practical importance, but we have absolutely no means, of a scientific or intellectual kind, by which to persuade either party that the other is in the right.[11]

There is a two-fold reply to this. Firstly, even if the premises of this argument were true, this would not necessarily prove the conclusion. The fact, if it is a fact, that moral disputes are undecidable is compatible with several other theories concerning the nature of moral judgments, e.g., with the theory that moral judgments *express* the speaker's attitude, or with the theory that moral judgments are objective claims but that the parties do not use ethical terms in the same senses. Secondly, the premise of the argument has been questioned on the ground that no *actual* moral dispute is ever a dispute concerning the "intrinsic" value of anything and that no *actual* moral judgment, occurring in a living context, is ever an "intrinsic" or "ultimate" moral judgment. I shall return to a discussion of this topic in Chapter VIII.

(iii) It is sometimes argued, among others by Westermarck, that since moral judgments are caused by emotions on their author's part, since they are thus "colored" by, "shot-through-and-through" with the speaker's feelings, they cannot have any claim to objective validity. Their emotional origin proves that they are merely subjective.

Now, it may readily be granted, as Hume emphasized again and again, that if human beings had no desires and never felt approval or disapproval, moral judgments would never have been made. It may be granted that emotions such as fear and envy play a very large part in the causation of the most formidable body of moral judgments, namely, those relating to sexual behavior. But all this in no way proves that the *subject matter* of moral judgments is the speaker's own attitude. The major premise implied in this argument—any statement which is the result of emotion is *about* the speaker's own feeling or attitude—is plainly false. Thus supposing X is a young philosopher who has been extremely successful and who is admired by most philosophers, young and old. Supposing,

---

11. *Religion and Science*, pp. 229-230.

further, that I am an intensely ambitious person with small gifts and that I am full of envy towards X. My envy may then cause me to start spreading vicious rumors about him. I might say, "He does not write his own books but engages me to write them for him. He seduces all the pretty girls in his classes. He got his present position because he married his Chairman's daughter whom nobody else wanted to take. He works for the FBI in his spare time and other philosophers tremble in his presence for fear he will pass in derogatory reports about them. He gives high grades to students who lavishly entertain him at fashionable restaurants." Supposing all these statements are complete fabrications due to nothing but my insane envy of X. In spite of this, they are *about* X and not about me. In the only relevant sense they are objective claims.

Furthermore, the fact that an objective claim is the result of emotion, even of pathological emotion, does not show that it is or is likely to be false. A great deal of what Nietzsche and Schopenhauer said about human beings and especially about their contemporaries was undoubtedly the outcome of their own diseased emotions. But a great deal of what they said was true. An unhappy man may wish everybody else to be unhappy also and this wish may cause him to say that X and Y and Z are miserable. Since most people are unhappy, he will frequently be right: in fact, his desire that everybody else be unhappy, is likely to make him perceive a great many things beneath the surface which a person not having his desire might miss.

The fact, therefore, that moral judgments have an emotional origin—itself not to be accepted without several qualifications—does nothing to show that they are merely subjective claims or that, if objective, they are likely to be false.

(iv) I finally come to what seems the strongest argument for naive subjectivism. Careful observation of the way in which people use language, it might be said, shows that very frequently, maybe always, when they make a moral judgment, they would quite willingly substitute for it a subjective claim. In fact, often they *actually* do so. Thus supposing a man has given a lecture on the "Justification of Mercy-Killing." He might conclude with the sentence, "For these reasons, ladies and gentlemen, I approve of

mercy-killing in the circumstances I describe." Or we might ask
a man who knew the late Homer Lane: "What sort of a man was
he?" The answer might be, "Lane was a profoundly good man"
or it might be, "I admired Lane very profoundly." The speaker
would be as ready to say the one thing as the other, and we, too,
would, in most circumstances, consider the two sentences to be
saying the same thing.

I hope to show later that this argument too, although it proves
something, does not prove naive subjectivism. However, it is impossible at this stage to make any useful comments upon it. This
will be possible only after certain general logical points have been
cleared up in Chapter V.

3. The Arguments
   against Naive Subjectivism

WE SHALL NOW CONSIDER the most powerful arguments against
naive subjectivism. (i) If two sentences, e.g., "Jones is a father"
and "Jones is a male parent," are synonymous in the sense of having the same referent, then the facts which make one of them true
ipso facto make the other one true and the facts which make one
of them false ipso facto make the other one false also. Conversely, if
there are facts which are sufficient to prove one sentence—e.g., "X is
a father"—but are not sufficient to prove another—e.g., "X is an old
man"—then the two sentences cannot be synonymous in the sense
in question.

Let m_1 be a typical moral judgment made by a person whom we
shall call Gangle. m_1 is the sentence, "Mercy-killing is always
wrong." Let a_1 be the sort of subjective statement which has frequently been claimed to be the correct translation of judgments
like m_1. Let a_1 then be the sentence, "I, Gangle, disapprove of
mercy-killing under all circumstances." A naive subjectivist, now,
would maintain that m_1 and a_1 are synonymous, that they have the
same referent. And this assertion is open to the following fatal
objection:[12] For Gangle to prove a_1 it would be sufficient for him

_____
12. The argument which follows is an elaboration in my own words of

to produce certain data *concerning himself*, e.g., the fact that he is a Catholic, that he demanded the death sentence for Dr. Sanders, that he regularly sends donations to the Society Against the Legalization of Euthanasia, etc. But neither he nor anybody else would consider this proof or indeed any kind of relevant evidence for m_1. In other words: the facts which make a_1 true do not make m_1 true. Again, a_1 could be disproven if it turned out that Gangle made the statement, "I disapprove of mercy-killing in all circumstances" only because his boss, a fanatical Catholic, happened to be in the company, but that he secretly works for the Euthanasia Society of America, that he sent money to the defense fund for Dr. Sanders, and so forth. But neither he nor anybody else would regard this as being a disproof of or any sort of evidence against m_1. In other words: the facts which make a_1 false do not make m_1 false.

Many people who hear this argument for the first time get the feeling that it is somehow unfair. I shall try to represent how an intelligent sympathizer with naive subjectivism might express this feeling: "You misunderstand and misrepresent naive subjectivism in this argument. According to naive subjectivism the question, 'Is mercy-killing ever right?' is incomplete as it stands and cannot therefore be answered. It has to be further qualified. It can be answered when it is completed, e.g., to read, 'Is mercy-killing ever right according to Sanders?' or, 'Is mercy-killing ever right according to Horn?' or, 'Is mercy-killing ever right according to Bertrand Russell?'[13] Naive subjectivism does not deal with incomplete statements like 'Mercy-killing is always wrong.' It deals with statements like 'Mercy-killing is always wrong, according to me,' as made by some specific individual. Your argument only shows that the former statements are not synonymous with subjective

---

several arguments contained in Ewing's *The Definition of Good*, pp. 4-7. There is a reply to Ewing by H. B. Acton in *Analysis* for October, 1948. But Ewing, in my opinion, properly disposes of this reply in his subsequent rejoinder.

13. I am very deliberately using "according to" and not "for." The latter expression is in this context dangerously ambiguous while the former is not. "X is good for Sanders" may mean (1) "X is good according to Sanders," but it would more frequently mean (2) "X has *good effects on* Sanders," which is something very different and something with which we have no concern in **this** discussion.

claims. It in no way proves that the latter are not synonymous with subjective statements."

This answer is disposed of as soon as we recall the distinction explained in Chapter I, Section 5, where I drew attention to the two very different functions of such phrases as "I think" or "I believe or "It is my opinion." In one context they serve merely as indications of the degree of assuredness with which an objective claim is asserted by the speaker. In another context they determine the subject matter of the statement. Let us recall our stock example and introduce a new piece of symbolism. In the sentence, "It is my conviction that war will break out within the next six months," as uttered by a political analyst at a public meeting, "It is my conviction" functions as an indication of the man's assuredness. The sentence itself is clearly an objective claim—a statement about the course of the world during the following six months. The same sentence, it will be remembered, when uttered to a psychiatrist in a clinical context, is a subjective claim and there the "It is my conviction" does help to indicate the subject matter of the statement. For the rest of this discussion we shall underline phrases like "I think" or "It is my opinion" in sentences which they make into subjective statements. In those sentences in which they occur but which are objective claims, we shall underline the words which give us the real subject matter and we shall put the autobiographical phrase in brackets. The concluding sentence of the political lecture we shall write as

"(It is my conviction that) *war will break out within six months.*"

The statement to the psychiatrist we shall write as:

"*It is my conviction* that war will break out within six months."

Keeping this distinction in mind, let us now look at the following three statements, each made by Gangle:

(i) Mercy-killing is always wrong.
(ii) (According to me) *mercy-killing is always wrong.*
(iii) *According to me* mercy-killing is always wrong.

Now, (i) and (ii) are clearly synonymous in the same way as "War will break out within six months" is synonymous with "It is my conviction that *war will break out within six months.*" But

(iii) is not synonymous with either of them, any more than "*It is my conviction* that war will break out within six months" is synonymous with "War will break out within six months" or with "It is my conviction that *war will break out within six months.*" Furthermore, (iii) is not really a moral judgment at all since "wrong" is not really its predicate, the sentence being synonymous with "*In me there exists* the belief that mercy-killing is always wrong."

To tell us something of interest concerning the meaning of function of moral judgments, naive subjectivism must be a theory about statements like (i) and (ii) and not about statements like (iii). In showing that m_1 and a_1 in the above example are not synonymous I was therefore arguing to the point. If naive subjectivism maintains merely that sentences like (iii) are synonymous with subjective claims many objectivists would agree with this. My argument would then be irrelevant, but the theory itself would cease to be a metaethic in our sense.

Granting for the moment that a_1 is a correct translation of "*According to me,* mercy-killing is always wrong," as asserted by Gangle, the argument against naive subjectivism may also be expressed in this way: m_1—i.e., "Mercy-killing is always wrong"—is not synonymous with "*According to me,* mercy-killing is always wrong." The facts which make the latter sentence true do not ipso facto make the former one true. By the way, a person who has been lecturing against mercy killing and concludes with the sentence, "In view of these considerations mercy-killing is always wrong" would not at all be willing to substitute for it the sentence, "In view of these considerations, mercy-killing is always wrong according to me," if the emphasis were placed on the phrase "according to me."

(ii) What is substantially the same argument may also be expressed in this way: If two sentences—e.g., "Jones is a father" and "Jones is a male parent"—really have the same referent, then the combination "Since Jones is a male parent, he is a father" is a tautology. If such a combination of two sentences does not produce a tautology then the two sentences cannot have the same referent. E.g., "Since Jones is an old man he is a father" is not a tautology and the sentences "Jones is a father" and "Jones is an old man" do not have the same referent. Now the appropriate combination of a_1 and m_1 is the sentence "Since I, Gangle, disapprove of mercy-killing under all circumstances, it is always wrong." This, so far from being a tautology, is "a piece of gross conceit."[14]

(iii) The following is an objection put forward by G. E. Moore:

It is commonly believed that some moral rules exhibit a higher morality than others; that, for instance a person who believes that it is our duty to do good to our enemies, has a higher moral belief, than one who believes that he has no such duty, but only a duty to do good to his friends or fellow-countrymen. And Westermarck himself believes that, some moral beliefs, "mark a stage of higher refinement in the evolution of the moral consciousness." . . . What then, could Westermarck mean by saying that A's morality is higher than B's? So far as I can see, what on his own views, he would have to mean is merely that he himself, Westermarck, shares A's morality and does not share B's: that it is true of him, as of A, that neglecting to do good to enemies excite his feelings of moral indignation and not true of him as it is of B, that it does not excite such feelings in him. In short, he would have to say that what he means by calling A's morality the higher is merely "A's morality is my morality, and B's is not." But it seems to me quite clear that when we say one morality is higher than another, we do not merely mean that it is our own. We are not merely asserting that it has a certain relation to our own feelings.[15]

Westermarck, in his later book, replies to this argument by saying:

I have no doubt that this is the case with most people's judgments, but this does not disprove my view that their assumed objectivity is an illusion. Leslie Stephen says each man thinks that his own morality is the right morality, and that any other standard is mistaken. But who could maintain that it is so, because it is thought to be so?[16]

This entirely misses the point and in effect concedes the validity of Moore's objection. For the only point at issue in the discussion of naive subjectivism is whether people *mean* by their moral judg-

---

14. Ewing, *op. cit.*, p. 6. This argument is really an application to naive subjectivism of Moore's famous argument against the so-called "naturalistic fallacy."

15. *Philosophical Studies*, pp. 334-335.

16. *Ethical Relativity*, p. 146.

ments something other or more than that they have a certain attitude. If, as Moore claims and Westermarck admits, they mean something more, then naive subjectivism is false, even if in fact all judgments of the form "This morality is higher than that" are mistaken. As usual, Westermarck replies by shifting to one of the other position he also holds, in this case to the error theory.

It is interesting to observe that Russell, in one of his latest and most elaborate discussions of the nature of moral judgments, shows himself very impressed with this objection.

But what are "good" desires? Are they anything more than desires that you share? Certainly there seems to be something more. Suppose, for example, that someone were to advocate the introduction of bull-fighting in this country. In opposing the proposal, I should feel not only that I was expressing my desires, but that my desires in the matter are *right*, whatever that may mean. As a matter of argument, I can, I think, show that I am not guilty of any logical inconsistency in holding to the above interpretation of ethics and at the same time expressing strong ethical preferences. But in feeling I am not satisfied.[17]

We shall have occasion to take up this passage from Russell again in Chapter IX, Section 3.

(iv) The next objection I wish to consider is due to Sir David Ross.

If something, without changing its nature, at some moment aroused for the first time the feeling in some mind, we should clearly judge not that the object had then first become good, but that its goodness had then first been apprehended.[18]

Again:

If I judge that Brutus did wrong in assassinating Caesar, I certainly do not think that his act first acquired his wrongness when I began to experience disapproval of it, or will cease to be wrong when I have ceased to do so.[19]

The same argument has also been advanced in several places by Brand Blanshard. Thus he writes:

---

17. *The Philosophy of Bertrand Russell,* p. 724.
18. *The Right and the Good,* p. 11, also pp. 82 ff.
19. *The Foundations of Ethics,* pp. 23-24.

Suppose that when we are away from home a pet dog gets caught in a trap, struggles long and vainly to get free, and is found dead on our return. We look back on what he must have gone through and put it down as a very bad thing that he should have suffered so. But according to the theory, the suffering was not bad at all, and all we are doing when we say it was bad is expressing our present feelings about it. Nothing in fact was bad until we came home and said our say; and if the dog had remained undiscovered, nothing bad would have happened at all; for it is only as people take up attitudes that good or bad comes into being. And if people could manage to delight in the suffering, once they discovered it, then it would be good. This conclusion has actually been held by able men; but it does small credit either to their heads or their hearts.[20]

Substantially the same argument is also contained in Moore's famous contrast of the exceedingly beautiful world with "the ugliest world you can imagine,"[21] where he argues that the former would be better than the latter even if no conscious being ever contemplated either world.

Maybe the following illustration will show what a very powerful objection this is. Like many other people, I believe that the Fair Employment Practices Bill, which had the support of President Truman but which Congress has for several years been refusing to consider, is a thoroughly just piece of legislation. Now whatever I actually mean by saying that the F.E.P.C. is a just piece of legislation, I do not mean anything which implies that if I suddenly died the F.E.P.C. would cease to be a just piece of legislation. I also do not mean anything which implies that if all people who believe that the F.E.P.C. is a just policy were exterminated and if no converts were ever again made to this belief, the F.E.P.C. would cease to be just.

Westermarck admits all of this but insists that it does not refute naive subjectivism:

I agree with Dr. Ross that if, for instance, some one were to become aware of an act of self-denial and admire it, he might "pronounce it

---

20. "Personal Ethics," in *Preface to Philosophy* (ed. W. P. Tolley), pp. 126-127; cf. also Blanshard's article, "The New Subjectivism in Ethics," *Philosophy and Phenomenological Research*, 1949, pp. 504 ff. Cf. Chapter IX, Section 1 of the present work for a discussion of various points raised in that article.

21. *Principia Ethica*, pp. 83-85.

had been good even when no one had been admiring it," inasmuch as he might attribute to himself a tendency to admire or, as I should say, approve of it, and consequently to the object a tendency to arouse in him the emotion of approval.[22]

The substitution of "A has a tendency to approve of x" for "A in fact approves of x" does not get at the heart of Ross' objection. When I say that the F.E.P.C. is a just bill I do not mean anything which implies that it would cease to be just once I died. This shows that I mean neither "I approve of the F.E.P.C." *nor* "I have a tendency to approve of the F.E.P.C." In the second part of Westermarck's reply we have another of his many shifts—this time to the theory we are calling "causal subjectivism."[23]

(v) I should like to mention, without discussing it, one further objection. Ross has stated it in the following words:

When I consider this emotion (the emotion of moral disapproval) it appears to me that it is not just a feeling which arises in us, we know not why, when we contemplate a right action. It seems to presuppose some insight into the nature of the action, as, for instance, that it is an action likely to redound to the general good, or a fulfilment of promise. It seems to be an intellectual emotion, presupposing the thought that the action is right, and right as being of a certain recognized character. And if this contention is correct, if the emotion of moral approval presupposes the thought that the action is right, it follows that we cannot mean by calling the action right that it awakes this emotion, since in order to have the emotion we must already be thinking of the action as right.[24]

I believe this objection to be substantially valid. I am also not aware of any place where a naive subjectivist has offered an intelligible answer to it. But, in the absence of distinctions to be introduced in Chapter V, it is impossible to say anything useful about it here.

---

22. *Ethical Relativity*, pp. 144-45.

23. It should be observed that this objection is without force against a "dispositional" form of subjectivism. Richard Brandt's view that "X is wrong" (roughly) means, "If I had all the facts about X clearly in mind and were ethically consistent, I would disapprove of X," is an example of such a theory.

24. *The Foundations of Ethics*, p. 23; cf. also *The Right and the Good*, p. 131.

4. Conclusions

IT WILL BE CONVENIENT to list here some of the conclusions to which we have been led in the discussions of this chapter:

1. Statements of the form, "X *is good* (according to me)" are by no means synonymous with statements of the form, "X is good, *according to me*." Even if the latter are synonymous with statements asserting the existence of the speaker's attitude towards X, the former are not.

2. When a person makes a statement of the form, "This morality is higher than that one" he does not mean or he does not merely mean, "I prefer this morality to that" or, "This is *my* morality, the other one is not."

3. When we say of something that it is right or good or ought to be done, whatever we do mean, we do not mean anything which implies that the object in question would cease to be good or right if we ceased to believe this.

4. Moral approval is an intellectual emotion in the sense that it presupposes beliefs of one kind or another concerning the nature of the object approved.

5. People *are* frequently, if not always, ready to substitute sentences such as "I cannot approve of this" or "I favor that" for moral judgments.

It may seem at first sight that conclusions 1. and 5. are mutually contradictory. I hope to show eventually that this is not so. In any case, it seems to me that an adequate metaethic must be able, among other things, to account for all the facts summarized in this section.

CONTENTS

Chapter III

The "Error Theory"

1. "The Great Mass of Moral Thought is Error"

FREQUENTLY when a person says that something is beautiful or that a certain action is right, he is met with the answer, "You mean *you* like it" or "You mean that *you* are for it." Naive subjectivism may be said to be an explicit formulation of the metaethic implicit in such remarks. The theory which I wish to discuss in this chapter may also be said to be an explicit formulation of a metaethic implicit in certain statements commonly made. These are also statements made in reply to the claims that something is beautiful or good or right. The remarks which one then sometimes encounters are: "All you have a right to say is that *you* like it" or "All that you are entitled to assert is that *you* approve of it."

The error theory has been given its fullest exposition in an article by the Australian philosopher John Mackie, published in 1946, which has been favorably quoted by several recent writers all over the world. Mackie's main points are: (1) that when people make moral judgments, they are asserting that an action or a person has a certain quality of goodness or rightness, or whatever it is, i.e., they are making objective claims, but (2) that, since there is no such "independent" quality, all moral judgments are false, and (3) this universal error is due to peoples' projection in a certain way

of their feelings of approval and disapproval onto the subject of
their judgment. The following are Mackie's own words:

We have only moral feelings but objectify these and think we are
recognizing objective facts and qualities.[1]
Moral terms do mean objective qualities, and every one who uses
them does so because he believes in objective facts.[2]
But there are no objective moral facts: the feelings are *all* that exists.[3]
The great mass of what is called moral thought is, not nonsense, but
error, the imagining of objective fact and qualities of external things
where there exists nothing but our feeling of desire and approval.[4]
In using moral terms we are as it were objectifying our own feelings,
thinking them into qualities existing independently of us. For example,
we may see a plant, say a fungus, that fills us with disgust, but instead
of stating that we have this feeling, or merely expressing and relieving
it by an exclamation, we may ascribe to the fungus a semimoral quality
of foulness, over and above all the qualities that a physical scientist
could find in it. Of course, in objectifying our feelings we are also turning them inside out: our feelings about the fungus is one of being dis-
gusted, while the foulness we ascribe to the fungus means that it is disgusting. The supposed objective quality is not simply the feeling itself
transferred to an external object, but is something that would inevitably
arouse that feeling. (No one would say, "That fungus is foul, but I feel
no disgust at it.") The feeling and the supposed quality are related as a
seal or a stamp and its impression.
This process of objectification is, I think, well known to psychologists
and is not new in philosophy. I believe that it resembles what Hume
says we do when we manufacture the idea of necessary connection out
of our feeling of being compelled, by the association of ideas, to pass
from cause to effect, though here the process of turning inside out does
not occur.[5]

Mackie gives the notion of economic value as another example of
this process of objectification:

Here value is created by demand—in fact a quality manufactured in
imagination out of the relation of being demanded by someone, the ab-
straction being the easier because the demand is not essentially that of

---

1. "The Refutation of Morals," *Australasian Journal of Psychology and
Philosophy*, 1946, p. 90.
2. *Ibid.*, p. 81.
3. *Ibid.*, p. 86.
4. *Ibid.*, p. 90.
5. *Ibid.*, pp. 81-82.

THE "ERROR THEORY" [69]

a single buyer, but of an indeterminate crowd of potential buyers: the analogy with the objectification of moral feelings, aided by their generality, is very plain.[6]

Mackie is here attacking what has sometimes been called the "pathetic fallacy." Perry has stated the same points at greater length:

Professor Laird appeals to the fact that there is an immediate objectivity in the appreciation of beauty, or in the admiration of conduct. These are not mere subjective states caused by an object; they present the object, clothed in its quality of charm or moral worth.

That feeling does somehow color its object is an undeniable fact of experience, and a fact recognized by common speech insofar as all of the familiar feelings assume the form of adjectives. We do speak of enticing greenness and delightful melodies. But if we were to trust such evidence of immediacy and accept the language of poetry for the prosaic purposes of science, we should be carried further than even Professor Laird, presumably, would care to go. We should be obliged to reduce feelings to bare sensibility, and to deny that the subject himself was in fact either enticed or delighted. It seems necessary at some point to admit that the qualities of feeling may be "referred" where they do not belong, or an object may for the summary purposes of poetic suggestion be endowed with characters that accurate judgment will attribute to their effects or to their context. A "coveted book" is evidently qualified by a relation to subjects. A "dull day," a "boresome meeting," a "tiresome place," a "hopeful situation," are less evidently so, but the clarification of the experience brings us in each case to the identification of the quality with a specific reaction of the subject. When, by an act of attention, we endeavour to localize the red of the cherry in the subject we fail. To call the red of the cherry a mode of the activity or process of seeing, or of the sentient organism, remains contrary to appearances no matter how carefully these are scrutinized. With the so-called "tertiary" or affective qualities, however, the reverse is true. The more closely these are examined the more clearly do they appear to be either modes of attitude or impulse, and thus motor or sensory qualia which are localized in the body. They rapidly *lose all semblance of that inherence in the object which becomes increasingly clear and unmistakable in the case of color.* In short, the attentive effort at localisation, whereas it unites the "secondary" qualities, and tends to unite them with the object, disassociates the alleged "tertiary" qualities, and tends to unite them with the sentient. It becomes less and less tol-

---

6. *Ibid.*, pp. 83-84.

erable to speak of a red or yellow organism, as it becomes more and more plausible to speak of one that is covetous, bored, tired, hopeful, enticed or delighted.[7]

In one passage, too, Kaplan makes the same point (I think inconsistently with his other contentions):

The statement that a concert is boring seems somehow more "objective" (hence "justifiable") than a confession—by a yawn, for example —that we are bored by it, though both express the same attitude. Value-expressions may therefore resemble propositions because, in Santayana's phrase, we objectify our emotions, and attribute corresponding "properties" to the object.[8]

Richard Robinson who advocates the same type of theory, with due acknowledgments to Mackie, calls it a form of the emotive theory. Ethical words, according to him, "name unanalyzable qualities belonging to certain acts or objects in complete independence of all human feelings and thoughts." But "in this descriptive use the ethical words involve an error, because nothing has such an unanalyzable independent attribute as they name."[9] Robinson's position differs from Mackie's firstly in that he does not commit himself to any theory of "objectification" and secondly in that he is more explicit concerning the nature of the property or properties whose presence people falsely assert when they make a moral judgment. Mackie says nothing concerning the properties except that they are objectifications of our feelings of approval or disapproval. Robinson is quite explicit that these properties are non-natural in the sense in which this is claimed by Ross and other intuitionists. It should be added that Ross and Carritt hold a view exactly similar to Robinson's concerning all statements whose predicate is the word "beautiful." By "beautiful" according to Ross,

. . . we mean something entirely resident in the object, apart from relation to a mind. I am suggesting that we are deceived in thinking that

---

7. *General Theory of Value*, pp. 31-32. My italics.
8. "Are Moral Judgments Assertions?" *Philosophical Review*, 1942, pp. 288-289.
9. "The Emotive Theory of Ethics," *Aristotelian Society* Suppl. Vol. XXII (1948), pp. 83-84.

beautiful things have any such common attribute over and above the power of producing this aesthetic enjoyment.[10]

So also Carrit:

Aesthetic judgments, assertions, i.e., that things are beautiful, also, I think, generally *mean* to attribute to the thing a quality independent of anybody's thoughts or feelings. But so far as they do assert this, there are reasons for thinking that perhaps none of them are true in the sense in which they are thus meant.[11]

2. Is the "Pathetic Fallacy" Really a Fallacy?

IN EXAMINING the error theory I shall concentrate on Mackie's version of it. It seems to me more defensible since it is free from the additional objections to which Robinson's version is exposed, in view of the latter's partial agreement with intuitionism. I shall confine myself to two points. I shall firstly try to show that Mackie has not succeeded in producing any instances of "inside-out-objectifying" and that in fact all his (and all of Perry's and Kaplan's) instances are objective claims of an empirical nature, which are often known to be true. I shall in this Chapter confine myself entirely to non-moral examples. What I shall say here will be a preparation to broadly similar remarks about moral judgments in Chapter VII. Secondly, I shall try to show that in the very statement of this theory, Mackie is guilty of a serious but also instructive confusion.

Our subsequent discussion will be simplified if we clearly distinguish at this stage between:

(1) statements which assert that a certain thing, x, has, in virtue of certain features, F_1-F_x, the power to produce a certain emotion or state of mind in people of a certain kind, and

(2) statements which assert that x has certain features, e.g., the features F_1-F_x, referred to in (1).

Let us refer to statements of the first kind as "power-statements"

---

10. *The Right and the Good,* p. 128, note.
11. *Ethical and Political Thinking,* p. 30.

and to those of the second kind as "feature-statements." The statement "Ljuba Welitsch, in virtue of her vocal and dramatic ability as well as her physical appearance, has the power to excite lovers of opera" is an example of a power-statement. The sentence "Erna Berger's voice is securely controlled, she has a perfectly equalized scale and a natural legato style" is an example of a feature-statement. It is clear that in the sense in which we are using "objective," statements of both kinds are objective claims.

Next, let us introduce the term "pathetic statement" to refer to any sentence whose predicate is one or other of the words mentioned by Perry and Mackie; i.e., words like "hopeful," "amusing," "tiresome," "enticing," "foul," etc. Using this terminology, what I now wish to show is that, in any usual circumstances, pathetic statements are either feature-statements or else power-statements. I shall also show that they are often known to be true.

As my first example, I shall take the case of a boring talk. Let us assume that Horn and I are two FBI men working as undercover agents in the Communist party. My assignment on a certain day, we shall assume, was to listen to a speech by cell-leader, Comrade Trinchitella. Horn asks me, as we have dinner that day, "How was Trinchitella's speech?" I answer, "It was very boring as usual." I then elaborate: "The same old stuff—that Wall Street is plotting a war against the Soviet Union and the Eastern democracies, that the common people of the United States do not support the Wall Street policy as carried out by Truman and Acheson, that we must wherever possible support isolationist sentiments; and of course the same old language—'the bourgeoisie in its death struggle,' 'the wreckers and Trotzkyites who co-operate with the bourgeoisie,' 'the stoolpigeons and saboteurs in the Trade Unions,' 'the treacherous Social Democrats'; the same old picture of eventual world-wide victory and salvation; the same appeal to the desire of the members to feel important. . . ."

Let s_t be the statement "Trinchitella's speech was boring" and let F_t be the features of the speech described in the last paragraph. Now what s_t *refers* to are the features, F_t, or features more or less like them. As I and many other people with the same tastes and the same general background use "boring" in such circumstances,

s_t is a true statement if the speech really has features like F_t. s_t would be false in that case if Trinchitella's speech had really been very different—if, e.g., it had been a description of Communist spy-cells in the Atomic Energy Commission, the White House, or the Pentagon.

This point is of great importance. I shall therefore, before further analyzing the Trinchitella case, consider another example which may throw light on the matter. Horn and I, in addition to being FBI agents, are very interested in philosophy. One evening, when Horn is on duty, I go to N.Y.U. where Professor von Künkel has been announced to give a talk on "Das Ich und das Weltall." The next evening Horn asks me, "How was von Künkel's talk?" I answer, "Very boring." I then elaborate: "Certainly he was different from all other philosophers I ever heard, with the possible exception of the late Professor Hallett. He began by saying that he was going to synthesize the views of Hegel, Goedel, and August Bebel, but unfortunately neither I nor anybody else understood a single word he said from then on. He talked a lot about the new laws of logic—the Law of Infinite Reiteration and the Law of Excluded Integration—but he never throughout his entire lecture gave a single concrete example of anything. He did not even make a violent attack on any other philosophy or on his notorious enemies, Sensenbrenner and Heffelfinger, each of whom claims to be the discoverer of the Law of Infinite Reiteration. His delivery, too, was quite monotonous."

Let us call my statement "von Künkel's talk was boring" s_k and let us refer to the features of his talk listed in my elaboration as F_k. Now "boring" seems here to be a shorthand description of F_k or features more or less like them. s_k, as I and many other people use it, is true if von Künkel's speech really has features F_k or other features more or less like them. If his speech was really lucid, original, full of concrete illustrations and jokes worthy of Bertrand Russell or Danny Kaye, then s_k is false.

To return now to s_t—the statement "Trinchitella's speech was boring." s_t *refers* to F_t or features like F_t. Although it *expresses* my boredom, the sentence does not *refer* to it. The sentence does not refer to my boredom, since "Trinchitella's speech was boring as usual, but *I* was not bored" is not a self-contradiction. I might, for instance, without being guilty of a self-contradiction say "Trinchitella's speech was the same boring stuff that you and I know so well by now—but I was in such an excited frame of mind that nothing, not even Trinchitella, could bore me."

The same point may perhaps be brought home with greater force by considering a slightly different example. Supposing I am Bob Hope's manager and script-writer. I meet a friend very late one night who asks me, "How was Bob tonight?" I might answer, "Very entertaining, as usual." Then, without in any way contradicting myself, I might add, "But I wasn't entertained. I was too much occupied with thoughts concerning the decline of American literature" or "But I was not entertained—I have been hearing these same jokes now for ten nights running."

s_t, furthermore, is not *referring* to boredom on the part of Trinchitella's audience. I could, without any self-contradiction, say, "Trinchitella's speech was boring as usual, but, as usual, it thrilled and delighted his audience." The same, of course, holds for the statement "Künkel's speech was boring." I might have developed the latter statement without any self-contradiction as follows: "Although Künkel's speech was really tremendously boring, the people there were on the verge of ecstasy. It turned out that most of them were members of the Local Chapter of the Gesellschaft für die Synthese der Transzendental-philosophie mit der symbolischen Logik."

In asserting s_t and s_k, then, I am referring to certain features of the talk and not to my own boredom and certainly not to the boredom of the audience. This is not to deny that if lectures having these features did not generally bore me, I would not call such lectures boring. It is perfectly true, that is to say, that the *cause* of my using the word "boring" with this referent and not some other, is the fact that lectures having these features tend to bore me. But this does not mean that *what* I refer to is my boredom or tendency to be bored. Exactly corresponding remarks apply to "exciting," "entertaining," "dull," and most of the "pathetic" words that Perry mentions.

If we define "polyguous expression" to mean "any term which

has a large number of referents" then it is easy to see that terms like "boring," "amusing," "hopeful" and many others are polyguous. Moreover, they may be said to be polyguous "in two directions." Thus, firstly, the same person or people with the same general tastes and sensibilities do not refer to exactly the same features when saying of *different* things that they are boring. When I call Trinchitella's speech boring, I referred to F_t; when I called Künkel's speech boring I referred to F_k; and when I call Maggie Teyte's programs boring, I refer to something else again. But, secondly, people with different tastes and sensibilities will tend to refer to different features. A fanatical symbolic logician, talking to another, refers to quite different features when he says that a lecture is boring or exciting from those to which a Communist or a Kantian or a follower of Korzybski or an atomic scientist refers. But all their statements are feature-statements and hence objective claims.

Perry, in the passage I quoted, says "They (the tertiary qualities) lose all semblance of that inherence in the object which becomes increasingly clear and unmistakable in the case of color." The answer to this is: if you first assume that they are simple qualities like redness or hardness you won't indeed find them. But this is a false assumption, based on the superstition that to every adjective there corresponds *one* property. *The boringness is in the lecture but it is not a "one"—it is a "many."* The boringness is constituted by several features and by different features on different occasions.

Two of Mackie's examples—those about the foulness of the fungus and the economic value of an object—are not, I think, feature-statements. But they very plainly seem to be power-statements. They are statements asserting that certain objects have a certain causal property. As such they are objective claims and many statements of both types are known to be true.

I conclude therefore that what is called the pathetic fallacy is not in general a fallacy and that the contrary view is due to the tacit false assumption that words like "amusing," "boring," "hopeful," and "foul" are used to refer to simple qualities. We have here a case of *ignoratio elenchi* similar to that frequently committed in discussions of induction. When the ordinary man says, e.g., that past instances of the sun's rising justify the prediction that the sun will again rise tomorrow, it has been argued, he is mistaken. For there is no self-contradiction in saying "the sun has risen every day till now, but it will not rise tomorrow." This argument against commonsense is fallacious since it rests on the false assumption that what the ordinary man means by "justify" is *deductive* justification. Similarly, the enemies of the "pathetic fallacy" assume that the ordinary man, in speaking e.g., about the boringness of a lecture, means some simple quality over and above the absence of any jokes, of concrete illustrations, the speaker's monotonous delivery, etc. Then, since no such simple quality is discovered, they conclude that the ordinary man is always wrong when making a statement of this kind. The critics of the "pathetic fallacy" are quite right in the latter contention just as the "critics of induction" are right in maintaining that "the sun has risen every day till now but it will not rise tomorrow" is not a self-contradiction. But they are wrong in thinking that the ordinary man refers to a simple quality when he says that a lecture is boring.

I shall return to the same general topic in Chapter V. I hope that if the reader has any misgivings about my remarks in this section, they will be removed by my later discussions.

I ought perhaps to add that in rejecting Mackie's contention I am in no way asserting that sentences with a subject-predicate structure are *always* objective claims. Sometimes, as we shall see in the next section, they have no referent at all. And sometimes they are subjective claims. Thus supposing Spurzheim is a logician with whom I have been discussing induction and necessary propositions and the Verification Theory many times during the last five years. Supposing that throughout our discussions he has shown himself to be a skillful advocate of the views of Ayer and Schlick. Supposing furthermore Riker is a close personal friend whose reputation for accuracy and truthfulness is such that I never doubt any report he brings me. One day, as I meet Riker, he says to me: "Guess what I found out. Spurzheim is a Roman Catholic who goes to Mass every Sunday morning." To this I reply, "No. He is not!" In this context, "No—he is not (a Roman Catholic)," although having the subject-predicate structure, is not an objective claim.

In this context it is synonymous with "I find it difficult to believe this."

3. Moral and Metamoral Mistakes

I NOW WISH to introduce a distinction which Mackie fails to make and which will help us in later chapters in evaluating certain claims made by intuitionists concerning the ordinary man's "moral views." I wish to distinguish between what, if anything, a person *actually refers* to by a certain statement, and the belief he holds concerning the referent of his statement. Let A be a man who has made a statement, s. Let F be the referent of this statement. A, that is to say, would consider s true if F existed while he would consider s false if F did not exist. Let us suppose that A holds a mistaken view concerning what is the referent of s, i.e., that he makes the statement, "the referent of s is G." Let us refer to this latter statement as m_s. Let us finally suppose that F really exists and that s is therefore true. In that event we would have the following situation: s would be true but m_s would be false; A would be making a true statement but he would be holding a false view concerning the referent of this statement.

Let us consider another case. B has uttered a sentence s_1, which has no referent. Having no referent, it can be neither true nor false. B, however, believes that s_1 has a referent although he fails to specify what the referent is. He expresses this belief by saying, "s_1 is meaningful," a statement which we shall call m_{s1}. Here we have the following situation: s_1 is not false but m_{s1} *is* false. B, in putting forward s_1, whatever else he may be charged with, is not saying something false, but in making the statement m_{s1} about s_1 he *is* saying something false.

Both types of cases, abstractly sketched in the preceding paragraphs, are not mere logical possibilities, but actually occur. I shall first produce a few actual cases illustrating the second type. Whether the Verification Theory is correct or not, there can be no reasonable doubt that on some occasions philosophers have been guilty of meaningless statements, in the sense of offering sentences without a referent. This much was generally admitted long before the Verification Theory was first put forward. Those who maintain that nobody ever seriously makes a statement which has no meaning either do not mean "referent" or else draw the invalid inference that because no one ever seriously makes a statement without "having something in mind" therefore nobody ever seriously makes a statement without a referent. Let us consider Locke's theory concerning the "material support" of sense-qualities. Berkeley, in discussing this assertion, pointed out firstly that the word "support" was here used as a metaphor and what is more, as a metaphor which was incapable of being eliminated in favor of a non-metaphorical expression. Secondly, he came close to pointing out that the presence of the word "support" was the reason why Locke and others failed to realize the meaninglessness of their statement. "Support" usually has a perfectly clear meaning and thus automatically calls up certain images:

It is said extension is a mode or accident of matter, and that matter, is the substratum that supports it. Now I desire that you would explain what is meant by matter's *supporting* extension. . . . It is evident *support* cannot here be taken in its usual or literal sense, as when we say that pillars support a building: in what sense therefore must it be taken? . . . If we inquire into what the most accurate philosophers declare themselves to mean by *material substance,* we shall find them acknowledge, they have no other meaning annexed to those sounds, but the idea of being in general, together with the relative notion of its supporting accidents. The general idea of being appeareth to me the most abstract and incomprehensible of all other; and as for its supporting accidents, this, as we have just now observed, cannot be understood in the common sense of these words; it must therefore be taken in some other sense, but what that is they do not explain. So that when I consider the two parts or branches which make the signification of the words *material substance,* I am convinced there is no distinct meaning annexed to them.[12]

Now, Locke obviously believed, since he believed it to be true, that the statement, "there is a material substance which supports the sense-qualities," has a referent. Since this statement has no referent, *it* was not mistaken, but his implicit view that it has a referent was mistaken. Very similar remarks apply to Kantian

---

12. *Principles of Human Knowledge,* §§ 16-17. In one place, Locke himself anticipates Berkeley's point.

statements concerning the noumena and also concerning the "contributory" activities of the transcendental unity of apperception, to Spencer's statements about the Unknowable, to various theological pronouncements about the "Infinite's erupting into the finite," etc., etc.

There are also many instances where a person makes a true statement but holds a mistaken view concerning the statement's referent, ending up by believing his own true statement to be false. Consider, for instance, statements about free actions. Normally, when we distinguish between an action which has been freely performed and one which has not been freely performed, what we mean is roughly[13] (i) that the agent's will-power was intact—e.g., that he had not been drugged or hypnotized; (ii) that if he had chosen to do something else, something else would have happened or tended to happen—e.g., "I acted freely in not going to hear Fabian and in staying at home instead" implies that I was not paralyzed or chained against the walls of my living room; and (iii) that I had a choice between alternatives more than one of which was not unreasonably painful. Now, there are many actions which are freely performed in this sense. Therefore there are many statements to this effect which are true. E.g., the statement, "last night at Barney's I acted freely in ordering a steak rather than turkey or veal chops" is true, if "free" is used in the familiar sense just explained. Yet many people can without much difficulty be made to think that what they mean by "x is an action which has been freely performed" is "x is uncaused," or "no matter how far back the causal history of x is traced, there can always be found a choice on the agent's part." Of course, once people believe this, they conclude that no actions are really free. The mistake here is not the original statement that the action in question was free. The mistake is the view the person comes to hold temporarily concerning what he means by "free."

My next illustration comes from discussions of perception, especially the perception of pain. I have had numerous students who, as a result of taking courses in psychology or psysiology or

---

13. The word "free" is of course used in more than one sense. But for the purpose of this discussion there is no need to enter into these finer points.

both, maintain with conviction that when ordinary people (including themselves in their non-theoretical moments) say that they have a pain in a certain tooth or in a toe or in their stomach, they are mistaken. For, so they go on, pains can only exist in the brain. This, by the way, is a statement found in several textbooks of psychology and physiology. Those who hold this view are obviously mistaken concerning what ordinary people and they themselves in non-theoretical contexts refer to by such statements as "the pain is right where you were knocking, Doc.—on the upper right side." To say that the pain is in a certain place, P_1, simply means that it is *felt* in P_1. In this sense, a statement that a pain is in a certain tooth is perfectly true if it is really felt to be in that tooth. By "the pain in P_1" we do *not* normally mean "the last causal antecedent of the pain is in P_1."[14]

The case of absolute certainty is another good illustration of the same phenomenon. However, I have dealt with that case elsewhere[15] and shall not therefore say anything about it here. In Chapters VI and VIII, when we expose the mistaken view that ought-statements never "follow from" is-statements, we shall see another instance of this phenomenon—where people first make statements which are perfectly true, but then as a result of mistaking their own meaning, believe these statements to be false.

Returning now to Mackie, I wish to point out that he totally fails to distinguish between two very different theories both of which are implicit in different of his remarks. On the one hand he seems to maintain

(I) the view that all *moral judgments* are false.

On the other hand he seems to maintain

(II) that what is false is not the moral judgment, but *the meta-moral view which invariably accompanies it* and according to which the moral judgment has an objective referent.

14. For a very illuminating discussion of this and similar "paradoxes of perception," allegedly based on the facts of physics and physiology, cf. Ernest Nagel's article "Russell's Philosophy of Science," in *The Philosophy of Bertrand Russell*.

15. "Absolute Certainty and Ordinary Language," *Philosophical Studies*, 1950.

Insofar as Mackie's statements commit him to the second view, it is not clear whether he would say that moral judgments really have no referent or that they are subjective statements.

My analysis of moral judgments in Chapter VII will show, I hope, that (I) is false. It will also show that (II) is false, i.e., that if the ordinary man believes concerning his moral judgments that they have an objective referent, he is not always mistaken. But in one respect (II) is, I think, more plausible than (I). It seems to me utterly fantastic to suppose that *all* moral judgments, whether they are superstitious and uncritical or whether they are the result of experimentation and reflection, are false. It seems to me fantastic to suppose, for instance, that when Margaret Sanger, after directly witnessing for years the effects of uncontrolled reproduction among the working classes, concluded that the use of contraceptives is morally justified, she was as much in error as an ignorant, abusive, and bigoted religious fanatic like ex-Congresswoman Mary Norton, who maintained that the use of contraceptives is always wrong. It seems to me equally fantastic to believe that when a great educational pioneer like A. S. Neill asserts, on the basis of a wealth of empirical data, that there is nothing wrong with masturbation, he is no less making a mistake than the guilt- and fear-ridden, conventional, old schoolmasters who can never get a child to open up to them and who, on the basis of no empirical evidence whatsoever, maintain that masturbation is wicked. On the other hand, it is not fantastic to say that when ordinary people have attempted to answer metamoral questions, they have so far always been mistaken. Metamoral questions may be very intricate and a person not trained in logic—and even one who is trained in logic—may easily fail to make a certain distinction and as a result totally misinterpret the nature of moral judgments. This is actually what has happened, if my remarks in Chapter II were correct, in the case of the people who say, "What you mean when you say 'x is good' is that *you* approve of it."

4. Conclusions

FROM THE DISCUSSIONS of this chapter we can learn several lessons which may be summed up as follows:

1. From the fact that a person holds a false metamoral theory it does not follow that his moral judgment is also false.

2. From the fact that a sentence contains only words which usually occur in sentences which have a referent, it does not follow that the sentence has a referent.

3. The mere fact that a sentence is of the subject-predicate form does not show that it is an objective claim.

4. "Pathetic statements" are usually objective claims. But their referent is not some special simple quality. It is either a causal property or a set of *natural* qualities.

5. The predicates of pathetic statements tend to refer to different sets of features when applied to different objects and also when used by people with different tastes and backgrounds.

6. Although pathetic statements are not *about* anybody's feelings or reactions, the features to which the statements refer in any given case are nevertheless determined by felings and reactions.

CONTENTS

Chapter IV

Intuitionism

1. Types of Intuitionism

OBJECTIVE NON-NATURALISM or intuitionism is a theory which is often too hastily dismissed. Although I hope to show in this chapter that it is an untenable theory, I also believe that, in the course of defending their theories and attacking rival doctrines, intuitionists have contributed much that is of great importance.

Intuitionists make the claim that in addition to the senses and introspection human beings possess a further faculty which discloses to them certain objectively existing qualities or relations. The ethical predicates designate these or certain of these qualities and relations. Most intuitionists would say, I think, that this faculty of moral intuition is possessed by men in general and not only by the intuitionists, though some men may have it more fully developed than others. I am sure that most intuitionists would maintain that even the philosophers who deny the existence of such a faculty possess it nonetheless. Indeed any other view on this topic would be most implausible since intuitionists and non-intuitionists are using the ethical predicates in much the same way and are frequently in complete agreement on specific moral issues.

Most intuitionists of the present century express their view by saying that one or more of the ethical predicates designate a simple, unanalyzable quality or else a simple, unanalyzable relation.

[85]

These predicates are said to be indefinable in the same sense in which, e.g., "yellow" or "hard" or "pleasure" or "being angry" are indefinable: no genus-differentia synonyms are obtainable for them. Other ethical predicates, while not definable in terms of expressions which designate natural qualities or relations, are definable in terms of the indefinable ethical predicate or predicates. According to Moore, the indefinable ethical predicate is the word "good";[1] according to Ross there are two indefinable terms, namely "good" and "right";[2] according to Ewing, the indefinable term is "ought";[3] and according to Raphael it is "obligation."[4]

Many of the recent intuitionists have emphasized the importance of the relation designated by the word "fitting," which they regard as a simple and non-natural relation. They have claimed that many if not all ethical terms can be at least partly defined in terms of fittingness. I shall cite a passage from Broad who has defended a view of this type:

When I speak of anything as "right," I am always thinking of it as a factor in a certain wider total situation and I mean that it is "appropriately" or "fittingly" related to the rest of the situation. When I speak of anything as "wrong," I am thinking of it as "inappropriately" or "unfittingly" related to the rest of the situation. This is quite explicit when we say that love is the right emotion to feel to one's parents, or that pity and help are the right kinds of emotion and action in presence of undeserved suffering. . . . Fittingness or unfittingness is a direct ethical relation between an action or emotion and the total course of events in which it takes place.[5]

Most intuitionists would deny that the special faculty of moral intuition is closely analogous to a sense like sight or hearing. But they frequently write *as if* it were just another sense and some of them have explicitly maintained such a position. Thus Reid writes:

---

1. *Principia Ethica*, pp. 6 ff. In later writings, Moore seems willing to allow another non-natural quality (cf. *The Philosophy of G. E. Moore*, pp. 510-511).
2. *The Right and the Good* and *The Foundations of Ethics*.
3. *The Definition of Good*.
4. *The Moral Sense*.
5. *Five Types of Ethical Theory*, pp. 164-165.

The testimony of our moral faculty, like that of the external senses, is the testimony of nature, and we have the same reason to rely upon it. . . .

When Mr. Hume derives moral distinctions from a moral sense, I agree with him in words, but we differ about the meaning of the word sense. Every power to which the name of a sense has been given, is a power of judging of the objects of that sense, and has been accounted such in all ages; the moral sense therefore is the power of judging in morals. But Mr. Hume will have the moral sense to be only a power of feeling, without judging: This I take to be an abuse of a word.

It has got this name of sense, no doubt from some analogy which it is conceived to bear to the external senses. And if we have just notions of the office of the external senses the analogy is very evident, and I see no reason to take offence, as some have done, at the name of the moral sense.

In its dignity it is, without doubt, far superior to every other power of the mind; but there is this analogy between it and the external senses. That as by them we have not only the original conceptions of the various qualities of bodies, but the original judgments that this body has such a quality, that such another; so by our moral faculty, we have both the original conceptions of right and wrong in conduct, of merit and demerit, and the original judgments that this conduct is right, that is wrong; that this character has worth, that, demerit.[6]

In their explicit formulations, however, most intuitionists give an account which differs greatly from Reid's. The faculty of moral intuition is said to resemble closely or in fact to be an instance of "*intellectual* intuition" or "apriori insight." It is the same faculty by whose means we apprehend (in their view) the principles of logic and mathematics. In Raphael's words:

The first principles of morals must be acknowledged to be perceived *by the understanding*.[7]

In the situation 'A is aware that B is in pain' there is a moral relation between A and B which can be expressed by saying 'It is fitting for A to help B' or by saying 'A is under an obligation to help B.' (I myself do not find the first form of expression as satisfactory as the second). This relation arises from elements in the existing situation, that is from the fact that B is in pain and that A knows it. It does not arise from a

6. *Essays on the Active Powers of Man*, iii, Part III, 6 and Part V, 7.
7. *Op. cit.*, p. 189. My italics.

possible future situation which does not now exist. Means and ends,
causes and probable effects, have nothing to do with this relation; it is
logically entailed by the existing situation.[8]

To quote Ross:

If we turn to ask how we come to know these fundamental moral
principles, the answer seems to be that it is in the same way in which
we come to know the axioms of mathematics. Both alike seem to be
both synthetic and apriori; that is to say, we see the predicate, though
not included in the definition of the subject, to belong necessarily to
anything which satisfies that definition. And as in mathematics, it is
by intuitive induction that we grasp the general truths. We see first, for
instance, that a particular imagined act, as being productive of pleasure
to another, has a claim on us, and it is a very short and inevitable step
from this to seeing that any act, as possessing the same constitutive character, must have the same resultant character of prima facie rightness.[9]

Several recent writers[10] have charged that intuitionism ignores
the "dynamic" and "expressive" function of moral judgments.
This is a fair criticism of certain champions of intuitionism. But it
is no refutation of intuitionism. There is no reason why an intuitionist should not admit everything concerning the dynamic and
expressive functions of moral judgments which has been claimed
by defenders of the emotive theory. An intuitionist could consistently maintain that moral judgments have more than one function and that intuitionism is a theory concerning the nature of one
of these, namely, their cognitive function.

Several intuitionists have in fact made explicit statements along
these lines. Thus J. B. Mabbott writes:

The positive work of Stevenson and his followers is interesting and
largely acceptable. It is their denials which remain in doubt.[11]

Ross and Moore, too, explicitly admit that ethical terms are used

8. *Op. cit.*, p. 41. My italics.
9. *The Foundations of Ethics*, p. 320. For a similar view concerning aesthetic
principles cf. G. H. Joyce, *Principles of Natural Theology*, p. 136.
10. Ayer, "On the Analysis of Moral Judgments," *Horizon*, September 1949,
p. 178. Also Margaret MacDonald, "Ethics and the Ceremonial Use of Language," in *Philosophical Analysis* (ed. Max Black), p. 215.
11. "True and False in Morals," *Proceedings of the Aristotelian Society*,
Vol. XLIX, p. 112.

not only to designate non-natural moral qualities, but also to express the speaker's feelings of approval or disapproval.[12] Sidgwick, furthermore, anticipated even some of the most recent pronouncements of the "dynamic" philosophers:

When I speak of the cognition or judgment that "X ought to be done—in the stricter ethical sense of the term "ought"—as "dictate" or "precept" of reason to the persons to whom it relates; I imply that in *rational beings as such this cognition gives an impulse or motive to action.*[13]

2. Is it Possible to "Refute" Intuitionism?

THERE MUST BE SOMETHING profoundly inconclusive about all disputes where one party claims, for itself as well as for its opponents, the existence of a faculty which is denied by the other side. It must be in principle impossible in any such case to prove by any direct test who is speaking the truth. For, supposing that all of us possessed what John Wisdom once called the power of "extended introspection" by means of which we can experience the contents of another person's mind with the same directness with which we experience the contents of our own mind. Supposing then that a non-intuitionist investigates the mind of an intuitionist to discover whether such a faculty as moral intuition really exists. This plainly would be of no avail since, according to intuitionism, his mind is not at all essentially different from the mind of the intuitionist. It offers as many opportunities for the discovery of the special faculty as the mind of the intuitionist, and if contemplating his own mind was not enough, contemplation of another mind will hardly do the trick.

In a sense, then, intuitionism cannot be refuted—in the sense, that is, in which many specific empirical statements can be refuted. However, in another very important sense, intuitionism *can* be refuted. For intuitionists are never satisfied simply to claim the existence of this faculty of moral intuition. They also invariably (1) liken it to or identify it with other faculties by whose means

---

12. Cf. the passages quoted in Chapter I, Section 2.
13. *The Methods of Ethics*, p. 36. My italics.

we admittedly or allegedly come to know certain truths; and (2) they claim that certain facts can be accounted for by intuitionism but by no other metaethical theory. Now, if it is possible to show that the alleged facts in question are not really facts or else that they can be explained without invoking any special faculty of moral intuition, intuitionism will be shown to be an unnecessary, a redundant theory. If, in addition to this, we can show that all the analogies which intuitionists have put forward between moral intuition and other cognitive instruments are open to fatal objections, we shall have given very strong reasons for supposing that the intuitionists are somehow guilty of self-deception, misinterpreting certain ordinary experiences.

In this connection two admissions by well-known intuitionists are of great significance. The first of these comes from Broad. He warns that

rules which really rest on custom and the opinion of the society in which we have been brought up (and on nothing more) may gain the appearance of moral axioms.[14]

Maybe then other moral rules which in Broad's view are synthetic a priori propositions can also be shown to be something else though not necessarily resting merely on custom and the opinion of society.

The second admission comes from J. D. Mabbott who first quotes a statement by Richard Robinson:

A great reason in favor of the emotive theory of ethics is economy. The occurrence of emotive language, and of human feelings of approval and disapproval, is a fact in any case. If this fact by itself will explain human behavior and speech in matters of morals and valuation, it is unreasonable to hypothesize any further fact consisting in the appearance from time to time of the non-natural qualities wrongness and badness and the rest.

To this Mabbott adds:

I agree entirely with this statement. All I would add is that the last sentence is an unfulfilled conditional.[15]

---

14. *Five Types of Ethical Theory*, p. 216.
15. *Op. cit.*, p. 142.

Maybe it can be shown that "human behavior and speech in matters of morals and valuation" can be explained not along Mr. Robinson's lines but nevertheless without the introduction of non-natural qualities.

3. The Arguments for Intuitionism

I NOW PROPOSE to enumerate the facts or alleged facts which are said to be explicable only by intuitionism and not by any other moral philosophy. It would be admitted by most intuitionists, I think, that some of these facts are compatible with other forms of objectivism and that other of these facts are compatible with forms of subjectivism and the emotive theory. But *all of them together* (and some by themselves) are compatible only with intuitionism.

(i) Firstly, there is a certain fact which was already discussed in Chapter II in connection with the arguments against naive subjectivism. When a person makes a statement like, "the F.E.P.C. is a just bill" he does not mean anything which implies that the F.E.P.C. would cease to be a just bill if he or if any of his supporters ceased to favor it. This fact, although compatible with objective naturalism, is not compatible with any form of subjectivism or of the emotive theory.

(ii) People constantly make judgments to the effect that a certain person is "morally blind" or "morally insane." They also frequently say such things as that one man has a finer moral sensibility than another. All these statements are intelligible and many of them are true. This fact, though compatible with intuitionism and objective naturalism, is incompatible with subjectivism and the emotive theory.

The most obvious examples of people who, on certain topics are morally insane, are political and religious fanatics. There are countless people in the world who protest against the persecution of minorities and the suppression of civil liberties by their political or religious opponents but who condone and in fact favor persecution and suppression when perpetrated by their political or religious associates. Paul Robeson, Harlow Shapley, the Dean of Canterbury, on one side of the fence; Dean Inge, Cardinal Spellman, Father

Coughlin on the other I would cite as instances falling under this heading.

A friend of mine once had a teacher whom many people would regard as morally blind. Among other things it appears that this man was a member of the Communist Party and a lover of handsome boys. He saw nothing wrong in giving high grades and prizes to people who were academically inferior provided they were members of the Communist Party or handsome, or both. He saw nothing wrong in consistently hurting defenseless girls whose only sin was that they were girls and defenseless. In calling such a man morally blind we would be making an intelligible objective statement which, if my account of the man's actions is accurate, would be a true statement.

Mabbott has stated the same point in a more general way:

Sometimes when I find a divergence it shakes me, sometimes it does not. A disapproves of what I approve. A is a man I respect. He seems to me to try to do what he believes to be right. I hesitate to say dogmatically my view is as good as his. B disapproves of what I approve. B is a man for whom I have no respect. He makes no effort to keep up even to his own moral standards. My difference with him shakes me not at all. C differs from me. He is a man of scruple. He has often spotted some subtle moral issue I might have otherwise missed. He sees the relevance of related issues. I hesitate to claim as great finality for my judgment, having heard his divergence from it. D differs from me. He has regularly shown himself a man of no moral discrimination at all. He sees no difference between obviously different cases. He sees no relation between obviously related cases. He disapproves of stealing the railway company's crockery but sees nothing wrong in travelling without a ticket. He defends free enterprise with an honest conviction of the value of the individual, and treats his own staff in a way which it would be polite to describe as feudal. My difference from him worries me little. E differs from me. He is a man of rich experience. No walls have sealed him off from his fellows. No restrictive education or narrow profession has blinded him to human motives and human feelings. He is of the world but not worldly. My difference from him will worry me. F differs from me. He is a narrow man, shut off by his upbringing and his profession from human contacts, with a nature obviously warped and embittered by these handicaps. My difference from him worries me less. G differs from me. He is a man of good practical sence. His views about people and policy, when they can be checked, are highly reliable. His general attitude to life is reasonable. He is alert, critical and sensible.

My difference from him worries me. H differs from me. His judgment on non-moral matters is hopelessly bad. He is silly and unpractical in choice, superstitious and credulous in belief, hasty and rash and almost always wrong in his predictions about people or policy. My difference from him does not worry me. . . . But all these contrasts (A-B, C-D, etc.) presuppose objectivity. They are all incompatible with the view that "good" and "right" are just names for what a speaker approves and tries to make others approve.[16]

(iii) There is a certain quality of "immediacy"[17] about the way in which we come to hold moral views, especially when a recognition of our duties or obligations is concerned.

When we consider a particular act as a lie, or as the breaking of a promise, or as a gratuitous infliction of pain, we do not need to, and do not, fall back on a remembered general principle; we see the individual act to be by its very nature wrong.[18]

This fact of the "immediacy" of our moral judgments, an intuitionist might argue, while it was realized and emphasized by Hume and while it may be compatible with subjectivism, is clearly at variance with objective naturalism—with views like those of Bentham, Spencer, or Dewey.

(iv) When people engage in a moral dispute, their disagreement is often genuine. Occasionally they disagree then even though they agree about the consequences, the causes, and the empirical qualities of the subject of their judgments. The former fact by itself is incompatible with subjectivism, the latter with subjectivism as well as with all forms of objective naturalism.

(v) No anti-intuitionist theory can

explain the fact of moral obligation. . . . Moral obligation is neither habit nor fear, neither custom nor obedience, neither fashion nor deference, and it is not the obscure feeling of these. For what do we mean when we say that we ought to do certain things, and ought not to do certain other things? Clearly we do not mean that we are forced to do the one and forced not to do the other. Our zeal for righteousness may perhaps constrain us but nothing else need: and righteousness itself includes obligation. Neither the enactments of our rulers with their sanctions in

---

16. *Op. cit.*, pp. 149-150.
17. Cf. Raphael, *op. cit.*, pp. 182-183.
18. Ross, *The Foundations of Ethics*, p. 173.

the police court, nor the commands of God with the carnal and spiritual penalties which the lawyerly minds of priests have devised, are moral obligation itself. And obligation is neither custom nor habit. There are customary obligations, it is true; and just men, I suppose, have formed the habit of walking uprightly; but there are obligations to non-conformity too, and these are felt and acted on.[19]

"What is experienced is an objective bindingness."[20]

(vi) Finally, there is the fact that ethical terms cannot be analyzed into non-ethical terms, whether the latter refer to natural qualities or relations like pleasure or aid in the struggle for survival or being approved by a human being, or to "metaphysical" properties like harmony with the Absolute or obedience to the will of God. This, it has been claimed, shows that the referents of ethical terms are *sui generis* and knowable only by a special cognitive instrument which is distinct both from sense-observation and introspecion.[21]

To sum up: the facts referred to under (i) and (ii) are incompatible with subjectivism and the emotive theory, (iii) with objective naturalism, (iv) with subjectivism and objective naturalism, and (v) and (vi) with all theories other than intuitionism. As against this, I shall try to show later in this volume that some of these alleged "facts" are not really facts and that those which are can be accounted for without invoking a special faculty of moral intuition.

4. Arguments against Moral Intuition Conceived as a "Sixth Sense"

IN THIS and the next section I shall try to show that both of the usual descriptions of the faculty of moral intuition are untenable. In this section I shall deal with the description of moral intuition as a kind of "sixth sense." In the next section I shall discuss the view that the moral faculty is identical with a priori insight.

19. Laird, *A Study in Realism,* p. 136.
20. S. Orr, "The Cambridge Approach to Philosophy," *Australasian Journal of Psychology and Philosophy,* 1946, p. 39.
21. Cf. Moore's *Principia Ethica* and various earlier writers listed in Prior's **very** informative book *Logic and the Basis of Ethics.*

(i) There is a very well-known objection to the view that the moral intuition resembles a sense like the sense of sight or hearing. Mackie has stated this objection in the following words:

Although at any one time, in a particular social group there is fairly complete agreement about what is right, in other classes, in other countries, and above all in other periods of history and other cultures, the actual moral judgments or feelings are almost completely different, though perhaps there are a few feelings so natural to man that they are found everywhere. Now feelings may well change with changing conditions, but a judgment about objective fact should be everywhere the same: If we have a faculty of moral perception, it must be an extremely faulty one, liable not only to temporary illusions, as sight is, but to great and lasting error.[22]

We saw in preceding chapters that the mere fact of widespread disagreement on a given topic does not imply that the judgments of the rival parties are not objective or that neither of them can be shown to speak the truth. But this fact does appear to be relevant against a theory which maintains that the statements in question ascribe *simple* qualities to objects. For as regards the simple sense-qualities of objects there is never any widespread disagreement and certainly not one which can be correlated with differences in cultural background. An Indian mystic and the average American will differ very strongly on the rightness of self-denial, but they will not differ as regard the color of apples or the comparative hardness of chemical substances. A man who at one time judged love and kindness to be the greatest goods may, as a result of failures and disappointments, come to think that power and the admiration of crowds are greater goods; but no amount of failure and disappointment will make him see physical objects differently colored.

Intuitionists have made two replies to this objection. Firstly, they have said, a great deal of what passes for moral disagreement is really disagreement about something else. According to Blanshard there is "an ultimate identity of values lying beneath the surface differences"[23] on moral questions. On the most ultimate

---

22. *Op. cit.*, p. 78. Cf. also Schlick, *Problems of Ethics*, pp. 106-7.
23. "Personal Ethics," *op. cit.*, p. 126; cf. also Duncker, "Ethical Relativity," *Mind*, 1939.

moral questions just about everybody, American and German alike, is in agreement. The differences are differences of means due to conflicting *non-moral* beliefs. According to other intuitionists, e.g., Laird and Ewing, in most *so-called* moral disputes, the disputants are not really talking about the same thing:

Consider, for instance, our appreciation of poetry. The rhythm and cadence of a poem, the images it suggests, the nuances of its theme, the associations of much of its diction—all these and much more are relevant to our aesthetic approbation. Is it even remotely plausible to hold that different readers, all of whom are stimulated by what we call the same black marks upon the same white paper, catch the same rhythm, the same associations, the same images? Is not each of them appreciating or depreciating, something different? If they are, they are not setting a different value upon the same thing.

The same is true of moral values. There could hardly be a greater difference than the conduct and ideals, say, of Torquemada regarding toleration and the conduct and ideals of Spinoza. And yet we may reasonably ask whether the two were thinking of the same thing. Torquemada saw, as he supposed, the confusion and impotence of Spain through an unholy alliance between Christians and infidels for the purposes of mere commercial gain. The remedy, as he saw it, was to unite Church and State by force. Hence the auto-da-fé, the prohibition laid upon Christians to supply any Jew with even the necessaries of life—and the conquest of the Moors. What was nationality to Spinoza, whose ancestors had been driven into exile from this very Spain? And what could he think of institutional religion, when this exiled community had expelled him with contumely from their own synagogue for holding what he could not but believe? Surely he and Torquemada thought very different things.[24]

So it may well be the case that all differences in people's judgments whether certain actions are right or wrong or certain things good or bad are due to factors other than irreducible difference in ethical intuition.[25]

Ewing, however, allows the possibility of "irreducible differences in ethical intuition." Laird also freely admits that a greater part but *not* the whole "of our most crucial ethical differences" can be explained in this way.

------

24. Laird, *The Idea of Value*, pp. 232-3; cf. also his *Study in Realism*, p. 132.
25. Ewing, *op. cit.*, p. 22.

As for the rest, the "irreducible differences in ethical intuition," all we need to keep in mind is that

ethical intuition, like our other capacities, is presumably a developing factor and therefore may be capable of error.[26]
Something may be self evidently true without being self evident to everyone. There is no need to distrust Einstein because there are bushmen or super-bushmen, who fail to follow him.[27]

The fact that a color-blind man would see an apple as a shade of gray which the normal man sees as red does not prove that the apple is not red or that seeing is not a cognitive instrument which gives us information about a world external to us.

There are several flaws in these defenses of intuitionism. It is true that there is no reason to distrust Einstein because a bushman cannot follow him. But Einstein is not merely reporting his observations of sense-qualities. If Einstein and the bushman claimed to see the same object differently colored there would be no antecedent reason for preferring Einstein's report.

Quite generally, the often-invoked analogy with color-blindness breaks down at the crucial points. In the case of color-blindness, there are certain tests, accepted by everybody concerned, which decide who is and who is not color-blind. The color-blind person not only accepts these tests without protest but actually welcomes them since among other things they reduce his chance of getting killed in a car accident. It is not obvious, to say the least, that corresponding tests exist in the case of "irreducible" moral disputes.

Furthermore, according to intuitionism, moral judgments are objective claims. If one man says, "A is good" and another says, "A is bad" and if they are really talking about the same A then they cannot both be speaking the truth. One of them is the victim of a pseudo-intuition. Now, while the person with normal eyesight is superior to the color-blind man in the sense that he can, while the color-blind man cannot, discriminate between certain objectively existing colors, the color-blind man is nevertheless *not* wrong so far as his seeing is concerned. He sees gray as genuinely

---

26. Ewing, *ibid.*
27. Blanshard, *op. cit.*, p. 125.

as the normal man sees red. He is *not* the victim of anything like a pseudo-intuition. The gray he sees is perfectly "objective" in the sense that he sees it whether he wants to or not and that everybody else having the same visual constitution as he would also see it from his spatial position. The color-blind man is wrong only if and insofar as he *infers* that people with normal sight would see the same color.

If moral disputes were likened to the differences between genuine sense-perceptions on the one hand, and dreams or hallucinations on the other, the former of these objections would hold just as much. In either case, too, the appeal does nothing to explain the difference we pointed out: that "disagreements" as regards simple sense qualities *do not* whereas moral differences *do* vary with cultural differences or differences in the person's success and happiness in life.

It is impossible to discuss the other reply of the intuitionist adequately at this stage. I shall do so in Chapter IX. Here I would like to make two comments. Firstly, as Strawson has pointed out,[28] intuitionists tend to have it both ways with moral disputes. When producing evidence for their theory or when arguing against rival theories, they are anxious to maintain that moral disputes are genuine, that the disputants are talking about the very same thing. When defending intuitionism against objections like the one we are considering, they are anxious to say that moral disputes are not really genuine or at least that they are not really *moral* disagreements.

Secondly, even if it were the case that people never disagree in their "basic" or "fundamental" moral judgments, there seems to be no doubt that they quite often genuinely disagree—and *not merely as regards means*—on other moral questions. This topic will be fully explored in Chapter VIII, Section 5. I there produce an actual case, typical of many others, which is an unresolvable moral dispute not about means and which yet is genuine in the sense that the disputants are judging about the very same action.

It should be added to all this that, to accomplish the task assigned

---

28. In his review of Ewing's *Definition of Good, Mind,* 1949, pp. 87-88.

to it by the intuitionists, the appeal to moral blindness would imply that in *every* irreducible moral dispute or in every dispute containing an irreducible element, one of the two parties is morally blind. This, if I am not mistaken, would take in a great many people who are not at all morally blind in the sense we shall analyze fully later on, in which political and religious fanatics like Paul Robeson or Father Coughlin may be said to be morally blind. Calling people morally blind who are not inconsistent in their valuations and who are not deficient in human sympathy surely sounds like a violent paradox.

(ii) If any of the ethical predicates really designated simple and directly apprehended qualities like "yellow" or "hard" or "being angry" or simple relations like "being larger than" or "being to the right of" it would be a mystery how there could be any or so many non-intuitionists. It would also then be quite inexplicable how intuitionist philosophers could occasionally have doubts about the existence of such a faculty, as Moore, for instance, has openly confessed. It would be inexplicable too how intuitionists can so strongly disagree amongst themselves as to which ethical predicate designates something simple and whether the simple something is a quality or a relation. Where simple qualities like "yellow" or "hard" are concerned, no such disagreement exists or has ever existed.

These facts would not be inexplicable if intuitionists claimed the possession of a faculty only for themselves and if their behavior differed in certain significant ways from that of the rest of mankind, the way in which for instance the behavior of certain animals who perceive ultraviolet rays differs from that of human beings. But the behavior of intuitionists does not in general differ from that of non-intuitionists. Nor, as already mentioned, do intuitionist philosophers claim the possession of the moral intuition only for themselves.

One final comment: Ewing, Ross, Blanshard, and several other intuitionists constantly write as if "the ordinary man" were clearly on their side. They assert that subjectivism, emotivism, and in fact all forms of non-intuitionism are views held only by a few philosophers and their following. They give the impression that the ordinary man is naturally an intuitionist in much the same way as he quite undoubtedly is a believer in the reality of space and time and motion.

It is noteworthy that none of these claims is ever supported by experimental evidence. All my own observations fail to bear them out. For a number of years now I have been teaching several sections of "Introduction to Ethics" each year. I do my very best to present intuitionism fairly, in the words of its defenders—sometimes so much so that my students think I am an intuitionist. Most of my students are complete beginners in philosophy and very few have any intention of taking the subject up professionally. I have found that, with the exception of a theologian here and there, just about all the students find intuitionism quite incredible. The following story typifies the reaction of students as I have found it. At the beginning of one course, during a discussion of perception, I had told the class of G. E. Moore's defense of common sense against the idealistic philosophers. Later, in the course of presenting intuitionism, I mentioned the fact that Moore was one of the most famous of contemporary intuitionists. Upon this one man in the class asked, in a sarcastic tone of voice, "Did you say earlier in the semester that Moore was a philosopher of common sense?"

If the moral intuition were a faculty like seeing or hearing, such responses would never occur. This objection would hold in full force even if my groups were unrepresentative and even if I had been very unfair in my statement of intuitionism. Imagine the response I would get from any group of students if I maintained that nobody possesses the faculty of seeing or hearing!

5. Arguments against Moral Intuition Conceived as A Priori Insight

(i) Against the view that moral truths, like the propositions of mathematics and logic,[29] are known by a priori insight, there is

---

29. Throughout this discussion I am allowing, *for the sake of argument*, that the principles of logic and mathematics are known by a priori intuition.

the following standard objection: No moral truth is a universal proposition in the sense in which, to be a priori, a proposition must be a universal proposition. It is possible to imagine if not indeed to find exceptions to every moral judgment. Thus it is wrong to lie, but not in all conceivable circumstances. If a lie were to save a man's life without materially hurting anybody then in that case it would not be wrong to lie. It is wrong to break one's promise but not in all circumstances. If breaking a given promise led to the avoidance of great suffering without causing much inconvenience then in that instance it would not be wrong to break the promise.

Recent intuitionists, especially Ross and Raphael, claim to have taken care of this objection by moderating the form of the moral truths which, according to them, are known by a priori intuition. We do not, by a priori intuition, see that any act which produces pleasure in another, to use one of Ross' examples, must be right. What we see by a priori intuition is that any such act has *prima facie* rightness, or what is the same thing, that it has *a tendency to be right*. We do not see that any act which is a case of breaking a promise must be wrong. All we see is that any such act *tends to be wrong*.

This revised version of intuitionism has been criticizezd by P. F. Strawson in one of the most brilliant articles on ethics published in recent years. The change from "is right" to "tends to be right," Strawson writes,

is incompatible with the account you gave of the way in which we come to know both the moral characteristics of individual actions and states, and the moral generalizations themselves. You said that we intuit the moral characteristics as *following from* some empirically ascertainable features of the action or state. True, if we did so, we should have implicitly learned a moral generalization. But it would be wrong *asserting without qualification* the entailment of the moral characteristic by these other features of the case. In other words, and to take your instance, if it *ever* follows from the fact that an act has the empirically ascertainable features described by the phrase "being an act of promise keeping," that act is right, then it *always* follows, from the fact that an act is of this kind, that it has this moral quality. If, then, it is true that we intuit moral characteristics as thus "following from" the others, it is false that the implied generalizations require the "trifling amendments"; and if it is true that they require the amendment, it is false that we so intuit moral characteristics.[30]

An intuitionist of the Ross-Raphael type would presumably reply to this objection that the older form of intuitionism requires to be amended not only as regards the universal moral truths which the a priori intuition discloses, but also concerning our cognition in a single case. In a single case, too, what is seen is not that this action, being an instance of producing pleasure, is right, but that, being an act which produces pleasure, it has a tendency to be right. That it is right and not merely *prima facie* right we could realize only if in addition to knowing that it produces pleasure we knew a great many other things about it.

Such an answer, however, presupposes the absurd view that tending-to-have-a-quality is itself a quality. To quote Strawson once more:

> When we say of swans that they tend to be white, we are not ascribing a certain quality, namely, "tending to be white," to each individual swan. We are saying that the number of swans which are white exceeds the number of those which are not, that if anything is a swan, the chances are that it will be white. When we say that Welshmen tend to be good singers, we mean that most Welshmen sing well; and when we say, of an *individual* Welshman, that *he* tends to sing well, we mean that he sings well, more often than not. In all such cases, we are talking of a *class* of things or occasions or events; and saying, not that *all* members of the class have the property of *tending-to-have* a certain characteristic, but that *most* members of the class do in fact have that characteristic. Nobody would accept the claim that a sentence of the form "*Most* As are Bs" expresses a necessary proposition. Is the claim made more plausible by rewriting the proposition in the form "All As tend to be Bs?"[31]

In other words, it is no more plausible to maintain that "Every action which produces pleasure in another has a tendency to be

---

30. "Ethical Intuitionism," *Philosophy*, 1949, pp. 29-30. Strawson's article is in the form of a dialogue. The "you" refers to the defender of the Ross-Raphael type of intuitionism.

31. *Op. cit.*, p. 29.

right" is known a priori than that *"most* actions which produce pleasure in others are right" is known a priori.

(ii) The objection from the fact of widespread disagreement on moral topics is I think no less fatal to the view that there is an a priori moral intuition than to the sixth-sense theory. For, in all other domains which, according to these philosophers, we know by a priori intuition, no such widespread disagreements exist. Where there are disagreements they tend to be temporary and are quickly removed by a fresh examination of the problem.

6. Conclusions

As IN THE LAST two chapters, we shall list the main new facts of which our discussions have made us aware.

1. It is meaningful and frequently true to say of a person that he is morally blind, of another that he is morally insane, and of a third that he has a well developed moral sensibility.

2. There is a quality of "immediacy" to many of our moral judgments very like that of judgments reporting immediate sense experiences or introspections.

3. When people seriously assert that they are obliged to do a certain thing, then whatever they may *express* by their statement, they mean to say that they are objectively bound to perform the action in question.

An adequate metaethic must take account of all these facts.

CONTENTS

Chapter V

"The Steak at Barney's
is Rather Nice"

BEFORE STATING my own answer to the three basic questions of this study, I wish to offer some remarks concerning firstly what might be called the logic of judgments of taste, and secondly the logic of imperatives. In this chapter I shall deal with judgments of taste; in the next chapter I shall deal with imperatives.

The topic I am about to discuss has hardly been treated at all by philosophers. This is a great misfortune since, as I hope to show, a thorough discussion of it throws very much light on the nature of moral judgments, making some famous theories quite incredible.

I propose to begin by spending a great deal of effort to determine the meanings of the word "nice," as applied to foods or dishes in different circumstances. Our conclusions about the meanings of "nice" will apply, with suitable modifications, to words like "fine," "splendid," "excellent," "awful," "mediocre," and many more, as used in connection with the same type of object.

1. Mr. Horn and the Steak
at Barney's

LET US CONSIDER the following situation (Situation I): Horn, a friend of mine who lives in Oklahoma, has arrived in New York

for a visit. Before deciding where to eat, he asks me the following
question: "What is the steak like at Barney's, the place we passed
on the way from the station?" It should be added that both Horn
and I are, at any rate as regards food, persons of very average
(Western) taste. Both of us, furthermore, know this about each
other. Now, each of the following three answers would, in the
circumstances, give useful information to Horn—the information
or at least the sort of information he wants to obtain:

Answer A: "The steak at Barney's is always tender, made of
very fresh meat, fairly thick but rather small in size, and it is done
to the exact degree of rareness or otherwise that the customer
desires."

Answer B: "The steak at Barney's is always rather nice."

Answer C: "I rather like the steak at Barney's."

It is important to be clear about the likenesses and differences
between answers A and B. If the steak at Barney's is really always
tender, made of the freshest meat, fairly thick but rather small,
and done to the exact degree of rareness that the customer desires,
then answer A would of course be a true statement. If on the other
hand the steak at Barney's is not always both tender and made of
the freshest meat, and fairly thick but rather small, and done to
the exact degree of rareness the customer desires, then answer A
is false, though if it only lacks one of these features we would still
say it came pretty close to the truth or that it was "nearly" or
"pretty" true.

The facts which would make answer A a true statement would
equally make answer B a true statement: if Horn were to eat steaks
regularly at Barney's and if he invariably found them to be tender,
made of the freshest meat, and so on, then he would undoubtedly
be willing to say that I had spoken the truth, that the steak at
Barney's is really rather nice. However, not all the sets of facts
which serve to falsify answer A would ipso facto falsify answer B.
Some would, others would not. In all the following sets of circumstances, answer A would be false.

(1) The steak at Barney's is always stale, peppery, thin, rather
small, and never done to the exact degree of rareness or otherwise
desired.

(2) It is always tough, stale, thick, large and done to the exact degree of rareness desired.

(3) It is always tender, fresh, thin but large, and done pretty much to the degree of rareness the customer desires.

(4) It is always tender, fairly fresh, middle thick and large and done to the exact degree of rareness desired.

Answer B on the other hand, would be false only in cases (1) and (2), but not in cases (3) and (4). A person with average taste calls a steak nice when it is tender, fresh, thin but large, and done pretty much to the degree of rareness desired as readily as when it is tender, made of the freshest meat, fairly thick but rather small in size and done to the exact degree of rareness the customer desires.

The relation between answer A and answer B is somewhat like the relation between the statement, "I shall get to the office not earlier than 3:59 and not later than 4:01" and the statement, "I shall get to the office around 4." The facts which would make the former statement true would ipso facto make the latter statement true: if, e.g., I came to the office at 3:59 sharp both statements would be true. Some of the facts, furthermore, which would make the former statement false would also make the latter statement false. Thus if I got to the office at 6:05 this would make both statements false. However some of the facts which would falsify the first statement would not falsify the second. For instance, if I got to the office at 4:04 this would make the first statement false but it would make the second statement true.

We may sum up the relations between these two statements by saying "I shall get the the office around 4" says, in an indefinite or less definite way, the same sort of thing as "I shall get to the office not earlier than 3:49 and not later than 4:01." Similarly, answer B says, in a vague way, the same sort of thing as answer A. "I shall get to the office around 4" is in most contexts equivalent to "I shall get to the office at 4 or at 3:59 or at 3:58 or at 3:57 or at 3:56 or at 4:01 or at 4:03, etc." Similarly, in the above context, answer B is equivalent to "The steak at Barney's is either tender, fresh, fairly thick but rather small, and done to the exact degree of rareness desired, or tender, fresh, thin but rather large, and done pretty much to the degree of rareness desired or tender, fresh, middle thick and large, and done more or less to the degree of rareness desired, etc."

This conclusion that "The steak at Barney's is nice" is a vague statement must not be misinterpreted in either of two ways: firstly, this in no way implies that it is a "subjective claim." On the contrary, it is clearly an objective claim, in the sense in which we decided to use this term in Chapter I, Section 5. It is not a statement *about* my feelings or attitude, but about the features of the steak at Barney's. If I suddenly came to dislike steaks which are tender, fresh, fairly thick but rather small, and done to the exact degree of rareness desired, or which are tender, fresh, fairly thin but rather large and more or less done to the degree of rareness desired, this would not falsify my statement "The steak at Barney's is nice," as meant at the time at which I made it, though presumably I would, from then on, start using the word "nice" in a different sense. In fact even if at the time at which I made the statement I really, contrary to Horn's belief, disliked steaks which are tender, fresh, and so on, my answer B would still not be false. For I might have deliberately adjusted by usage of "nice" to that of the person of average taste.

The following parallel may help to make this clear: on a midsummer day my friend Riker pays me a visit. Both of us are accustomed to living in what geographers call the temperate zones —in climate such as prevails in New York City. Both of us are people with a fairly average constitution and we know this about each other. As he enters my apartment, I ask Riker: "What is it like outside?" He answers: "It's terribly hot." This statement of his is obviously an objective claim meaning something like "The temperature is well above 85 degrees." If the temperature were in fact 45 degrees the statement would clearly be false. I also have a friend by the name of Mittelmann who, until very recently, spent his life near the equator, i.e., in what is called the torrid zone. He never feels hot unless the temperature is well over 105 degrees. Supposing now Mittelmann visits me one day when the temperature is in fact 95 degrees, but he does not feel hot at all and to my question, "What is it like outside?" he replies, "It's warm, but no more." His statement, too, is obviously an objective claim having

more or less the same referent as Riker's statement "It's terribly
hot." However, Mittelman might very well have discovered by the
time he visits me that locals like myself refer to temperatures which
he calls "warm" as "terribly hot" and then he might well answer
my question in the same way as Riker answered it—by saying "It's
terribly hot outside." He would then be using the word "terribly
hot" in a sense different from that in which he used it while living
in equatorial regions, but his statement would, as before, be an
objective claim.

The fact that answer B, as given in a situation like Situation I, is
an objective claim can also be made apparent in the following way:
supposing Horn and I—both of us, it will be remembered, are persons of average Western taste—stand outside the Red Coach Grill
debating whether we should go inside and order a steak. Neither
of us has ever before had a meal at the Red Coach Grill. Horn
says, "I venture the guess that the steak is rather nice here" to which
I retort, "I venture to guess that it is absolutely awful." Now, supposing the steak at the Red Coach Grill is always tough, stale, thin,
small and done to a degree of rareness which was not desired, then
undoubtedly my statement will be true, and Horn's will be false.
On the other hand, if the steak at the Red Coach Grill is always
either tender, fresh, thin but large and done to the exact degree of
rareness desired, or else tender, fresh, thick but not large, and more
or less done to the degree of rareness desired, his statement would
be true and mine would be false. Of course both of us might be
wrong, but at least one of us must be wrong. Our statements are
logically incompatible. Thus we cannot both be making autobiographical or subjective claims.

I hope I have made it clear that in saying answer B is indefinite
or vague one does not imply that it is a subjective claim. I now
have to make it clear also that to say answer B is indefinite in no
way implies that it is useless. If the steak at Barney's is in fact
tender, fresh, fairly thick but rather small and done to the exact
degree of rareness desired, then undoubtedly answer A would provide Horn with more information than answer B. But even then
answer B would not be useless. It would give him a general, rough
idea of what the steak is like—all that he might need in order to

decide whether to try Barney's or not. Supposing however that
sometimes at Barney's the steak is tender, fresh, thick but small
and done to the exact degree of rareness desired and at other times
it is tender, fairly fresh, thin but large and done to the exact degree
of rareness desired and that on many occasions it is tender, fresh,
fairly thick and large, but done only very approximately to the
degree of rareness desired. Under those circumstances, answer A
would mislead Horn while answer B would not mislead him. Under
those circumstances answer B would be the only reasonably brief
way of giving him the information he is seeking.

Answer B differs from answer A not only in saying the same
sort of thing more indefinitely. Answer A *expresses* only the
speaker's belief that the steak has the features mentioned without
also expressing a favorable or unfavorable attitude on his part towards the steak. Answer B on the other hand expresses not only a
belief of this sort but also a favorable attitude. Of course together
with a certain tone or in a certain context, answer A may express
this attitude also, but answer B does it simply in virtue of the use
of the word "nice."

It is necessary to insist on the following point with the greatest
possible emphasis: although it is our taste, our likes and dislikes
which determine what features we refer to when we call a steak
(or some other dish) nice, a statement like answer B is an objective
claim. It asserts that these features belong to the steak at Barney's.
It does not *assert* that we like steaks having these features.

One further remark concerning answer B must here be added.
Although many features of the steak are relevant to its niceness
or otherwise, some certainly are not. Thus, for instance, its shape
is not relevant. If it is tender and fresh and done to the exact degree
of rareness desired then it is nice whether it has an elliptical, a
rectangular, or a rhomboid shape. If it is tough, stale and not done
to the degree of rareness desired then it is not nice, no matter what
its shape may be. Supposing people started liking steaks only if
among other things, they had a rectangular shape. Then their shape
would become relevant to their niceness. At the same time, however, the meaning of "nice" would have changed. As "nice" is
used now by members of the Western taste-community, the shape

of a steak is irrelevant to its niceness. We shall make use of these facts when discussing the question of moral arguments in Chapter VIII.

Let $F_1 \ldots F_x$ be the features to one or other set of which answer B refers—i.e., the steak's tenderness, its freshness, etc. Now, it is very interesting to observe that if somebody were to ask, "What *reasons* are there for saying that the steak at Barney's is nice?" one perfectly appropriate answer would be an enumeration of one or other set of $F_1 \ldots F_x$. It is interesting to notice this because unless one keeps in mind two facts, one may here easily be tempted into the view that the steak's niceness is some special quality over and above $F_1 \ldots F_x$. Not to fall into this temptation all we have to do is to remember firstly that answer B, in addition to referring to $F_1 \ldots F_x$, also expresses the speaker's pro-attitude towards the steak at Barney's, and secondly that, as we pointed out in Chapter I, Section 6, there is such a thing as a reason for an attitude or an emotion.

The question, "What reasons are there for saying that the steak at Barney's is nice?" may then either mean (i) "What reasons are there for supposing that the steak really has the features referred to in answer B?" or (ii) "What are the features of the steak which are the reasons for your favorable attitude expressed by answer B?" If the features have not yet been enumerated the question can only mean (ii). The fact then that $F_1 \ldots F_x$ can be the reason for the steak's niceness does not show that the referent of answer B is something other than these features. What it shows is that the same features which are the referent of answer B are also the reasons of the attitude which the sentence expresses.

I next wish to return to a discussion of answer C—i.e., the statement, "I rather like the steak at Barney's," made in reply to Horn's question, "What is the steak like at Barney's?" I wish to throw light on the "logic" of this type of statement and its relation to answer B.

The main point to be observed here is that while in a somewhat narrow sense the two statements are not synonymous, in a broader sense, which it is not difficult to describe, they do mean the same. Answers B and C do not mean the same in the sense that their referents are not identical. "I like the steak at Barney's" is not false

even if the steak there is always tough and stale and small and is
never done to the degree of rareness desired. It *is* false if I don't
really like the steak there, even though it always is tender, and
fresh and thick and done to the exact degree of rareness desired.

However, the two statements do mean the same in the sense that
they have *the same force or do the same work*: they both, if true,
equally give Horn the information he wants *concerning the steak
at Barney's* and they both, if false, equally mislead him concerning
the steak there. The reason for this is, of course, the fact that answer
C, in what in Chapter I, Section 6 we called sense (3) of the word,
implies answer B. Being a member of the Western taste-community,
I would not like a steak unless it is either tender, made of fresh
meat, thick but rather small, and done to the exact degree of rareness desired, or unless it is tender, fresh, thin but large and done
pretty much to the degree of rareness desired or . . .

That answers B and C are in this way synonymous is also apparent from the fact that Horn might instead of using the words,
"What is the steak like at Barney's?" just as appropriately have
framed his question as, "How do you like the steak at Barney's?"
In contexts like Situation I we use these two forms of speech quite
interchangeably to express our desire for information concerning
certain events or objects: "How was last night's concert?" and
"How did you like the concert last night?" or "How was Truman's
speech?" and "How did you like Truman's speech?", and so forth.

Observing this synonymity between statements like "The steak
at Barney's is nice" and "I like the steak at Barney's," many people
have inferred that statements of the former type are "merely subjective," that they are merely assertions about or expressions of the
speaker's taste. Countless people, including many philosophers,
have thus taken for granted that a theory corresponding to naive
subjectivism is a correct account of statements like answer B—
statements concerning the niceness or otherwise of food, the excellence or otherwise of drink, and the like. It is not difficult to see,
however, that what the synonymity between statements like answer B and statements like answer C proves is not that statements
of the B-type are "merely subjective." It proves that, contrary to

linguistic appearances, statements of the C-type are *not* merely subjective.

It is a fact, which philosophers have unduly neglected, that sentences with an autobiographical referent are frequently offered for the purpose of giving *non*-autobiographical information. Often of course, autobiographical sentences *are* used to give autobiographical information. Thus a man who is treated by a doctor for lack of appetite may one day come in and relate with satisfaction, "This week for the first time I enjoyed a dish. I really liked the steak at Barney's last Monday and every evening at seven I feel a genuine desire to go back to Barney's and each time I order a steak and like it." Or a man, filling in a questionnaire in connection with applying for a position, may write: "I don't approve of gambling, drinking or loose women and I do not believe that Negroes or Jews are the equals of white Christians." The Objective of the autobiographical statements in *these* cases is to give information, maybe inaccurate information, concerning the person who makes them. But in many other cases, statements with an autobiographical referent have a different Objective.

Thus supposing a Communist, who has never before heard of Ambassador Davies' book about the Soviet Union, sees it displayed in the window of a bookshop. He is not familiar with the political views of the owner of the shop. At the next meeting he asks the leader of his cell: "This book about the Soviet Union by Ambassador Davies—what is it like?" The leader answers, "I liked it very much indeed." This answer, although it has an autobiographical referent and although the questioner wanted information concerning the book and not concerning the leader, is perfectly appropriate. It is perfectly appropriate because it serves to give the questioner the sort of information he wants—in this case obviously that the book is a pro Soviet book. Countless similar examples could be given.

Autobiographical sentences such as answer C have a certain resemblance to sentences like "It is my conviction that war will break out between Russia and America within six months," when they are employed as *objective* statements. In both cases the linguistic

form is typical of autobiographical statements and yet in both
cases the Objective is the giving of non-autobiographical information. But here the resemblance ends. Sentences like answer C
have, while sentences like "It is my conviction that war will break
out between Russia and America within six months" do not have,
an autobiographical referent.

2. Mr. Ved and the Steak at the Pen and Pencil

WE SHALL NOW PROCEED to consider another instructive case which
we shall call Situation II. Ved Perkasch Managdala, for short Ved,
is the son of a rich New Delhi family now studying economics at
Columbia University in New York. His schooling at home was
conducted in the English language which he knows better than
Hindustani. Like most Indians, he likes steak only if it is tough,
peppery, thin and burnt. If it lacks one of these features he does
not like it and if it lacks all of them he detests it. For many months
all the steaks Ved tried in New York, whether he went to the Old
Brew House or the Press Box, to the Brass Rail or to Barney's,
turned out to be what he refers to as "awful" steaks. A few days
ago he chanced to go to the Pen and Pencil, a place favored by
members of the Indian delegation to the United Nations and by
Indian journalists. There, to his pleasant surprise, he got a steak
which was peppery, tough, thin and burnt. He has been going
back there every day since and he always comes back murmuring,
"At the Pen and Pencil they serve a steak which is rather nice—
almost as nice as the steaks I used to get at home." Yesterday he
persuaded Horn to go to the Pen and Pencil with him. I joined
them as they were drinking their coffee.

Horn: This was the most awful steak I ever saw or tasted.

Ved: It was rather a nice steak.

Horn: But it was so tough!

Ved: It sure was. That's one of the things that made it nice.

Horn: It was so seasoned, so peppery! I don't understand you
taking me here.

Ved: The pepper made it delicious.

Let us call Ved's statement, "The steak at the Pen and Pencil is rather nice" answer D and let us refer to Horn's (or my) statement, "The steak at the Pen and Pencil is not nice" as answer E. Several points are quite plain after what has already been said: Ved's answer D is as much an objective claim as my answer B— "The steak at Barney's is nice." Both of us, when we say that a steak is nice, assert something about the steak's features and, though we also *express* something concerning ourselves, we are both making objective claims but *different* claims. Our statements have different referents. Thus answers D and E are not at all logically incompatible, although both are objective claims.

3. The Vegetable Salad at the President Cafeteria

IN SITUATION I we were dealing with people who came from the same "taste-community." In Situation II we were dealing with people coming from different taste-communities. In Situation III, to which we now turn, we are again confining our attention to people from the same general taste-community.

Horn, Hedemacher and Belotti are three business men from Oklahoma, who recently visited New York, staying at the Lexington Hotel on 48th Street and Lexington Avenue. One evening, after their return to Oklahoma, the Belottis are visiting the Horns. Mrs. Horn is asking questions about the food in New York. After reports concerning turkey, meat, and dessert, Horn at last turns to the topic of salads:

HORN: There is a place near Lexington Avenue, called the President Cafeteria, where they have a truly splendid vegetable salad. The vegetable salad there contains, of course, a large variety of fresh vegetables. But in with the vegetables they give you chunks of Virginia ham and Romano cheese. The salad is adorned with radishes and green peppers and the whole thing is soaked in strong vinegar sauce specially imported from Munzenmeyer's famous factory in Kramatneusiedl.

BELOTTI: I don't know what has come over you, Horn! The vegetable salad at the President Cafeteria was awful stuff. I distinctly remember you complaining the last time we went to the President about the

fact that their vegetable salads are so plain, that they contained no
ham or cheese, and that they are so dreadfully dry. The dish you
painted I never once saw or tasted at the President Cafeteria.

HORN: You have got the places all mixed up. The place you are talking
about, where I complained about the dullness of the vegetable salad,
is the Lexington Cafeteria. I don't think you ever went to the
President. That's the one ten blocks away from our hotel to which
I went on my own on the day you had to see Lord Crook of the
British delegation.

Assuming that Belotti was really confusing the Lexington with
the President, it is clear that he was making a false statement when
he said that the vegetable salad at the President was awful, while
Horn was making a true statement when he said that the vegetable
salad was wonderful there. Horn and Belotti used "wonderful" and
"awful" in the same or substantially the same sense here and thus
their statements were mutually incompatible.

The next evening, the Horns visit the Hedemachers. The topic
of discussion is again the food in New York. But Hedemacher,
like Horn, does not confuse any of the places at which he ate.

HORN: There is a place in New York you must not miss when you go
there next year, Mrs. Hedemacher! It's called the President Cafeteria and their vegetable salad is superior indeed.

HEDEMACHER: Don't listen to him—it's awful stuff.

HORN: I don't understand you, Hedemacher. Have you forgotten the
pieces of aged Romano cheese and lean Virginia ham, the pieces
of chopped egg and the finely cut onions which enhanced the well
varied vegetables? Have you forgotten that strong vinegar sauce
imported from Austria? I suppose you prefer the dull tasteless
leaves at Hans Jager's, or the Wisconsin Swiss Cheese they throw
into the salads at Patricia Murphy's.

HEDEMACHER: Unfortunately I have not even now forgotten the so-
called "enhancements" of the vegetable salad at the President.
Onions and chopped egg, Romano cheese and Virginia ham, however delicious they may be in conjunction with other things, spoil
a vegetable salad. I eat a vegetable salad to enjoy the vegetables.
At the President the taste of the vegetables is drowned out by all
these so-called enhancements. As for the vinegar sauce, I cannot
stand it. The one thing I really like at the President Cafeteria is
their Russian dressing, but instead of letting me pour this over the
vegetable salad, they had to spoil it with that awful vinegar sauce.

Horn's "dispute" with Hedemacher is of the same sort as his dispute with Ved over the niceness of the steak at the Pen and Pencil. Horn and Hedemacher do *not* mean the same by "wonderful" and "awful," when these terms are applied to vegetable salads. Their statements, "The salad in splendid" and "The salad is awful" are therefore logically compatible, although both are objective claims.

4. Broiled Chinchilla
Soaked in Vermouth

WE SHALL NOW CONSIDER Situation IV—a situation which is very different from all the others we so far considered. Gangle is a man with a reputation for having very bizarre tastes in food. He hates steak, chicken and duck, for instance, but likes horse flesh, roasted pigeons, fried rats on hovis toast, and particularly filet of bear. Mrs. Horn, herself a person of average Western taste, is famed for her accurate perception of qualities perceived through the sense of taste. Gangle is invited for dinner at the Horns. He knows that Mrs. Horn never misses the feature of any dish and she knows that his tastes are very strange. She is trying to prepare the most bizarre possible dish, and finally, after carefully tasting different candidates for the position, she decides upon broiled chinchilla soaked in vermouth. After everybody has finished with the chinchilla, Mrs. Horn turns to Gangle and asks him: "Well Mr. Gangle, how was the chinchilla?" Gangle sincerely answers: "It was very nice."

Let us call this statement of Gangle's answer F. Gangle, when he gave this answer, knew that Mrs. Horn was not asking for information concerning the features of the chinchilla, for she knew these as well if not better than anybody else. She was interested in whether he, Gangle, liked it or not. His answer, "It was very nice," assuming Gangle to be sincere about the matter, is perfectly to the point. It gives Mrs. Horn the desired information, i.e., that he liked it.

Now, I do not think the rules governing the usage of the word "meaning" in its sense of "referent" are sufficiently definite to determine whether answer F *refers* to any features of the chinchilla. What *is* clear beyond any doubt is that the Objective of answer F is the conveying of the information that Gangle himself liked the chinchilla. The emphasis here is clearly on his liking and not on the features of the dish which is liked.

Nevertheless, the features of the chinchilla enter into the situation even here. For if somebody asked Gangle, "What are the reasons for maintaining that the chinchilla was nice?" he would undoubtedly enumerate certain of its features. And on another occasion, if somebody asked him, "What is the chinchilla like at Horn's?" he might answer, "It is very nice," this time *referring to* the features which he before gave as reasons.

It should be added that there are many actual cases which resemble Situation IV in that what is in question is the attitude of the speaker and not the features of the object.

5. Summary of Conclusions

LET US NOW TRY and sum up all that we have learned concerning the meanings of "nice" as applied to dishes. Let us refer to sentences of the form "x is nice," where x stands for some food or other, as "food-evaluations"; and let us refer to the situations in which such statements are made as "taste-situations." In all taste-situations, we came across (1) *dishes having certain features* and (2) *favorable or unfavorable attitudes* toward these dishes on the part of the various people involved. The features in question are, one and all, observable, empirical features. At no stage was there the least need to appeal to "non-natural" features.

The word "nice," we also found, has meaning in all three senses of the word and its meaning, in all senses, varies a great deal from type of situation to type of situation. To be more specific:

1. The Objective of food-evaluations differs greatly. In some of our cases it was the giving of information concerning the features of the dish. In other cases the Objective is the supplying of information concerning the author of the statement.

2. Food evaluations are always either equivalent to or else imply in sense (2) or (3) statements concerning the features of the dish

in question. In other words, they either are or else imply objective claims.

3. The features of a dish referred to or implied by a food-evaluation tend to vary from taste-community to taste-community. And even within the same general taste-community they may vary as between different persons. That is to say, even in the same general taste-community there need not be, with regard to the very same dish, one set of rules governing the correct usage of terms like "nice."[1]

4. "Nice" does not mean the same for all values of x in "x is nice." The features referred to by an average Westerner when he says, "The steak at Barney's is nice" are quite different from the features he refers to when saying, "The orange juice at the Plaza Drug Store is nice" or "the wine you get at Ryan's cellar is nice."

5. The objective statements to which food-evaluations are equivalent or which they imply are somewhat indefinite without however being useless on that account.

6. Food-evaluations always express an attitude on the speaker's part towards the dish in question. When the Objective of the statement is the giving of information concerning the dish, this tends to be incidental. When the purpose of the statement is the giving of information concerning the speaker's attitude, it becomes of primary importance.

7. "Nice" always expresses a favorable attitude. Thus, although, in the sense of referent, "The steak is nice" does *not* mean the same irrespective of the author of the sentence, in the sense of what the sentence expresses, it does mean the same no matter who the author may be.

6. Niceness and "Nice-Making Characteristics"

I SHOULD NOW LIKE to consider in greater detail one point relating

---

1. The following is an interesting point which I did not work out in the text: even where people agree that a certain set of features makes or tends to make a dish nice, they do *not* usually agree as to the exact importance of each feature.

to answer B of Situation I: my statement to Horn, "The steak at
Barney's is rather nice." This, we found, so far as referential meaning is concerned, means

The steak at Barney's is tender, made of the freshest meat, fairly
thick but rather small in size, and done to the exact degree of
rareness the customer desires; or

The steak at Barney's is tender, fresh, thin but large, and
done pretty much to the degree of rareness desired; or

The steak at Barney's is tender, fairly fresh, middle thick and
large, and more or less done to the degree of rareness desired,
or, . . . etc.

Following a suggestion made by Broad in a slightly different
connection,[2] I shall introduce the word "nice-*making* characteristic" to mean any characteristic which a person would mention
in reply to the question, "What makes it nice?" Following Ross,
we could speak of "*grounds* of a dish's niceness." We shall here
stick to the former language. The tenderness or the freshness of
the meat would be examples of nice-making characteristics in the
above illustration. If Horn had asked me, "What makes the steak
at Barney's nice?" I would have undoubtedly said something like,
"The fact that it is always tender" or "the fact that it is always
tender and that the meat is always fresh."

In the light of our discussion, I wish to insist on the following
points:

(i) the niceness belongs to, is "located" in the steak, not in me
or my feelings;

(ii) the niceness of the steak is *not* identical with any one or any
one set of nice-making characteristics;

(iii) although niceness is objective there is no feature or set of
features to which one can point and say, "This is niceness";

(iv) nevertheless niceness is not something distinct from or over
and above these features—it *disjunctively* refers to an indefinite set
of them.

---

2. "Certain Features of Moore's Ethical Doctrines," in *The Philosophy of
G. E. Moore*, p. 60.

CONTENTS

Chapter VI

Imperatives and
Their Justification

1. Some General Properties
of Imperatives

ACCORDING TO a widely supported contemporary theory, moral judgments are equivalent to or closely resemble commands. They are prescriptive and not descriptive, imperatives and not assertions. I believe that this theory contains a great deal of truth, but it is also very apt to be misunderstood, sometimes by its own supporters. We shall avoid these misunderstandings if we first become clear concerning the nature of imperatives in general, and their relations to other types of discourse.

Let us consider a few imperatives as they occur in actual situations and see what features they have in common.

(i) A teacher wants to begin his lecture and, looking at a group of students at the back of the classroom, he says: "Please stop talking now!"

(ii) Mr. Horn, before leaving for the office in the morning asks his wife: "Shall I get you something on the way home?" She replies, "Yes, please get a dozen eggs."

(iii) A doctor, telling his patient what to do to put on some weight, concludes with the statement: "And don't forget to drink a glass of milk every night before retiring!"

The first thing we notice in each of these three cases is that at least two people or parties are involved—the party issuing the imperative and the party to whom it is issued. This is true of most, though not of all imperatives. Thus a man who knows that he has a tendency to say things he later regrets may catch himself in the middle of a conversation and silently say to himself: "Shut up, you fool!" But, in a sense, in this case too, there are two parties involved —his rational and his foolish or compulsive self. Hofstadter and McKinsey make a distinction between what they call "directives" and what they call "fiats." By a "directive" they mean "an imperative which includes an indication of the agent who is to carry it out," while by a "fiat" they mean "an imperative which includes no reference to an agent who is to carry it out."[1] So far as the syntax of imperatives is concerned, this may be a useful distinction and Hofstadter and McKinsey were only concerned with that. But it should be observed that fiats in the sense defined are quite pointless. What at first sight seem to be fiats are often really directives of a certain kind. Thus I might call out, on finding myself locked in somewhere, "Please help me!" I would not then be addressing myself to any *particular* person. But the imperative is nevertheless a directive. For I *am* addressing myself to another party—to whoever may hear me. God, when he said, "Let there be light!" if he was doing any more than expressing a desire, was addressing *himself*. "Let there be light!" roughly meant "Go on, Big Boss, make light!"

Secondly, all our three imperatives express, in the sense defined in Chapter I, a desire or demand on the speaker's part. These desires and demands may be satisfied or they may fail to be satisfied. The people having the desires may be obeyed or disobeyed. By a familiar linguistic device we shall from now on say that an imperative itself is satisfied if the desire or demand which it expresses is satisfied; and we shall say that the imperative is not satisfied if the desire or the demand it expresses is not satisfied. We shall also say that an imperative is obeyed if the person who has the desire or issues the demand in question is obeyed; and we shall say that the imperative is disobeyed if the person is disobeyed. Using this

---

1. "On the Logic of Imperatives," *Philosophy of Science*, 1939, p. 446.

terminology,[2] we can express the second feature of our three imperatives by saying that in each case the speaker would be considered insincere if he did not really desire or demand the state of affairs which will satisfy or obey the imperative.

The third feature we have to notice is that none of our three imperatives can be said to be true or false in any sense in which these terms are commonly used. There is no conceivable state of affairs which would make "Please stop talking!" true. If the people in question do stop talking this would satisfy the imperative, but it would not make it true. Similarly, there is no conceivable state of affairs which would make it false. If the people at the back did not stop talking, the imperative would be disobeyed or unsatisfied, but it would not be false. From this it follows that in the sense of referent, imperatives have no meaning.

This seemingly obvious point has been challenged by C. H. Langford who protests against the view,

sometimes stated in textbooks on logic that to give a command is not to express anything true or false.[3] Consider, [he says] a command of the form, "John, close the door," and suppose this command actually to be given on a certain occasion. Suppose, further, that on the same occasion someone remarks, "He will close the door." When we consider what observations would determine whether or not this command was obeyed, and what observations would determine whether or not the corresponding prediction was true, we see that these are indistinguishable, and that in fact the two sentences have the same sense, or express the same idea, namely, that of John's closing the door. To be sure, if John did not close the door, we should say that the person who made the prediction had been in error, but should not say this of the person who gave the command. That, however, is because the indicative mood signifies that the speaker believes what he expresses, whereas the imperative mood does not, and we must distinguish between error, which pertains to beliefs, and falsehood, which pertains to propositions. Now the sense of an indicative sentence is a proposition, and therefore the sense of an imperative sentence is a proposition. Hence, to give a command is to express a proposition.[4]

And hence, commands can be true or false.

---

2. Cf. Hofstadter and McKinsey, *op. cit.*, p. 447.
3. "The Notion of Analysis in Moore's Philosophy," *The Philosophy of G. E. Moore*, p. 332.
4. *Op. cit.*, pp. 333-334.

This is a truly amazing argument. To expose Langford's fallacy, let us first of all note that when we say about a pair of sentences that they "have the same sense" what we very often mean is that they have the same referent. In this sense, "Jones is a father," for instance, has the same sense as "Jones is a male parent." Let us call this sense (1) of "have the same sense." This sense has to be distinguished from another sense in which Langford uses the phrase in the passage I quoted. According to that sense, two sentences mean the same if the referent of one is identical with the Objective of the other. Let us call this sense (2) of "have the same sense." Next, let us refer to the sentence, "John will close the door" as s_1 and to the sentence, "John, close the door!" as s_2. Now, Langford is perfectly right in maintaining that the facts which make s_1 true are the very same facts which make s_2 obeyed. And from this it follows that in sense (2) of the word s_1 and s_2 "have the same sense." From that, however, it in no way follows that s_1 and s_2 "have the same sense" in sense (1). But only if they had the same sense in sense (1) would it follow that s_2, like s_1, has a referent— that it too can be true or false. Of course independent examination shows that s_2, like other commands, is not true or false. If John does close the door, this does not, in any known sense, make s_2 true, and if he does not close the door this does not make it false.

2. The Justification of Requests

FROM THE FACT that an imperative cannot be true or false it does *not* follow that it is capricious. Of course many imperatives are capricious in the sense that their authors are not willing to support them with *reasons*. The commands which a concentration camp guard or any of the usual type of guard in a prison bellows at the inmates are cases in point. Many imperatives of parents and "educators" also fall into this class. However, there are also many imperatives which their authors support or are willing to support with reasons. Partly following terminology suggested by Barnes,[5] I shall refer to the former as "blind imperatives" and to the latter

---

5. *Op. cit.,* p. 16.

as "persuasives." It will also be convenient to distinguish between persuasives, such as requests and exhortations, where the speaker's desire or demand is somehow central to the situation and those persuasives, such as suggestions and pieces of advice, where the desire of the person to whom the imperative is addressed is central. I shall call the former persuasives of class (I), the latter persuasives of class (II).

We commonly use the terms "good reason" and "bad reason" in talking about the statements which are brought forward to support persuasives. We also commonly characterize some imperatives as rational, sound, or sensible, and others as irrational, unsound, or senseless. It is important that we inquire what is meant by these expressions. I shall begin with an analysis of "rational request."

We shall consider a typical request like that of Mrs. Horn in our example (ii): "Get me a dozen eggs on the way home!" Let us describe the situation more fully: there are no eggs left in the house and Mrs. Horn wishes to bake a fruit-cake for which she needs anything from eight to twelve eggs. She and her husband like fruit-cake and they are expecting guests who are also fond of it. Furthermore, Mrs. Horn usually makes very fine fruit-cakes, and enjoys making them. Mr. Horn can easily afford to buy the twelve eggs and buying them on the way home does not mean much trouble to him.

Now, when we say that a request is "rational" we may be using the word in one of two senses. The first of these—to be called sense (i)—is the narrower, the more common, and the only one of real importance to us. In this sense a request is rational if (1) it can be satisfied—i.e., if its satisfaction is "practically possible," (2) if its satisfaction is the satisfaction of a desire on the part of the person who makes the request or a necessary or at least a convenient means toward the satisfaction of that desire, and (3), if the desire is "rational" in a way to be explained a little later on. We call a request "rational" in this first and main sense if, and only if, all these three conditions are fulfilled and thus in the situation described in the preceding paragraph we would consider Mrs. Horn's request rational.

Supposing, however, Mrs. Horn knew that her husband did not

have enough money to buy a dozen eggs and that nobody would give him the eggs for nothing. In that case, assuming everything else to be unchanged, we would not consider her request "rational"— condition (1) would be absent. Again supposing that Mr. Horn does have the money to buy the eggs but that, as Mrs. Horn well knows, he is already going to be overloaded with parcels by the time he can go to the grocer and supposing furthermore that the grocer is going to make a home-delivery the same afternoon anyway. In that event, too, we should call Mrs. Horn's request "irrational"—condition (2) would be unfulfilled. Finally, we shall assume that Mr. Horn has enough money and that his buying the eggs on the way home is the most convenient method of obtaining them. Supposing, however, that Mrs. Horn wanted the eggs not to bake a fruit-cake but to add to her "egg-treasury and library." Supposing, that is, she has already filled all her drawers and cupboards with eggs and has now begun to fill her book-shelves with eggs also—in that case too we would call her request "irrational." We would do so because we regard a desire for something like an "egg-library" as irrational, to put it mildly. Condition (3) would not be satisfied.

We very commonly call some desires rational and others irrational. We say, for instance, that a man's desire to be a musician is rational if he is very gifted and his prospects for a brilliant career are great. We call it irrational if he has no gift and no hope of success. It is impossible, I believe, to give one simple definition of the phrase "rational desire" for much the same reason as in the case of the phrase "nice steak." The features designated by "rational" tend to vary a great deal. However, the word does very generally *express* the same favorable attitude. Although no simple definition of "rational desire" can be given, in very many actual instances it is not at all difficult to determine what the phrase refers to. Thus in the above example of the gifted person's desire to be a professional musician what is meant is roughly that the desire, if acted on, will bring him a great deal of happiness.

In the broader sense—which we shall call sense (ii)—we call a request rational, irrespective of whether the desire is itself rational. What we mean is simply (1) that the satisfaction of the request is practically possible and (2) that it is the satisfaction or a convenient or necessary means to the satisfaction of a desire on the part of the author of the request. Thus supposing Mrs. Horn needs exactly twelve more eggs to fill the bottom shelf of her egg-library and supposing she feels that she absolutely must fill the bottom shelf before the day is gone. We would say then that in a sense, i.e., in relation to her "needs," her request is rational. It is rational in a sense in which then "get me six eggs" or "get me a dozen bananas" would not be rational.

I hope I have now clarified the meaning of "rational" and "irrational," as applied to requests. But I yet have to clarify what is meant by calling a statement a good or a bad reason for a request. It is worth mentioning in this connection that we also commonly refer to some factual statements as being *relevant* to an imperative and to others as being irrelevant. In clarifying the meaning of "good reason" we shall at the same time clear up the meaning of "relevant" in a context like this.

We call a statement a good reason for a request if, given a certain rational desire on the person's part, the statement truthfully asserts or is evidence for the fact that the satisfaction of the request is a necessary or convenient means to the satisfaction of the desire. Or else we call it a good reason if, given that the satisfaction of the request is a necessary or convenient means to the satisfaction of a rational desire, the statement truthfully asserts that the person has this desire. Thus if we knew that Mrs. Horn wants to bake a fruit-cake her statements, "There are no eggs left in the house" or "The grocer cannot make any home-deliveries today" would, if true, be good reasons for her request. Or again, if it is known that there are no eggs in the house and that Mr. Horn's buying them is the most convenient method of getting them home, her statement, "I want to bake a fruit-cake" would, if true, be a good reason for her request.

Fairly similar remarks apply to the meaning of "relevant," as applied to attempts to support a request. A statement is relevant to a request if, given the person has a certain desire, it asserts or is evidence for the assertion that the satisfaction of the request is a necessary or convenient means to the satisfaction of the desire; or

if, given the latter, it asserts the existence of the desire. It is noteworthy that in the case of relevance no provision is necessary either
concerning the "rational" character of the desire or concerning the
truth of the statement. As in other contexts, a statement may be
relevant even though it is false.

In Chapter I, Section 6, we lumped together certain words under
the title of "evidence-words." It is interesting to observe that in
talking about certain relations between requests and the statements
which are brought up to support them, we use some but do not use
others of these evidence-words. In the case of deductive and inductive reasoning the situation is different. The fact that Bjoerling
is a Swede is not only a *good reason* for our saying that he is a
Scandinavian. It also *justifies* the latter statement. It *proves* and
implies it, although it would be an abuse of ordinary language to
say that it is *evidence* for it. The statement that Bjoerling is a
Scandinavian also *follows* from the statement that he is a Swede.
The fact that the sun has risen every day for so many days is
similarly not only a *good reason* for the statement that it will again
rise tomorrow. It also *justifies* the latter statement and is *evidence*
for it. In the case of inductive arguments we are somewhat hesitant
about using "prove," "imply," and "follows from," but we sometimes do. In the case of requests, on the other hand, it is correct to
use "good reason" and "justify" but *none* of the other evidence-
words. As language is used at present, it would be senseless to say
the fact that no eggs were left in the house is evidence for—or
proves or implies—Mrs. Horn's request, "Please get me a dozen
eggs on the way home."

It has to be emphasized that the relations to which "good reason"
or "justify" refer in the case of requests are rather different from
both those referred to by these phrases in the case of deductive and
also from those referred to in the case of inductive arguments. As
in the case of inductive and deductive argument, we have here one
sentence which is supported by another sentence or set of sentences. But unlike the conclusions of inductive arguments the request does not assert anything at all—it has no referent; and unlike
deductive arguments it does not repeat part of what is asserted or
more generally what is done by the sentences which are its reasons

in a sense in which the conclusions of a valid deduction must always repeat part of what is said in the premises.

In other words, "good reason" and "justify" are ambiguous expressions which mean one thing in the case of deductive reasoning, another in the case of inductive reasoning and yet another in the case of the supporting of requests. If there is anybody who argues that requests cannot possibly be justified by any set of factual statements because the assertion of the factual statements together with the denial of the request can never yield a formal contradiction, he is obviously proceeding on the false assumption that "justify" means the same in the case of requests as it does in the case of deductive arguments. His argument may also be described as a case of *ignoratio elenchi* if aimed against the "common-sense" view that requests can often be justified by reference to factual statements. I.e., it is true that in the sense of "deductive justification" no set of factual statements ever provides a justification for a request. But when an ordinary person claims that a certain request is justified by a certain set of factual statements he does not mean "deductively justified."

Supposing somebody were to argue that since requests can be justified and since, like other imperatives, they do not refer to anything observable, they must therefore have an unobservable or non-natural referent. This argument, too, would be based on the false assumption that "justify" means the same in the case of requests as it does in the case of inductive or deductive arguments.

The upshot of our discussion is very simple but also, as we shall find in the next chapter, very important: *requests can be justified although they have no referent.*

Let us now turn to persuasives of class (II): imperatives like suggestions and advice. These, too, are often characterized as on the one hand rational, sensible, and sound, and on the other hand as senseless, irrational or unsound. A great deal of what we said in this connection about the Persuasives of class (I) applies here. The desire of the person who issued the imperative is however replaced now by the desire of the person to whom the imperative is issued.

Let us recall example (iii) of page 123. A doctor there said to a patient who wants to put on weight, "Drink a glass of milk every night before going to bed!" Now, if drinking milk is likely to make the patient put on weight, the doctor's advice is "rational." To say that an advice is "rational" simply means that its satisfaction is a necessary or convenient means to the satisfaction of a certain desire on the part of the person to whom the advice is given. The same applies to all other persuasives of class (II). Of course many complications arise when more than one desire is involved.

3. A Note on Categorical Imperatives

IT IS STILL widely held[6] among empiricists (1) that there are no such things as (meaningful) categorical imperatives and (2) that the admission that there are categorical imperatives would constitute a surrender to intuitionism. In my opinion both these views are plainly false. In a perfectly familiar sense of "categorical," there are millions of imperatives which are categorical and perfectly meaningful.

Let us consider a simple example. There are two roads connecting Salzburg with Bad Gastein. One of them, R_1, goes along magnificent scenery and is easy and pleasant to ride on, but it takes four hours to get to Salzburg along this road, even with fairly speedy driving. The other road, R_2, is very bumpy and goes through extremely dull countryside. Along R_2, however, it only takes two hours to get to Salzburg. Horn, Hedemacher and I are staying at Bad Gastein. It is noon and Horn comes to me saying, "I have to give a lecture in Salzburg at 2:30. Which road shall I take?" I of course answer, "Take R_2!" Later Hedemacher comes along and says to me, "I would like to drive to Salzburg today. Which road would you recommend?" This time I appropriately answer, "If you want to have an enjoyable ride along magnificent scenery, take R_1!" My answer to Hedemacher is obviously a hypothetical imperative, but my answer to Horn equally clearly is not. Hedemacher did *not* inform me whether he desired to get to Salzburg as quickly as possible or whether he preferred a pleasant drive. Horn did inform me that he was in a great hurry. The

---

6. E.g., Schlick, *op. cit.*, Ch. V, Section 6.

if-clause is therefore appropriate in the one case but not in the other. The absence of the if-clause in "Take R_2!" marks the fact that Horn's desire is known. The same applies to all other cases where the questioner's desire is known. In all these cases we have *categorical* and not hypothetical imperatives. But of course the fact that they are categorical in no way implies that they refer to some special "non-natural realm" or that they are not based on or determined by human desires.

4. "Should-Persuasives"

IN DISCUSSING persuasives of class (I) we found that while it is perfectly correct to say that they may be supported by good reasons or that certain factual statements may justify them, it is never correct to say, as language is used at present, that they *follow from* or are *implied by* these statements. I now wish to show that there is a sub-class of persuasives of class (II), including categorical as well as hypothetical imperatives, about which it is perfectly meaningful to say that they follow from or are implied by certain factual statements. The persuasives in question are those containing the word "should" or "ought" in what would generally be recognized as a "non-moral" sense. I do not contend that the same does not apply to cases where "should" and "ought" are used in a moral sense. Far from it. But I do not wish to discuss that topic as yet. I shall only consider categorical imperatives since it is more likely that my statement would be disputed in their case than in the case of hypothetical imperatives.

Let us suppose that the doctor, in the above example, had said, "You *should* drink a glass of milk every night before going to bed!" instead of saying, "Drink a glass of milk every night before going to bed!" Now it would be very odd to say: "From the fact that X desires to put on weight and that drinking a glass of milk every night is a convenient way of putting on weight *it follows* that 'X: drank a glass of milk every night!' " But it would not at all be odd to say: "From the fact that X desires to put on weight and that drinking a glass of milk every night is a convenient way of putting on weight it follows that X should drink a glass of milk

every night." Again it would be odd to say: "The fact that X
desires to put on weight and that drinking a glass of milk every
night is a convenient way of putting on weight *implies* 'X: drink
a glass of milk every night!'." But it is not at all odd to say: "The
fact that X desires to put on weight and that drinking a glass of
milk every night is a convenient way of putting on weight implies
that X should drink a glass of milk every night."

In the case of the "should"-persuasives, then, the relation between
"follows from" and "implies" on the one hand and "good reason"
and "justify" on the other, with which we are familiar in the case
of deductive and to some extent also in the case of inductive arguments, is reestablished. To say that the two statements, "X desires
to put on weight" and "Drinking a glass of milk every night is a
convenient way of putting on weight" justify or constitute a good
reason for the imperative, "X, you should drink a glass of milk
every night!" is equivalent to saying that they imply the imperative or that the imperative follows from them. But of course, just
as "good reason" and "justify" do not mean in cases when imperatives are being supported what they mean in the case of deductive
or inductive arguments, so "follow from" and "imply" do not
in the case of should-persuasives mean what they mean in the case
of deductive or inductive arguments. To say that a should-persuasive
follows from a set of factual statements simply means that these
statements assert (1) that the person to whom the imperative is
addressed has a certain desire and (2) that the satisfaction of the
imperative is a necessary or convenient method of bringing about
the satisfaction of that desire. Where (1) is known or obvious, we
tend to say simply that the imperative follows from (2). It follows from (2) together with "the situation itself."[7]

It will be convenient to distinguish this sense of "follows from"
from the sense in which the conclusion of a valid deduction follows from its premise and also from the sense in which the conclusion of an inductive argument is sometimes said to follow from
certain premises. We shall from now on call it sense (3) of the word.

---

7. Thoughts along this line were suggested to me by a passage in Sidney
Hook's "The Desirable and Emotive in Dewey's Ethics," in *John Dewey:
Philosopher of Science and Freedom* (ed. Hook) p. 204-205.

There are two other interesting respects in which should-persuasives differ from all other imperatives. Firstly, it is possible in the case of a should-persuasive to *accept* the imperative without obeying it. In the case of all other imperatives, the only sense in which it is possible to accept or reject them is to obey or disobey, satisfy or fail to satisfy them. Here this is not the case. For instance: I accept the doctor's, "You should drink a glass of milk every night!" if I adopt a certain attitude toward the drinking of a glass of milk in cases where people want to put on weight—e.g., if I sincerely give the same advice to others who are in similar circumstances, if I genuinely desire to be myself the sort of person who can drink a glass of milk, and if I feel displeased with myself when I fail to drink milk. If I act and feel in this way, I am accepting the doctor's persuasive although I may in fact fail to obey it.

Secondly, unlike in the case of all other imperatives, should-persuasives can be about a third person and they can also be in the past tense. Thus the doctor in our example might have said, "You should drink a glass of milk every night and so should that thin brother of yours who keeps on throwing stones at my windows! And your mother should have drunk three glasses of milk every night. She would still be alive if she had."

It has sometimes been maintained that should-persuasives must have a referent since the Objectives of a trio of sentences like

"You should do x"

"A should do x"

"B should have done x"

are plainly different while the *meaning* of "should" in them is the same. The answer to this is that when we say that the meaning of "should" is the same in the three sentences, we are referring to what in Chapter I, Section 6, we called sense (4) of "meaning." We are referring to the facts referred to by the factual statements which are the reasons for the persuasive and from which it follows.

It should be emphasized that this sense (4) of "meaning" is not an artificial construction of my own. On the contrary it is an exceedingly common usage, although philosophers have hardly ever recognized it. We constantly use "meaning" and other related expressions in this sense when justifying or explaining the reasons for our feelings or attitudes and also when giving reasons for advice, requests, or indeed almost any kind of imperative. I already gave several illustrations in Chapter I in connection with the justification of feelings. I shall here add one involving an imperative. Supposing a neurotic girl of twenty-two is consulting a doctor about her dyspepsia and her constant feelings of exhaustion. The doctors happens to know something about her surroundings at home. He knows that the mother is a puritanical old hag, full of jealousy and hate, while the father, who really loves the girl, is weak and overprotective. Being a sensitive and intelligent man, the doctor dispenses with the usual injections, vitamin pills, thyroid tablets, tonics, and the half-witted advice "to stop working so hard." Instead, he says to the girl: "Move away from home and get your own apartment!" The girl, taken aback, asks: "What do you *mean*?" He replies: "What I mean is that you'll begin to live; a terrible burden will be taken off your shoulders. You'll enjoy looking after your own place where you can entertain your friends. You'll be able to come and go as you please without any jealous watchdog. You'll blossom out and all your dyspepsia and weariness will be gone before you know it." It is evident that the "meaning" of the original sentence—"Move away from home!"—is the *reasons* given for it, or, to be more exact, the referent of the sentences offered as reasons or justification. Countless similar cases could be cited.

The expression "descriptive meaning" has frequently been used to mean what we in this book call "referent." This, it seems to me, has led to much confusion in implying that sentences can give objective information only if they have a referent. We have seen that this is not so. I propose therefore from now on to use "descriptive meaning" as a blanket term to mean, "meaning in the sense of referent or in sense (4)." Using this terminology, persuasives may be said to have descriptive meaning without having a referent.

It will also be convenient and in keeping with ordinary usage slightly to widen our usage of "objective claim" or "objective statement." We shall mean by this from now on any sentence which either asserts or else implies, either in sense (2) or in sense (3) of the word, something other than the speaker's state of mind.

I hope I have made it clear in this chapter that, whatever else can be said against it, a theory according to which moral judgments are disguised or undisguised imperatives, does not imply that all moral judgments are equally irrational or equally valid. It does not imply that moral judgments cannot be supported with reasons and it also does not imply that moral judgments can never follow from factual statements.

CONTENTS

Chapter VII

The Logic of
Moral Discourse (I)

1. Statement of My Theory

IN THIS and the next two chapters I shall state and defend my own metaethic, my own answers to the three questions which form the subject matter of this inquiry. I am advancing my theory in a purely experimental spirit, to be modified or discarded as new evidence becomes available. I believe it to be a strong theory mainly for two reasons. Firstly, it is compatible with and indeed explains all the facts concerning moral judgments which we noticed in the course of our various discussions and many of which are incompatible with other metaethical theories. Secondly, it fits all the examples of moral judgments, disputes and arguments I have had occasion to analyze. It is entirely possible, however, that the examples I have studied are not sufficiently representative.

The main features of my metaethic are summarized in the following six propositions: (1) most moral judgments are objective claims either in the narrow sense of Chapter I, Section 5, or else in the broader sense, defined at the end of Chapter VI; (2) moral judgments, so far as their descriptive meaning is concerned, tend to be polyguous like statements about the niceness of food or the boringness of lectures; (3) the features to which moral judgments refer or which they imply are no more non-natural than the features to which judgments about the niceness of foods refer; (4) certain moral judgments *resemble* commands and requests in certain respects, but they *are not* commands or requests—they are *sui generis* and also differ from commands and requests in various significant ways; and some moral judgments do not even resemble commands and requests in *any* significant way; (5) many moral disputes are, within certain limits, capable of settlement in the same sense or a sense closely analogous to that in which scientific disputes can be settled; (6) many moral judgments "follow from" non-moral judgments in the only sense in which any ordinary person ever meant to assert this.

The direction of many of my discussions will be clearer if I pause here to say a few words about the *naturalistic* character of my theory and the way in which it differs from other forms of naturalism.

Let us call a situation in which a moral judgment is made a "moral situation." Now, according to intuitionism, four types of entities enter into most if not all moral situations:

(1) Attitudes or emotions or demands on the part of the person who makes the moral judgment;

(2) Attitudes or emotions on the part of the person to whom the judgment is addressed;

(3) Natural features of the subject of the moral judgment; and

(4) Non-natural features of the subject of the moral judgment.

As against this, naturalists of various types have held that only (1), (2), and (3) enter into moral situations. In this, I think, they have been entirely right.

At the same time I do not know of any naturalistic theory, from Hobbes to Stevenson, which has successfully withstood the critical fire of intuitionists or of rival naturalists. The reason for this, it seems to me, is not that naturalism as such is false. The reason is rather that the ethical predicates function in a very strange and perplexing fashion: their relations, on the one hand, to the attitudes and emotions which enter into moral situations, and on the other to the natural features of the subject of the moral judgment, are manifold and frequently very variable. Now, some forms of naturalism, like naive subjectivism, have been altogether mistaken about these relations. But other theories such as, e.g., the theories of Ayer and Stevenson or those of Dewey and Mill, while they succeeded in bringing out some of these relations, failed to bring out others that are equally important.

Assuming that my theory, too, will turn out to be open to decisive objections, my study of the subject has nevertheless convinced me that this will be due not to any inherent error in naturalism, but to my inability to track down with sufficient care the manifold varieties in the usages of the ethical predicates.

My exposition will be greatly simplified if I distinguish at this stage between two classes of moral judgments. Following suggestions made by Broad[1] and Findlay,[2] I shall distinguish between "value-judgments" and "judgments of obligation." Judgments having as their predicate "good," "desirable," "worthwhile," are instances of the former. Sentences containing "ought," "oblige," or "duty" are instances of the latter.

In my exposition I shall confine myself to one sub-class of each of these classes of moral judgments. I shall single out judgments containing "good" as their predicate from the class of value-judgments and I shall select sentences containing "ought" from the obligation-judgments. I shall from now on, call the former "good-judgments" and the latter "ought-judgments." I am confident that what we shall discover about these will apply, without major qualifications, to moral judgments not explicitly considered in this work.

2. "Good and Nice"

THERE ARE MANY highly interesting likenesses between the functions of the word "good" as applied to actions and characters and the word "nice" as applied to foods.

(A) OBJECTIVITY AND POLYGUITY

Like "nice," "good" usually *both* refers to certain qualities of the

---

1. *Five Types of Ethical Theory*, pp. 277 ff.
2. *Op. cit.*, pp. 154-156.

thing judged to be good and expresses a favorable attitude on the part of the person who makes the judgment. As in the case of "nice," the emphasis is sometimes on the one, sometimes on the other. Like "nice," furthermore, "good" is polyguous so far as its referent is concerned. People belonging to different groups and also, though far less so, different people belonging to the same group, tend to refer to more or less different features when they use the word "good." Like "nice," too, "good" tends to be rather vague. There are also some significant differences between the usage of "good" and that of "nice." For the moment, however, I shall confine myself to the likenesses.

Example I. Not long ago at a party I was, in misanthropic fashion, talking somewhat along the following lines: "The average man is a liar and a thief. His dearest aim is to get something for nothing. He is anxious to please and be pleased, but never to have the truth about himself or the people he euphemistically calls his 'friends.' Full of envy and fear, he destroys the life in his children whom he thus fashions in his own image. . . ." As I was proceeding in this vein, reciting case after case, someone interrupted me with the question: "Well, have you ever met a good person?" I thought for a moment and then I said, quite sincerely: "Yes. X.Y. is a good person." Let us call this statement m₁.

Now X.Y. is a close friend of mine and a very remarkable person. She is one of the very, very few people in the world whose organism is wholly free from repressed fear and anger and she is entirely devoid of neurotic traits. People like X.Y. are so rare that we do not have an adequate vocabulary to describe their positive qualities. I can only say that she is completely open and has contact with everything around her. When she meets another person she immediately establishes rapport with whatever is open and living in that person. She is incapable of lying, having none of the neurotic fears which make people into liars. She is completely devoid of envy and thus has no desire to wreck whatever happiness others may possess. She is cruel neither in an open way nor in the underhand fashion in which so many intellectuals get out their sadism. She has a little boy whom she brings up in as com-

plete freedom as external conditions allow, including a degree of
sexual freedom which would appal more conventional parents and
teachers. Even relatively blind people cannot help noticing the remarkable relationship of honest, straightforward love between her
and the boy. Like her, he is devoid of neurotic anxieties and the
sadistic traits which are so common in children that ignorant psychologists and novelists consider them hereditary. I ought to add
that X.Y., being free from irrational fears, does not recognize any of
the sexual taboos which are fostered by traditional religion and
which are deep inside even most of those who have intellectually
broken with religion. I do not consider her "promiscuous" though
I suppose some people would call her that. But in any case I want
to mention, since it is relevant to theoretical points I shall try to
illustrate shortly, that X.Y. has not been married for four years but
has not for that reason refrained from sexual relations. It is further
relevant that she feels no guilt about her conduct and would only
pity somebody who did.

I ought to mention one other thing about X.Y. which will be
material to our discussion. She was at one time a member of the
Communist Party. But her motive for joining that organization
was not, as in so many cases, the ambition to be a leader or the
desire to feel important or any longing for salvation, but simply her
desire to help the underdog. After a while she simply could not
stand the people in the Party. She found them, one and all, so
"hard, stiff, and sick." She also discovered many other things about
the Party which made her oppose it strenuously, so far as she
still takes an interest in politics. She favors the United States intervention in Korea and I think she would even go so far as to support the ousting of Communist teachers and the banning of the
Communist Party.

Now, when I said, "X.Y. is a good person" I referred to some
though not to all of X.Y.'s qualities which I mentioned in the last
paragraph. One of the things I meant was that X.Y. is gentle and
loving; another that she does not lie; a third that she is free from
envy and ambition; a fourth that the happiness of her child means
more to her than the opinion of her neighbors or the growth of

any political movement. Let us for the moment, for the sake of simplicity, assume that these are the only features of X.Y. to which I referred in m_1.

It seems to me beyond any question that m_1 is, in the sense in which we are using the term, an objective statement. If somebody were to doubt m_1 and if I thought it worth the trouble, I would take him to meet X.Y., so that he could see for himself that she is gentle and loving, that she does not lie, that she is free from envy, etc. I would have proven m_1 if I could show that X.Y. really had these qualities. If, on the other hand, it turned out that she does not really have these qualities, that I had been consistently taken in by a clever act, I would have to admit that m_1 was a mistake.

I know many people who would contend that X.Y. is a bad person. Or if they did not go so far as that, they would at least maintain that she was not a good person. A rigid Catholic, for instance, even if he is not so blind as to miss her warmth and gentleness and some of her other qualities, would nevertheless say "X.Y. is a bad person." It is I think fairly plain what he would refer to by saying that X.Y. is a bad person. He would mean that, in being sexually free, she was giving in to her own selfish desires and defying "the laws of God and man." He would also mean that, by bringing up her little boy the way she does, she was encouraging the violation of "the laws of God and man" and failing to impart such qualities as discipline and self-control.

I also know some rigid Communists who would quite sincerely say of X.Y. that she is a bad person. Here, too, I think, it is clear what they would mean. They would mean that, in favoring United States intervention in Korea and even more in favoring a ban on the Communist Party, she was hampering the spread of Communism and helping to postpone "The Revolution." They would also mean that in bringing up her child the way she does, she was making him into a useless if not actually harmful person from the point of view of the struggle for Communism.

Example II. Z.Z. is a member of the League Against Vice and Moral Corruption in the Australian town of Shepparton. She has a little boy whom she brings up in strict discipline, "cleanliness," and fear of God. Her cruelty comes out in a thousand ways. Even

Australian judges, the most brutal outside the Soviet Union, are too lenient for her taste. There is not enough corporal punishment either in prisons or in the schools. She herself, to impart to her son the maxim that "cleanliness is next to godliness," beats him mercilessly every time he gets himself dirty. Every serious question her boy asks her she answers with a lie or an evasion. Although Z.Z.'s husband is quite wealthy, she takes in a boarder who happens to be the present writer. In her zeal for holiness she peers through his keyholes and carefully watches his comings and goings. She is in the forefront of every movement to ban a book or movie. She contributes regularly to religious causes and is one of the pillars of her congregation. Her chastity is unrivalled.

Now the members of the League Against Vice and Moral Corruption, who would call X.Y. of Example I a bad person, would call Z.Z. a good person. Let us use "m_2" as an abbreviation for their statement, "Z.Z. is a good person." What they refer to by m_2 is Z.Z.'s chastity and self-denials, her devotion to holy causes, her bringing up her child according to the "laws of God," etc. I do not suppose they would actually use "good" to refer to her cruelty. But they would certainly say that her cruelty is more than outweighed by her other features.

Example III. C.C. is a lecturer in philosophy and psychology at some such institution as the Jefferson School of Lies and Forgeries. He originally joined the Party partly out of genuine conviction and partly because he had powerful desires to be a hero and a celebrity. With other groups he could not cut much ice since he was neither very intelligent nor particularly charming. But he found that if he bellowed "Fascist," "Trotzkyite," "wrecker and saboteur," very often and at the top of his voice at people who were out of favor with the "most progressive section of the working-class," he was certain to get thunderous applause from a certain quarter. So he became a "Party-philosopher." By now he is very deep in the soup—his "refutations" of logical positivism, bourgeois psychology, and mechanical materialism have been translated into sixty-four languages and are quoted by distinguished men from Vladivostok to Kubishev and from Peking to Sofia. By now he believes, on the surface layer of his soul at any rate, so strongly in the rightness of "The Cause" that he is willing to undergo a great deal of suffering in its service. This is one feature of C.C. But his character has also many other features which should not be suppressed in this survey. Thus he is a pathological liar. His demonstration of the "Fascist Character of Bertrand Russell's Outlook" and similar performances are one long string of deliberate lies and misquotations. In his classes at the X School of Lies and Forgeries, he will stop at nothing in his "parodies" to get a few laughs. He has read the Dewey exposure of the Trotzky trials and some of the literature on the slave labor camps, all of which has given him some slight uneasiness. But neither the truth nor the sufferings of millions means anything to him, so long as he can go on feeling important. He is tremendously ambitious and he dreams of the day when, in the Red Square in Washington or London, he will address a crowd of millions all of whom have come to pay homage to the wise and courageous Hero of Socialist Labor.

Now, many people who would call X.Y. a bad person would refer to C.C. as a good man. Let us call this statement of theirs "m_3." By m_3, it is clear, they simply refer to C.C.'s contributions to "The Cause" and his readiness to make sacrifices on its behalf.

m_1, m_2, and m_3, although they no doubt *express* their author's approval, are not statements about these attitudes. They are objective statements. They can be and commonly are proven by an appeal to facts concerning the persons who are said to be good. But the features to which I refer in m_1 are different from those referred to by the authors of m_2 and different again from those referred to by the authors of m_3. If we use the term "good-making feature" to mean a feature of something to which a person refers when he calls it good, then we may express the last point by saying that the good-making features referred to in m_1 are different from those referred to in m_2, and also from those referred to in m_3. Under "feature" I shall from now on include not only what are sometimes called "inherent qualities" but also causal properties.

I noted at the beginning of Chapter III that ordinary people sometimes make metamoral comments which are equivalent to naive subjectivism and that they sometimes also make comments implying the error theory. It may be worth pointing out that they occasionally make comments which are in harmony with the theory just proposed. They do quite often say things like, "Well, it all depends what you mean by 'good' here" or "Well, I can see that your moral standards are different from mine."

If this account is correct then the usage of "good" resembles that of "nice" in the following respects: (i) the sentences in which it is used as predicate are, frequently at any rate, objective claims and (ii) their meaning tends to vary with the person or group of the person who employs them.

Some further resemblances can be brought out by contrasting the two statements, made by me:

"X.Y. is gentle, loving, does not lie, and is free from envy and malice," and,
"X.Y. is a good person,"

or by contrasting the two statements, both made by a puritanical fanatic:

"Z.Z. is a devout believer, leads a chaste life, and brings her child up in strict discipline and devotion," and,
"Z.Z. is a good woman."

In both cases, the second statement, which is in our sense a moral judgment, says the *same sort* of thing as the first, but more indefinitely. In both cases, too, the second statement expresses the speaker's attitude of approval or admiration while the first does not or not so definitely. It is true that words like "gentle" and "kind" and "truthful" are very generally accompanied by approval, but not nearly as generally as "good." We may express the difference by saying that while "good" expresses the speaker's approval, "kind" and "gentle" and "truthful" only *tend to* express his approval. As for "Z.Z. brings up her child in strict discipline," this nowadays hardly even tends to express approval.

It is worth our while now to recall another point which I emphasized in Chapter V. I there pointed out that when, in circumstances like Situation I, I say, "the steak at Barney's is nice" my taste determines what features in a steak I refer to by "nice," but the statement itself refers to the features and not to my taste.

Similarly, what causes me to call X.Y. a good person is my favorable attitude to gentleness and truthfulness and freedom from envy. But what I refer to when I say, "X.Y. is a good person" are these features in X.Y. and not my approval. Similarly in the other two cases and in plenty of others which we have not analyzed: what determines one to regard a person or an action as good is one's approval of certain of the qualities of that person or action, but in saying that the person or the action is good one refers to the qualities and not to the approval. This is the most important point of my whole treatise. I shall therefore state it once more in slightly different language: *the referent of the moral judgment is determined by the speaker's attitude, but it is not that attitude.*

Although then the subjectivists were mistaken in denying the "objectivity" of moral judgments, they did get hold of one very essential feature of the whole situation. When a person makes such statements as, "It is going to rain tomorrow" or "the pressure exerted by a liquid is exactly proportional to its density," it is quite unnecessary to know anything about his emotion or attitude in order to know what he is asserting. On the other hand, in the case of moral judgments it is necessary to know this. "It will rain tomorrow" and "X.Y. is a profoundly good person" are both objective statements. But to know what the first refers to one needs to make no investigation concerning the author's approvals and disapprovals. To know what the second refers to one must know something about the author's approvals and disapprovals.

To guard the above formulations against misunderstanding, I should like to cite and defend a passage from Hume which, in one crucial respect at least, advocates the same doctrine:

When a man denominates another, his enemy, his rival, his antagonist, his adversary, he is understood to speak the language of self-love, and to express sentiments, peculiar to himself, and arising from his particular circumstances and situation. But when he bestows on any man the epithets of vicious or odious or depraved, he then speaks another language, and expresses sentiments, in which he expects all his audience are to concur with him. He must here, therefore, depart from his private and particular situation, and must choose a point of view, common to him with others; he must move some universal principle of the human frame, and touch a string to which all mankind have an accord and sympathy.

If he means, therefore, to express that this man *possesses qualities,* whose tendency is pernicious to society, he has chosen this common point of view, and has touched the principle of humanity, in which every man, in some degree, concurs.[3]

This passage has often been misunderstood to be equivalent to the view that "X is vicious" is synonymous with, "X is disapproved by all or most men," i.e., to the view we called public subjectivism. Now, whatever Hume may have said on other occasions, the wording of this passage gives no warrant for such an interpretation. It follows from the words I italicized that according to Hume "X is vicious" means, "X possesses certain qualities—namely qualities which are pernicious to society." "X is vicious" is an objective statement in our sense. It is not a statement about the author's disapproval and it is not about the disapproval of other people either: *it is about X's qualities.* The disapproval of mankind, on Hume's view, determines what qualities "vicious" refers to. But the referent of "vicious" are X's qualities and not the disapproval of mankind.

(B) REASONS AND REFERENT

Supposing somebody, who once casually met X.Y. of Example I, and who knows that I know her well, asks me, "What sort of a person is X.Y.?" Suppose I reply, "She is a very wonderful person—above all she is really good." Not satisfied with this answer, he asks me, "What reasons do you have for saying that she is really good?" One appropriate answer would then be a citation of instances of her behavior. But an equally appropriate answer would be an enumeration of the very same qualities which in our earlier discussion I claimed to be the referent of "X.Y. is a good person" —her gentleness, her truthfulness, her freedom from envy and ambition, etc. Let us refer to these features as G_1-G_x.

The fact, now, that G_1-G_x can be adduced as the reasons for X.Y.'s goodness may seem to falsify my earlier claim that they *are* her goodness. It may seem to make plausible the assertion, "X.Y.'s possession of G_1-G_x are the grounds or the reasons for saying that X.Y. is a good person, but her goodness is a further quality over

---

3. *Enquiry,* IX, i. My italics.

and above G_1-G_x." However, in view of our various distinctions and similar comments in the case of "niceness," the answer to this is plain: "What reasons do you have for saying that X.Y. is a good person?" is in the above case taken to mean, "What are X.Y.'s features which are the *reasons for your favorable attitude* towards her?" The fact that in one context G_1-G_x are the referent of m_1 while in another they are its reason shows nothing more than that m_1, in addition to having an objective referent, expresses the author's favorable attitude to the object having the features referred to and *that these features are the reasons for that attitude*.

(C) VAGUENESS AND INDEFINITENESS

Something must now be said about a subject which I have glossed over up to now. The good-judgments made by fanatics tend to be fairly definite since a fanatic tends to approve very few features for their own sake. But other good-judgments are both indefinite *and* vague. In Chapter V, I used "indefinite" and "vague" synonymously. But that was an over-simplification. There is a difference here which I shall now explain.

Let us look at the following four statements:

(1) The steak at Barney's is very tender, very fresh and fairly large;

(2) The steak at Barney's is fairly tender, very fresh and very large;

(3) The steak at Barney's is very tender, fairly fresh and fairly large; and

(4) The steak at Barney's is either very tender, very fresh and fairly large, or fairly tender, very fresh, and very large, or very tender, fairly fresh, and fairly large.

It is easy to see what I mean when I say (4) is more indefinite or less definite than any of (1)-(3). (1) asserts that the steak at Barney's has a certain set of features, (2) asserts that it has another set of features, (3) asserts yet another set. (4) then asserts that it has one or other of these three sets of features.

By saying that one word, w_1, is vaguer than another, w_2, we mean that there is a larger range of situations in the case of w_1

than in the case of w_2 for which language provides us with no rules to decide whether or not the word can be correctly applied. In this sense (4) is no vaguer than (1)-(3). Now, the statement, "The steak at Barney's is rather nice" is *both* more indefinite and vaguer than (1)-(3). It differs from them not only in saying that the steak has one *or* other of certain sets of features. It also differs in that there is usually a very considerable "area of linguistic indeterminacy"[4] here. There is usually in the case of "nice" a sizeable region of situations where the speaker himself is unable to say whether the steak is nice or whether a certain feature is relevant to its niceness.

Exactly the same holds for a great many good-judgments. They are both more indefinite *and* vaguer than statements such as "X.Y. is gentle and loving, truthful, and free from envy and ambition." When I say that somebody is a good person I refer to one or other of certain sets of features. But in most cases, there are some features where my usage of "good" is simply not sufficiently fixed for me to say whether or not I am referring to them. E.g., X.Y.'s truthfulness and freedom from envy are clearly relevant to her goodness as I use the term. Her figure and her pronunciation of the English language are clearly irrelevant. But I simply cannot tell whether, e.g., the fact that she never hits back at people who annoy or even harm her is relevant. I am sure that my usage of "good" is in this respect very representative of many other peoples' usage.

One further remark in this connection to correct or supplement something I said earlier: when I say about a particular person, e.g., X.Y., that she is good, I have of course *certain* features in mind. But in the sense in which we defined "refer" I am not referring to them as such but to any of a large number of possible sets. For, as I use "good," *any* one of a large number of sets of features would make my statement true.

There is nothing in what I have been saying which implies that moral judgments are necessarily "uncritical" or "irrational." What is meant by a "critical moral judgment," I am assuming, is a

---

4. What von Mises calls "Unbestimmtheitszone," in his *Kleines Lehrbuch des Positivismus* (The Hague: Van Stockum and Zoon, 1939), pp. 23-25.

moral judgment based on an investigation of the features of the object judged. In this sense many moral judgments are of course uncritical. Thus when an ignorant and anxiety-filled parent moralizes against masturbation or when Mary Norton condemns birthcontrol, their moral judgments are certainly uncritical. For their disapprovals are not based on any investigation into the nature and consequences of what is judged bad. However, if a parent investigates the consequences both of masturbation and of its suppression in children or if somebody informs himself of the effects both of the use of contraceptives and of unrestricted reproduction before arriving at his moral view on the subject, then the moral judgment so formed would be critical.

My view also does not imply that moral judgments are "emotional" in the sense of expressing momentary fits of emotion. What they express are attitudes and attitudes have what is somewhat pompously called "an element of universality." When I said, "X.Y. is a good person" I did not express my approval of X.Y., period. I expressed my approval or admiration of her *as being* a person who is gentle and truthful and free from envy: I imply that, other things being equal, I would approve of anybody else insofar as he possesses these qualities. People do occasionally express momentary fits of emotion by using the word "good." But such sentences, though "moral judgments" in our artificially broad sense, would not usually be considered to be moral judgments.

(d) TYPES OF MORAL ATTITUDES AND OBJECTIVES

Approval and disapproval are sometimes called "the moral emotions" or "the moral attitudes." I should like to point out in this connection that, whether they are in fact always expressed by moral judgments or not, there seem to be other emotions and attitudes which are occasionally at least also expressed by a moral judgment. I shall give two examples to substantiate this assertion.

Consider first the case of Gottfried Eisinger. Gottfried has been a leading Communist for over twenty-five years now. He is of the tough, hard-boiled variety. Whatever he may have once believed, he believes nothing now. He is an efficient instrument in a machine whose justice he neither questions nor cares to question.

He is absolutely pitiless, but he is still full of envy of people whom
he deems happy and also of those who never surrendered their
integrity. Gottfried is responsible for more deaths and deporta-
tions among the German and Austrian refugees who settled in the
Soviet Union than any other single person. Several of the leading
figures in the Trotzky trials were accused because of the "information" which he passed on to the OGPU. During the period of the
Russo-German friendship pact he made sure that some of his worst
personal enemies were handed over to the Gestapo. Gottfried
Eisinger I call an evil man and what I am expressing here is not
just disapproval, but *impersonal* hatred. I hate him not because
he has done me any harm personally. He has not. I hate him because his character has certain qualities. I would hate *anybody*
with a character of the same kind.

My second case is that of Martin Sekierer. Sekierer is a sadist
and pornographer with a cleanliness-neurosis. He also lives in
constant fear that people may take him for a homosexual. He sees
dirt where nobody else can see it. When he goes to a restaurant
he never stops complaining about the glasses and cups and plates.
He prides himself on taking three baths daily and on spending six
hours every Saturday to clean his apartment. He is too tense and
neurotic to settle down to any work. So most of his waking activity,
prior to a recent conversion to religion, is taken up with telling
pornographic stories, drawing pornographic figures, and "spot-
ting" homosexuals. All this I would not mind so much. However,
the moment he detects—and on this score he has an unfailing eye—
a person's soft spot he hits at it with all his might. If it happens
to be a girl who is not good-looking and obviously feels touchy
on this subject, our dear Martin will know how to bring the conversation to the subject of the overwhelming importance of a
girl's good looks in our society. "It's a sad fact—but what am I
to do—that intelligence, a pleasant disposition, even money, are of
no avail if a girl doesn't have a pretty face. That's how the world
is! I know—I didn't make the world. Take for instance my cousin
Paula. . . ." Or supposing Martin sees that a person feels touchy
because he speaks English with a heavy accent. Martin will come
in as follows: "You know, America is a funny country. A person,

unless he is a magician, can be as gifted and charming as anything.
He still won't get on if he does not properly acclimatize himself.
Take a seemingly trivial thing like pronunciation. . . ." Martin
Sekierer is too insignificant for me to call him evil. The terms I
usually apply to him are unprintable. When I use printable terms
I call him a vile stinker. Here what I am expressing, in addition
to disapproval and a certain modicum of impersonal hatred, is
contempt and disgust.

There are, then, emotions and attitudes besides approval and
disapproval which moral judgments express. Similarly, the Objective of good-judgments may vary greatly from case to case. Sometimes the Objective of a good-judgment is simply the giving of
information. When, in the example on page 149, I was asked, "what
sort of a person is X.Y.?" at least part of my Objective was the
giving of information concerning X.Y. It is true that in many
such cases I also aim at influencing the questioner in a certain
way; and sometimes this is the whole of my Objective. But it is
important to insist, as against some recent writers, that sometimes
the Objective of the author is simply the giving of information.
Thus if Martin Sekierer had asked me, "What sort of a person is
X.Y.?" I would have answered, "She is a very good person" and
this, since he knows me well enough for that, would give him, in a
rough way, the information he wanted. In giving my answer, I
would not care one whit whether he is going to like X.Y. or not.
I am no proselytizer, reformer or humanitarian and I have not the
least desire to influence his character or interfere in any way in
his life.

Sometimes, but not very often, the Objective of a good-judgment is the venting of one's feelings. Thus supposing I am alone,
reading Rauschning's fascinating book, *Hitler Speaks*. As I read
descriptions—which have been amply proven since—of Hitler's
complete indifference to human suffering, his ruthlessness and
mercilessness, of the cynical way in which he planned the construction of concentration camps for his enemies, of his deliberate
employment of fear to conquer the world, I speak out loud, "my
word, that man was an evil specimen of the human race!" Here
the Objective of my statement is clearly not the giving of informa-

tion to anybody. Nor can it be the influencing of anybody. There is nobody else around and I am already as hostile before the statement as I shall be after making it. The Objective here is simply getting into the open and out of my system some of the anger and revulsion which accumulated as I read Rauschning's descriptions. It should be noted that even when, alone and only in order to vent my own feelings, I say, "my word, Hitler was a very evil man," I assert or imply that Hitler had certain features and I also *express* not merely a feeling but an attitude of disapproval towards him as being a man who had these qualities.

I may have given the impression in what I said concerning the polyguity of "good" that when two people with a different background argue about the goodness of a person, they are engaged in a purely verbal disagreement and that their dispute is therefore a "pseudo-dispute." I shall deal with this point more fully in Chapter VIII. But I should like to say at once that this is only a small part of my view concerning moral disputes. The disputants do indeed, in such a case, "speak different languages,"[5] but their linguistic differences are the signs or effects of *non-verbal* disagreements.

3. "Ought"[6]

IT IS IMPOSSIBLE to give an adequate account of the functions of the word "ought" or of ought-judgments without a discussion of moral disputes. Prior to that discussion we shall have to confine ourselves to a few simple and obvious points.

Supposing I lived in a state where there is a law against the sale and use of contraceptives. Supposing a certain legislator has just introduced a bill, to be referred to as "the Contraception Bill," which would legalize the sale and use of contraceptives. In the course of a conversation I make the statement, "The bill ought to be passed by the legislature." I shall call this statement n_1.

---

5. Cf. Hampshire, *op. cit.*, pp. 477-478.

6. In this section and in the next chapter I shall assume, in order to simplify my presentation, that approval and disapproval are the only moral emotions or attitudes. As already pointed out in the last section, this is not really the case.

It will be very instructive to compare and contrast n_1 with my statement m_1, discussed in the last section—"X.Y. is a good person." It will also be interesting to compare n_1 with the doctor's advice— "you should drink a glass of milk every night before going to bed"— to the patient who wanted to put on weight. We shall from now on refer to the doctor's persuasive as "p."

(i) Both n_1 and m_1 express the author's approval. (ii) n_1 is like p in that both have as their Objective the performance of a certain action or certain actions. (iii) n_1 differs from m_1 and resembles p in that it has no referent, that it cannot possibly be said to be either true or false. (iv) n_1, next, resembles m_1 and differs from p in that what determines its author to regard a factual statement as "relevant" or "reason" for n_1 are his own approvals and disapprovals and not any desires on the part of the person whom he is addressing. We must now elaborate the last two points.

It is clear, to begin with, that n_1 has no referent. No state of affairs, actual or possible, would make it correct to say "n_1 is true" or "n_1 is false." If the Contraception Bill were passed, this would not make n_1 true; and if the bill were not passed, this would not make n_1 false. If I stop approving of the bill, I might no longer address myself to anybody with n_1, but n_1 would not be false. If I change my belief about the consequences of the bill, I might conclude that it is not really justified and that it ought not to be enacted. But such a change could not be properly described as, "I came to believe that n_1 is false." I am confident that any observation of how people use "true" and "false" in connection with situations like this will confirm what I have said.

Although n_1 has no meaning in the sense of referent, it does have descriptive meaning and thus, in the extended sense explained in Chapter VI, it is an objective claim. For it does clearly have meaning in what we decided to call sense (4) of the term: I am willing to defend n_1 by appealing to certain factual statements. I am willing to give up or moderate n_1 if these factual statements could be shown to be false. n_1, then, although it does not refer to the referent of these factual statements, is nevertheless corrigible by and "based upon" them.

Suppose I were engaged in a public debate in defense of n_1. I might very well talk along the following lines: "If this bill is passed, it will lessen the pains and sufferings of countless women in our state who do not wish to have more than two or three children. It would lessen the financial burden of countless fathers. It would also give the children of these families a far greater chance for happiness. It would prevent the conclusion of marriages which are often certain to be unhappy, formed as they are for the only purpose of legalizing an unwanted child. Finally, it would reduce the income of quack-abortionists and the cost of the upkeep of foundling hospitals." It will be convenient to refer to these statements from now on as "$s_1 \ldots s_6$."

Each of $s_1 \ldots s_6$ I would consider as a reason for n_1. The features of the bill to which $s_1 \ldots s_6$ refer I would regard as being *relevant* to n_1. I consider these features relevent because I approve or tend to approve of anything which has them. The bill has many other features which I do not consider relevant. Thus it is likely to lead to an increase in the income of gynecologists and the manufacturers of contraceptives; and it is likely to lead to a decrease in the income of the manufacturers of baby-clothes and toys. I do not consider these features relevant and the corresponding factual statements to be reasons because I neither approve nor disapprove of them.

It is important to insist that although my approval of the features in question makes $s_1 \ldots s_6$ into reasons for n_1, *the statements themselves are objective claims*. My approval makes them into reasons, but it does not make them true or false. They are true if certain facts, totally distinct from my approval, exist, and they are false if these facts do not exist. In this respect n_1 resembles p. For in that case the patient's desire made the statement "Drinking milk regularly is a convenient way of putting on weight" into a reason for the advice, but it did not make it true or false.

An interesting point about ought-judgments is their "flavor of holiness." By this I mean the speaker's implication, "I make this statement although I do not stand to *gain* by its satisfaction" or "I would say this even if its satisfaction would not bring me any personal benefit." In many cases of advice something of this flavor is also present, but rarely to the same extent as in ought-judgments.

It should also be noted that while the Objective of (non-moral) imperatives is always the performance of some *action* or other, the Objective of ought-judgments is sometimes the adoption of a certain *attitude* rather than the performance of any action. Thus, a Catholic priest, in denouncing immorality to Valletutti, a notoriously "immoral" man, may know in advance that nothing he can say will stop Valletutti from having sexual relations with women other than his own wife. Yet he will be very pleased with himself if he succeeds in strengthening Valletutti's tendency to *feel guilt* about his behavior or if he succeeds in getting Valletutti to bring up his children according to "the laws of God."

Like good-judgments, ought-judgments tend to be rather vague. That is to say, there will usually be a fairly wide range of features of an action concerning which a person will not be able definitely to say either that they are or that they are not relevant to the ought-judgment concerning the action. My discussion in preceding paragraphs may have given the impression that people always either definitely approve or definitely disapprove of a given feature or definitely adopt an attitude of moral indifference. I hasten to add now that this is not the case. Observation quite plainly shows that there are varying degrees of approval and indifference.

The question will undoubtedly be raised: are ought-judgments polyguous, so far as their descriptive meaning is concerned? Since different people tend to approve and disapprove of different features are you willing to maintain that moral disputes are really verbal disputes only and therefore pseudo-disputes? I must now face these questions. To this end the whole subject of the nature of moral disputes has to be investigated.

CONTENTS

Chapter VIII

The Logic of
Moral Discourse (II)

1. First- and Second-Order Reasons

THE DISTINCTION BETWEEN what I shall call "first-order reasons" and what I shall call "second-order reasons" will be of some importance in subsequent discussions in this chapter. Let us for a moment return to n_1—"The bill legalizing birth control ought to be passed." Suppose that in defending n_1 I offered $s_1 \ldots s_6$ as reasons. Let us suppose, furthermore, that these are absolutely all the reasons I could ever give. Now, supposing somebody were to demand a justification for regarding one of these statements as a reason for n_1. Supposing, e.g., he were to ask: "Why should the income of quack abortionists be decreased?" In answer to this question I would again be willing to offer certain factual statements as reasons: e.g., "Quack abortionists use their income to corrupt legislators and the police" (t_1) and "Quack abortionists escape paying income tax thus raising the income taxes of other people" (t_2). To offer statements like t_1 or t_2 as reasons for regarding "It will decrease the income of quack abortionists" as a reason for n_1 would be a perfectly natural procedure. On the other hand it would be most unusual, to say the least, to offer t_1 and t_2 as reasons for n_1. They may properly be called "reasons for regarding a certain statement as a reason for n_1" but not "reasons for n_1." Now, I propose to refer to the reasons for an ought-judgment as "first-order reasons" for it and to reasons for considering a statement as a reason for an ought-judgment as "second-order reasons" for it. If this process were continued we would also meet "third-order reasons," "fourth-order reasons," etc. The features referred to in a first-order reason we shall call "first-order features" and the features referred to in a second-order reason we shall call "second-order features."

2. Model Disputes

To THROW some light on the nature of moral disputes I shall begin by constructing and analyzing several artificial cases which I shall call "models." This done, we shall consider how far actual moral disputes resemble and how far they differ from these artificial disputes.

Model I. A and B are people who approve and disapprove and feel morally indifferent towards exactly the same features and in exactly the same degrees. Supposing x is an action which has two and only two features.[1] One of these features is H. Neither A or B have any doubts about x's possession of H. Both of them are morally indifferent toward H. As regards the other feature, A believes it to be F_a—which both of them approve—while B believes it to be F_b which both of them disapprove. A maintains that x ought to be done. B maintains that x ought not to be done.

In this case A and B disagree in their attitude towards x and in their Objective since A desires x to be performed while B desires it not to be performed. Since they also mean the same by "x ought to be done," so far as the descriptive meaning of the sentence is concerned, they disagree in belief. They disagree as to whether x has feature F_a or feature F_b. Is their dispute capable of settlement in any sense other than what we called sense (2)?[2] The answer is plainly "Yes." It can also be settled in sense (3).[3] That is to say:

---

1. Throughout Model I "features" means "first-order-features."
2. Cf. Chapter I, Section 3.
3. Cf. Chapter I, Section 6.

if it can be shown that x really has F_a, A will be shown to be "in the right" and B "in the wrong"; while if x can be shown to have F_b, B will be shown to be in the right and A in the wrong. In the former case, A's attitude will be shown to be appropriate and B's inappropriate; in the latter case the reverse will be true.

When I say that the dispute has been settled in A's favor in sense (3), this in no way means or implies that A has succeeded in getting B to adopt his attitude. Similarly, anything which tends to show that x has or does not have F_a or F_b is relevant to the dispute whether the consideration moves the parties or not.

Before going any further, I should like to introduce the notion of "ought-making feature," corresponding to some extent to the notion of "good-making feature," introduced in Section 2 of Chapter VII. A man will be said to regard a feature, say F_o, as an ought-making feature if and in so far as he is willing to defend his recommendation that something, say x, be done on the ground that x possesses F_o. Conversely, we shall say that somebody regard F_p as an anti-ought-making feature if and in so far as he bases his recommendation that something, y, ought not to be done on y's possession of F_p. As before we are using "feature" very broadly to include inherent qualities as well as causal properties. Corresponding to first-, second- and higher-order reasons, it is also possible to distinguish first-, second- and higher-order ought-making and anti-ought-making features.

Using this terminology the situation of Model I may be described as follows: A and B here agree completely concerning which features are and which features are not ought-making. They disagree whether x really possesses the feature they both regard as ought-making.

Model II. A again maintains that x ought to be done. B again maintains that x ought not to be done. x again has two (first-order) features. This time A and B are in complete agreement as to what these features are. They are G and H. Towards H, A and B feel morally indifferent. But towards G their attitudes conflict. A approves of it while B disapproves of it. Here then there is no disagreement concerning what are x's first-order features but rather whether one of them is ought-making.

Let us suppose also that both A and B approve of what in this context would be a second-order feature, G_1, and disapprove of the second-order feature G_2. A furthermore believes that anything which has G also has G_1. B on the other hand believes that anything which has G does not have G_1 but G_2.

In what sense other than sense (2) can this dispute be settled? I think the answer is clear. If the disputants stick to first-order reasons the dispute is incapable of settlement in any sense other than sense (2). However, if they proceed to take into account second-order reasons the dispute can be settled in sense (3). If it can be shown that anything that has G necessarily has G_1 also, A will be shown to be in the right and B in the wrong. If it can be shown that anything which has G necessarily has G_2 and cannot have G_1 then B will be shown to be in the right and A in the wrong.

About Model II it might be said that the parties *do not mean the same* by "ought" so far as the descriptive meaning of the word is concerned. This will be true in the sense that they do not give the same first-order reasons for their ought-judgments. But to leave it at that would be very misleading. Their difference in meaning is only a symptom or result of their disagreement concerning the non-verbal issue: does anything which has G also have G_1 or G_2?

Model III. A again says, "x ought to be done" and B again says, "x ought not to be done." x, as before, has only two features. A and B agree that these features are F_1 and F_2. A approves of F_1 and disapproves of F_2; B approves of F_2 and disapproves of F_1. This time, however, they also agree concerning the connections between F_1 and other features and between F_2 and other features. They agree that anything which has F_1 has also F_{11} and further that anything which has F_{11} has F_{21}, etc. They also agree that anything which has F_2 has F_{12} and anything which has F_{12} has F_{22}, etc. But while A approves of F_{11} and F_{21} and disapproves of F_{12} and F_{22}, B approves of F_{12} and F_{22} and disapproves of F_{11} and F_{21}

Can this dispute be settled in some other than sense (2)? Here the answer is clearly "No": No appeal to any facts is of any avail.

We must now turn to an investigation of some actual moral disputes. I have chosen three cases, two of them dealing with topics which are much discussed at the present time, while the third is a dispute of a more personal nature which seems to me very instructive.

3. "Should Communists be Allowed to Teach in Universities?"

As MY FIRST actual case I have chosen the discussion as to whether members of the Communist Party ought to be allowed to teach in universities. Sidney Hook has lucidly stated the case that as a general policy they ought not to be allowed to teach,[4] while Irving Howe has ably presented the case that they ought to be allowed to teach.[5]

Hook, in support of his conclusion, mainly relies on the following factual assertions: (1) Teachers who are members of the Communist Party are instructed to take advantage of their position to indoctrinate their students with the party line on any topic they may have occasion to discuss. (2) It is extremely improbable that a member of the Communist Party is inactive since inactivity is a sufficient reason for expulsion. Control Commissions exist which periodically purge the Party of inactive and unreliable members. (3) A member of the Communist Party is not allowed to have doubts concerning any aspect of the party line. Divisions such as that between Thomists and Augustinians in the Catholic Church are not tolerated. (4) Communist teachers are themselves aware that they are violating accepted notions of academic responsibility.

In addition to supporting his conclusions with these and similar factual statements, including documentation of Communist directives and activities, Hook considers it necessary to make it clear

---

4. "Academic Freedom and Communism," *New York Times Magazine*, February 27, 1949. Hook's position was subsequently spelled out in great detail in other articles and in his book *Heresy Yes, Conspiracy No*. Readers are referred to this book for a complete statement of Hook's viewpoint. Hook does not maintain, as is often supposed, that membership in the Communist Party should *automatically* bar an individual from teaching but that it should be considered as *prima facie* unfitness to teach. It should be sufficient to indict rather than to convict. Faculty committees would then, in the light of the evidence, determine whether a dismissal is justified.

5. "Intellectual Freedom and the Stalinist Teachers," *The New International*, December 1949.

that certain types of teachers ought not to be dismissed. He also considers it necessary to attack a certain counter-proposal. To be more specific: (5) "Fellow-travellers" ought not to be dismissed just because they are fellow-travellers.

The term "fellow-traveller" is hopelessly vague. "Fellow-travellers" come and go. They are of all varieties. No one is wise enough to pick out the dumb, innocent sheep from the cunning and dishonest goats. So long as they are not under the discipline of the Communist Party, they may still be sensitive to the results of honest inquiry. Whatever harm they do is incomparably less than the harm that would result from any attempt to purge them. Without the steel core of the Communist party faction on the campus to magnetize them, they will fly off in all the directions their scattered wits take them.

(6) Catholics too ought not to be dismissed:

There is no evidence whatsoever of the operation of Catholic cells in nonsectarion universities which impose a party line in all the arts and sciences that must be followed by all Catholic teachers on pain of excommunication.

Catholics, when living in a country in which they are in the minority

. . . have Papal justification to live under and even enforce certain laws which run counter to Catholic dogma. For example, Catholic judges on the bench in New York State grant divorces even to Catholics and recognize that they have a duty both to the standards of their profession and to the laws of the state, insofar as it is not a Catholic law or a Catholic state under which they live. The same "absolution" is granted to Catholic teachers who are good members of the church insofar as they are members of non-Catholic institutions. They are supposed to fulfill their obligations and duties as a member of the non-Catholic academic community and prescribe readings, for example, for their students which are on the Catholic index even when their students are Catholics.

(7) Hook, finally, opposes the view that Communist party members must be

. . . judged by their individual actions in the classroom; they must, so to speak, be "caught in the act" of inculcating the party line in the minds of their students.

This has two fatal difficulties. It would require spying in every classroom to detect the party line, and disorganize or intimidate not only Communist party members but the entire faculty, since a member of the

Communist party admits membership only when faced with a charge of perjury, and not always then. The academic community would wrathfully and rightfully repudiate any such practice.

Second, it would be very difficult to determine when a teacher was defending a conclusion because he honestly believed it followed from the evidence, and when he was carrying out his task as a good soldier in the party cause.

Howe argues explicitly against Hook. I shall present his position, so far as possible as a series of comments or replies to the seven points listed in my exposition of Hook's case. Howe fully agrees with (1) and (4) of Hook's assertions:

It would be absurd to deny that teachers who join the CP usually cease to function as free teachers should. To keep them in the faculty of a school means to risk the possibility that they will convert a few students, perhaps capture a little pocket of power here and there, etc.

However, he denies, in part or in whole, (2) and (3):

How do Stalinist teachers actually behave? It is hard to say in any generalized way, for there seem to be wide variations. But it is quite certain that they are seldom the party line automata the CP resolution quoted by Hook directs them to be and as Hook assumes they are. It must be remembered that many CP teachers are men quite competent in their fields, with a certain training in the methods of free intellectual inquiry. They are not ordinary Stalinist hacks.

Hook offers two objections to this proposed procedure: it would involve spying on teachers and it would be difficult to distinguish CP members from fellow-travellers. If it is necessary to "spy" on a teacher to find out if he is misusing the classroom, then the overwhelming likelihood is that he is not; consequently, there is no reason to discharge him. When teachers act as petty tyrants, the news travels very quickly in the universities. As for Hook's second objection, it is meaningful only if one's premise is that the automatic elimination of all CP members from the campus is desirable. But if one judges teachers by their individual behavior, then it is quite conceivable that a fellow-traveller might merit expulsion while a CP teacher might not. The essential criterion is: how does this teacher behave in the classroom, not what he thinks.

Howe next questions whether Hook can consistently maintain (5) and (6).

Hook, of course, is quite right in saying that doctrinal impositions, whatever their source, affect adversely the work of a teacher. But then we must notice that doctrinal impositions are the work not only of Stalinist teachers but of a great variety of other teachers: Catholics, NAM economic teachers, etc. Hook counters this view by saying that there is "no evidence whatsoever of the operation of Catholic cells in non-sectarian universities," as there is of CP cells. Hook's statement is true but irrelevant, for doctrinal imposition is not contingent on the existence of party cells: one can exist without the other.

It is true that the Catholics have no cells in the universities; they long ago abandoned such crude methods of operation. (I suppose, however, one could maintain that their cells meet regularly every Sunday morning.) The Catholic teachers generally don't need the spur of cells, their intellectual discipline and coherence being products of centuries-long tradition and training. This intellectual discipline—or more accurately, as Hook puts it, doctrinal imposition—is often as extensive and severe as that of the Stalinist movement. (I speak of the genuine believers, not the fellow-travelling "sleepers" of the faith.) And this doctrinal imposition is no less real because Catholic teachers in any given university never hold "fraction" meetings.

He also attacks Hook's arguments against the proposal that Communist Party members should not be dismissed till they are "caught in the act."

In the U.S. the CP is not in a position to enforce the kind of intellectual discipline from its teacher-members that Stalinist movements can in those countries where it has state power. And since the CP knows this it allows its teacher-members a greater degree of latitude in the expression of opinion than it does other members.

Finally, Howe accuses Hook of having ignored certain considerations which have an important bearing on the issue. Firstly, he says, Hook has ignored the social context which gave rise to the whole discussion—the attempt of reactionary groups to suppress the expression of heretical views, Communist or otherwise. Secondly, Howe maintains, a policy of dismissing Communist teachers is likely to drive the nicer type of Communist or Communist sympathizer closer to the Party.

It is necessary to understand that the CP is not merely a totalitarian organization, though it is that, but that it is also a movement which peculiarly bases itself on and exploits the legitimate dissatisfactions of workers and intellectuals. And those power agencies which today attack the CP have no particular reason to distinguish the pseudo-radical from the genuinely radical. To support such suppression is to help strengthen the adherence to the CP of those of its followers who should be won away from it—for the best CP supporters, the most sincere and idealistic ones, will draw closer to it when it is persecuted, only the middle-brow riff-raff will run in fright.

So far as I know Howe did not ever again take up this subject in print. Hook did not explicitly reply to Howe's article but in his book he replied in detail to several of the points made by Howe which were also made by other critics of his position. Hook also offered some explicit objections to Howe's article in correspondence with myself from which I have permission to quote the relevant comments.

Among other things Hook is concerned to maintain in his rejoinders that, so far from weakening the position of heretical teachers in general, the policy he recommends is in the total social context the one most likely to make their position secure. While the "cold war" is raging between Russia and the United States the elected representatives of the community would not for long tolerate the continued presence of Communist teachers in public colleges, knowing that their sympathies are with Russia and that the Communist Party is primarily an instrument of Soviet policy. If Communist teachers are eliminated by the universities, acting through their own faculties, great care can be taken that nobody will be dismissed merely on the ground of holding heretical views. For then the question will be handled by men who are devoted to academic freedom and who are not inspired by motives of political gain. If, on the other hand, Communist teachers are not dealt with in this way, ignorant and unscrupulous politicians who very possibly have no concern for academic freedom are liable to take over the job. Then a great many people who are not part of the Communist conspiracy but whose views happen to be offensive to this or that politician may also suffer.

Hook is also concerned to reinforce point (7) above—that any attempt to base one's policy towards Communist teachers exclusively on their class-room acts rather than the fact of their membership and other campus activities must lead to a system of almost continuous classroom supervision or worse. "Howe believes in something worse. For he says that when 'teachers act as petty tyrants, the news travels very quickly.' In other words he would give credence to and act upon mere rumors. . . . How would Howe know that the rumors were true? At some point he would have to check up on the teacher's performance, by questioning students and doing the things for which 'spying' is a generic term." Even if we could rely on students to detect and report skilful indoctrination, "it would be a sad day in the history of American education if we used students in this way or encouraged them to stoop to the techniques of a police state. Far better to leave Communist Party teachers to do as they please than to degrade their students by impressing them into the kind of service made so notorious in countries behind the Iron Curtain."

I have presented this dispute at some length since it seems to me a mine of information to the student of the logic of moral discourse. I shall confine myself, however, strictly to the points bearing on the questions of our inquiry.

(i) Although the dispute is not capable of settlement in sense (1), since there is no state of affairs which would make Hook's ought-statement true and Howe's ought-statement false, or vice versa, the dispute is *within certain limits* capable of settlement in sense (3). Hook, in saying what he says, is clearly committing himself to the following position: if it could be shown that CP members invariably defy party instructions to indoctrinate their students, or if it could be shown that my descriptions of the CP and its attitude to academic institutions is altogether mistaken—if their attitude is really like that of the American Association of University Professors—or again if it could be shown that the dismissal of CP members would, certainly or very probably, lead to the dismissal of numbers of non-Communist teachers who hold heretical views, then CP members ought not to be dismissed. Similarly, Howe is committing himself to some such position as the following: if it could be shown that teachers who are CP members always or very commonly follow the instructions of the Party in the classroom and if it could also be shown that the dismissal of CP members, so far from making the position of heretical teachers more difficult, would actually result in more freedom of expression, then, other things being equal, CP members ought to be dismissed. The dispute between Hook and Howe, then, resembles Model I at least to this extent: Hook and Howe agree to a large extent as to what in the situation are ought-making and what are anti-ought-making features. They disagree as to whether these features are present or not. If they are, one of them is in the right; if they are not, the other one is in the right. Given the original attitude of the disputants, which of them is in the right is decided by the facts and not by their success in converting the opponent.

(ii) There is a very considerable range of situations for which the disputants have not "provided." By this I mean that their commitments are not sufficiently definite for us to be able to say, in quite a number of possible situations, in whose favor the dispute has been settled—in sense (3) of the word. Thus supporting it could be shown that exactly 85%, though not all, CP members followed the party's instructions in the classroom; and suppose also that the position of heretical teachers would, as a result of the dismissal of Communists, become slightly but *only* slightly more precarious. In this eventuality we would be unable to say, on the basis of the statement of the disputants, who, if anybody, is in the right. The same applies to many other possible situations.

Supposing that in the circumstances just imagined, Hook and Howe stuck to their original recommendations. In that case obviously their disagreement would not be capable of settlement in sense (3) by an appeal to first-order features. For they now agree as to what these features are, but disagree whether they are ought-making. Nevertheless it is still quite possible that the dispute is capable of settlement in sense (3) by an appeal to second-order features or generally to higher-order features. Thus Hook might elaborate the position we are assuming him to adopt by saying: "The conquest of the world by Stalinism is certain to result in destruction, for many centuries, of all the most precious things in life including those without which any genuine happiness for the human race is impossible: living without the fear of arbitrary arrest and being spied on, free science and philosophy and art, etc., etc. The strengthening of the forces of Stalinism which is certain to be the result of the activities of CP instructors is more likely to

lead to the death of democratic institutions than the slight increase
in the difficulty of heretical teachers to maintain their position in
the universities." Howe on the other hand might very well take
the following position: "The conquest of the world by Stalinists
would have all the effects that Hook mentioned. But other events
may also lead in the same direction and making the position of
heretical teachers even slightly more difficult is going to undermine
democratic institutions more than the slight strengthening of the
forces of Stalinism inside the United States."

If this were the positions of the two disputants, the dispute could
in principle be settled in sense (3) by an appeal to second-order
features. To this extent, the dispute would resemble Model II and
not Model I.

(iii) It is very interesting to observe that Howe does not content
himself with challenging some of Hook's factual assertions but *adds*
factual considerations which he claims to be relevant and which
Hook did not take into account in the magazine articles which
constituted his original statement. Similarly, Hook in his rebuttals
and especially in his book introduces still further facts which he
had not introduced in his original statement. The same of course
would apply to further rebuttals by both parties.

4. "Should Mercy-Killing be Legalized?"

EXAMPLE II. My next example concerns the topic of euthanasia
or mercy-killing. "Euthanasia" means "the termination of human
life by painless means for the purpose of ending severe suffering."
The Euthanasia Society of America has for many years been trying to get a law passed which will make euthanasia legal in certain
types of cases. Section 30 of the proposed bill reads:

> Any person of sound mind over 21 years of age who is suffering from
> severe physical pain caused by a disease for which no remedy affording
> lasting relief or recovery is at the time known to medical science may
> have euthanasia administered.

This bill has been violently opposed by dignitaries of the
Roman Catholic Church and also by some other people whose
religious affiliations are unknown to me. The Catholic position has

been stated in two pamphlets by the Rt. Rev. Msgr. Robert E. McCormick.[6] I shall present the views of the opposing parties in the form of a debate, basing myself on the official literature of the Euthanasia Society of America[7] and Msgr. McCormick's two pamphlets.

Defender of Euthanasia: (1) In spite of the advances of medical science, there are still several diseases which are incurable. Many of these are exceedingly painful and often last for several years before they finally kill the patient. The patient's life becomes a long nightmare of torture. (2) Again and again he requests his friends or his doctor to put an end to his suffering.

Sometimes the patient himself, knowing that he faces months of agony and unable to secure a painless, sure means of merciful release, resorts to a crude method—jumps from a window, slashes his wrists, gulps down a searing disinfectant, or turns on the gas-jets, the last method resulting in injury and death to others

(3) So great is the suffering of so many a patient that their doctor, although he thereby risks a trial for murder, surgically administers a lethal dose of narcotic. In fact "what might be called 'boot-leg' euthanasia" has become a growing practice. (4) Euthanasia moreover, is not contrary to the principles of Christianity. A group of non-Catholic ministers of New York has stated:

In our opinion, voluntary euthanasia should not be regarded as contrary to the teachings of Christ or to the principles of Christianity.
"I cannot believe," said a Catholic physician who is a member of the Euthanasia Society, "that the Prince of Peace who said 'blessed are the merciful,' would condone unnecessary suffering."

(5) A man may be punished for cruelty if he does not put a horse or dog out of its misery but is liable to be prosecuted for murder if he helps a cancer patient to an overdose of morphine. This is an intolerable situation in which the suffering of human beings is treated more lightly than the suffering of animals.

Catholic: (1) Euthanasia is a "pagan concept." It is based on the

6. *Legalized "Mercy" Killing—Moral or Immoral?* (New York: The Catholic Information Society, 1947) and *So-called "Mercy" Killing* (New York: The Catholic Information Society, 1947).
7. *Merciful Release* (The Euthanasia Society of America, Inc., 1950).

view that, "physical pleasure and happiness are the main purpose
and sum-total of life." A by-product of this philosophy is:

a great fear of physical suffering. Some people think that they are great
philanthropists and humanitarians if they can curtail human physical
suffering, even if it means disregarding the general code of morality
accepted by civilized nations for many centuries.

As against this

Catholic teaching holds that sufferings have their place in God's plan,
for the salvation of the individual soul. This is evident from the example
of Christ Himself, who suffered the scourging at the pillar and the
agony and death upon the Cross for the sole purpose of redeeming man
from his sins and giving him the means of the salvation of his soul.
Christ Himself said, 'He that taketh not up his cross and followeth Me
is not worthy of Me' (Matt. X, 38). St. Paul says, 'Whom the Lord
loveth, He chastiseth' (Heb. XII, 6).

(2) Euthanasia is simply murder; medical murder, it is true, but
murder nonetheless.

The practitioners of euthanasia have of course a more delicate approach to the problem of committing murder than had Bluebeard,
whose technique was rather crude and gory. The euthanasians do the
job cleanly and painlessly. These seem to be only practical advantages
of medical murder. The net result however is just the same, for when
the affair is over the patient is decidedly dead.

(3) As for the admission of various doctors that they commonly
practice euthanasia, this "boomerangs" since it

is a recognized principle of all law that a person should not profit by
his own fraud or have his past crimes sanctioned by new legislation.

(4) How any minister of the Christian Protestant denominations
can support legalized voluntary euthanasia is beyond comprehen-
sion because it is definitely against the natural law, the innate
moral code, the teachers in the Old Testament of the Jewish law,
and the teachings of Christ.

That suicide and murder are against the very law of nature is evident
from the fact that God, who created the human being, gave to him a
highly-developed nervous system which instinctively acts immediately
to ward off or escape any danger to life.

When we come to the pronouncements of Our Lord, Jesus Christ, there can be no doubt that He condemned suicide and murder, for He said in the words of today's text that He had come not to destroy but to fulfill the Jewish law and the Prophecies. Our Lord stated in no uncertain terms, 'You have heard that it was said to them of old, Thou shalt Not Kill. And whosoever shall kill shall be in danger of the judgment.' (Matt. V, 21)

There is a metaphysical justification for Christ's statement:

The reason that suicide and murder are condemned by God in the Old Law and Christ in the New is that destruction is an act of dominion, and a man does not have dominion either over his own life or that of any other person. Only God, the Creator, Who made man in His own image, has that dominion. Hence, suicide and murder are both horrible crimes because they invade the supreme and exclusive dominion and right of God Himself. Moreover, they destroy a creature belonging to God.

(5) There is no inconsistency in allowing mercy-killing for animals but not for human beings. For unlike "brute animals," human beings have immortal souls.

(6) Finally

If we allow the state to legalize voluntary "mercy killing," we will permit the government to usurp a divine prerogative and abrogate a divine law which prohibits the killing of the innocent. The passage of this bill will indicate that our Legislature has adopted the principle that man-made law takes precedence over the natural law. There will no longer be any inalienable rights of human beings or any immutable standards in basic ethics. A thing will be right or wrong only because the civil law says that it is right or wrong. This of course will mean utilitarianism in law. What seems opportune to the majority of the Legislature at the time will be made the law regardless of its basic morality, and this will also become the mode of interpretation for the courts.

If the legislature can disregard the commandment "Thou shalt not kill," sanctioned by Jewish and Christian civilization since the time of Moses, it can also set aside the commandments "Thou shalt not steal" and "Thou shalt not bear false witness." In that event personal and property rights will be invaded without hope of redress, and courts will find it difficult to render justice because legal oaths will be meaningless.

Defender of Euthanasia: In reply to the charge that euthanasia is murder I wish to point out that

Murder is the "illegal killing of another person with malice afore-thought." But euthanasia is administered in mercy, not malice; and it will not be illegal when the proposed law is enacted. Therefore it is not murder.

In reply to the charge that euthanasia is against the Biblical command "Thou shalt not kill," it is proper to insist that

Those who justify war and capital punishment (as the Christian Church has done through all the ages) cannot reasonably condemn euthanasia on this ground.

To those who say that the ethics of the medical profession for-bids the physician to destroy life, we answer:

There are exceptions to this rule. The physician may perform an abortion if his colleagues agree that the mother's health or sanity is imperiled. At childbirth he may sacrifice the baby to save the mother's life. If euthanasia is sanctioned by law, there will be no more stigma attached to its administration than there is now to the therapeutic inter-ruption of pregnancy.

It has also been said that

Suffering is part of the Divine Plan for the good of man's soul, and must not be interfered with.

In that case,

. . . we should not countenance the use of anaesthetics or any relief of suffering by the medical profession. "Blessed are the merciful—All things whatsoever you would that men should do unto you, do you even so to them."

Catholic: You are wrong in what you say about war and capital punishment. For the principle of self-defence enters into the situa-tion in that case and all people recognize the right of self-defence.

The motive of Voluntary Euthanasia is not self-defence but the direct opposite—SELF-DESTRUCTION. Nor can they claim parity in capital punishment, for civil rulers have the duty to promote the com-mon good of society, and must have the means at their disposal for the safety of the citizens and the public order. Especially must they impede such crimes as homicide, but frequently this cannot be accom-plished except by the death penalty.

The killing of a man is not intrinsically evil except insofar as it is unjust. To God alone belong the full and direct power over life of a man (Wisdom, XVI, 13), but He can, and does, delegate it to the civil authority which has the right to impose capital punishment for heinous crimes. Thus the civil rulers do not act by their own authority but as representatives of God on earth.

This does not mean that the Catholic Church advocates capital punishment, for she believes in the correction of the culprit rather than his death, but she does say that civil rulers are not acting outside their authority in imposing capital punishment when the crime warrants it for the common good. But certainly legalized voluntary euthanasia is not necessary for the common good unless the euthanasians absurdly hold that the patient is a menace to the state and his citizens merely because he is the victim of a painful and incurable disease.

This dispute is even more complex than the last one. I shall again confine myself to points directly relevant to the topic of our inquiry.

(i) The dispute is at least to some extent capable of settlement in cense (3). For in producing certain factual considerations as reasons for their ought-judgments—where "factual" is used broadly so as to include theological as well as empirical assertions—both parties are committing themselves to the statement that if the facts were other than what they claim them to be, their ought-judgments would be less strongly supported. If, e.g., there is no God, or if there is a God but if suicide and murder do not "invade the supreme and exclusive domain and right of God Himself" or if the legalization of euthanasia would not lead to perjury and the destruction of personal and property rights, but on the contrary to less perjury and greater respect for the law, then McCormick's ought-judgment would obviously be weakened. If on the other hand, it could be shown that the legalization of euthanasia would lead to a brutalization of the medical profession and of people in general, the ought-judgment of the defenders of euthanasia would be weakened. At the risk of wearisome repetition, I wish to emphasize that "weaken" does *not* here mean, "has a tendency to change the favorable attitude of the author of the moral judgment."

(ii) As in the previous case the commitments of the disputants are not sufficiently definite to cover all possible situations. Thus supposing it could be shown that (a) there is no God, (b) that human beings have no immortal souls, (c) that the legalization of euthanasia would not lead to "the invasion without redress of personal and property rights," but (d) that every year say one hundred people who have no desire to die will be done away with by their greedy relatives as a result of clever abuses of the new law. On the data before us, it is impossible to say who would have been shown to be in the right in that case. The same applies to many other possible situations.

(iii) It appears here, even more clearly than in the previous example, that there is no closed set of facts which can be described as "the facts of the situation." McCormick in replying to the defender of mercy-killing, introduces the consideration that legalization of euthanasia would lead to perjury and "the invasion of property and personal rights." A defender of euthanasia, on his part, could introduce, apropos of McCormick's remarks on suffering, all the enormous quantity of psychological and anthropological evidence concerning the effect of pain and frustration on the human organism. Similarly, a great many other factual considerations not actually brought up by the disputants in the pamphlets from which I quoted, are relevant in sense (3). In this respect, both our Examples I and II are altogether different from all of Models I-III.

5. "The Seating at Camp T."

EXAMPLE III. The following is a true story and I am sure many more along the same lines could be produced. My friend S. and I agree as closely on practically all important questions in life as two people can. One summer some years ago, we went to Camp T. for a weekend. The first morning we found ourselves seated with six other people each of whom we immediately disliked. The girls were stiff and humorless, the men tough and unintelligent. After the second meal I suggested that we ask to be seated at another table. My friend disagreed although we were in complete agreement both that by leaving we would in all probability offend some or all the six people at the table where we were now seated and that, whatever new company we got, it could hardly be worse than the one we had now. We finally did move to another table where we met some delightful people. We later saw some of the old company who were quite obviously peeved by our leaving them. To this day I maintain that we were right in moving while my friend maintains that we were wrong. Before discussing this example I should like to emphasize that both my friend S. and I are opposed to any doctrine of self-sacrifice and asceticism and that we are also both opposed to any doctrine that says that only one's own pleasure matters. If it had been certain that our leaving the table would result in the death of one or more of the people seated there, I would have unhesitatingly said that we ought not to leave. Conversely, if it had been certain that at another table both or one of us would meet a person destined to make us very happy, my friend would have said that we ought to leave.

With this introduction I should now like to point out the following features of this case: (i) It seems highly probable that here we have a closed set of facts which are *"the facts of the situation"* or at any rate that any further factual considerations, which are relevant in sense (3), would be accepted or rejected by both disputants alike. (ii) The parties are in entire agreement as to what the features of the case are. (iii) They also agree as to what features are *in general* ought-making and what features are in general anti-ought-making in cases of this sort. But (iv) in this particular case, they do not agree as to whether the *combination* of features present is ought-making or not. (v) This disagreement does not seem to be resolvable in sense (3) even by an appeal to second- or generally higher-order features.

6. Summary and Conclusions

FROM THE EXAMINATION of these three cases we may, I submit, draw the following conclusions:

1. Many, though not all, moral disputes are *within certain limits* capable of settlement in sense (3) and not only in sense (2). They are capable of settlement, that is to say, by an appeal to *facts*, whether these facts move the disputants or not. In this respect they resemble scientific disputes.

2. The commitments of the disputants are frequently rather

indefinite. There is often quite a large range of possible situations concerning which it is impossible to say in whose favor the dispute has been settled.

3. In moral disputes we are rarely faced with a closed set of facts. The facts of the situation tend to be "open" in the sense that "they cannot be uniquely described and finally circumscribed. Situations do not present themselves with their labels attached to them."[8]

If this account is correct, then Stevenson's theory concerning the nature of moral disputes is altogether mistaken. Thus he writes:

> *Any* statements about *any* matter of fact which *any* speaker considers likely to alter attitudes may be adduced as a reason for or against an ethical judgment.[9]

Again:

> Both disagreement in attitude and disagreement in belief are involved, but the former predominates in that (1) it determines what sort of disagreement in belief is relevantly disputed in a given ethical argument, and (2) *it determines by its continued presence or its resolution, whether or not the argument has been settled.* We may see further how intimately the two sorts of disagreement are related: since attitudes are often functions of beliefs, an agreement in belief may lead people, as a matter of psychological fact, to agree in attitude.[10]

There are also other views found in Stevenson, but the passages I have quoted represent the dominant theory in his writings. Expressed in our terminology, his theory states that moral disputes cannot be settled in any sense except sense (2) and that similarly factual considerations cannot be relevant to a moral judgment in any sense except sense (2).

The paradoxical consequences of this view have been pointed out by several recent writers. In the words of Brandt:

> On the emotive theory, a factual belief can be relevant to an ethical attitude or utterance only in the sense of being a causal ancestor of it.

---

8. Hampshire, *op. cit.*, p. 476.
9. *Ethics and Language*, p. 114. Stevenson's italics.
10. "The Nature of Ethical Disagreement," in *Readings in Philosophical Analysis* (ed. Feigl and Sellars), p. 500. My italics.

And causal relevance, of course, is entirely different from logical relevance.

. . . We all do want to be able to say that sometimes a person's ethical beliefs or attitudes are influenced by objectively irrelevant considerations. But if "relevance" merely means "causal relevance," this would be impossible. On the emotive theory, if one comes to believe about an action A that some person, for him prestigeful, disapproves A, and if that belief makes him inclined to disapprove A too, he has been moved by a perfectly relevant consideration. Again, if one is moved to disapprove socialized medicine by the thought that any expression of approval would oust him from his favorite club, he has been moved, according to the emotive theory, by as ethically relevant a consideration as any other he might have thought of. Now, I do not think this describes ordinary ethical thinking; we think some persuasive beliefs are distinctly *ir*relevant.[11]

Stevenson is obviously operating here on the assumption that if factual statements cannot be relevant in sense (1) the only other sense in which they can be relevant is sense (2).[12] But this, as I hope to have shown, is a complete mistake. Properly to describe "ordinary ethical thinking," "to enable us to make the distinction we all want to make," we do not need to invoke some non-natural realm; nor do we need to restate some form of private subjectivism, as Brandt suggests. All we need to do is recognize a further sense or set of senses of "settle" and "relevant."

We are now in position to deal with the questions which we raised at the end of Chapter VII: are ought-judgments polyguous in the same way as good-judgments? Are moral disputes, when the parties do not approve the same features, pseudo-disputes? To the first question the answer is plain now: ought-judgments are just as polyguous as good-judgments in the sense that their descriptive meaning varies a great deal from topic to topic. Thus the features which people imply when they say that mercy-killing ought or ought not to be legalized, are very different from those they imply when contending that Communists ought or ought not to be per-

---

11. "The Emotive Theory of Ethics," *The Philosophical Review*, 1950, pp. 312-313. Brandt's italics.

12. The same holds for Ayer who writes: "What are accounted reasons for our moral judgments are reasons only in the sense that they determine attitudes." *Op. cit.*, p. 175.

mitted to teach in colleges. They are also polyguous in the sense that when talking about the same subject different people do *not always* imply the same features when using the word "ought." Presumably—though this is a point which we did not investigate—this polyguity becomes very striking where people from widely different cultures are concerned.

It would seem to follow from this that when the disputants do not refer to the same feature by "good" and do not imply the same features by "ought," moral disputes are a species of pseudo-disputes, i.e., that they are merely verbal disputes. This, it would rightly be added, is an incredible consequence.

In reply, I should like to point out that there are many "verbal disagreements" which are not *merely* verbal differences. The verbal disagreement is there, but as a symptom of a different type of disagreement. The use of "healthy" by different schools of psychiatry is one of numerous cases which could be cited in this connection. Reich and Horney, for example, refer to very different sets of features by the term. But this verbal difference is among other things the result of disagreements concerning the cause as well as the most effective treatment of neurotic symptoms and personality problems in general.

Very much the same applies to moral disputes. I do not refer to the same features by "good" as a Catholic. Among other things, this is due to factual disagreement concerning the existence of God, the trustworthiness of the Bible, the effects of suffering, etc. Even in those cases, as in Example III above, where there seemingly was no factual disagreement at all, the disagreement was nevertheless, not merely verbal. The verbal difference in that case was the effect of a disagreement in attitude.

7. Fundamental Moral Judgments

I have so far omitted any discussion of one peculiar kind of moral judgment which must be exempted from the objectivism advocated in this work. I am referring to what are sometimes called "fundamental" or "basic" moral judgments. When a man is unable or unwilling to support a moral judgment with anything that would be considered a reason, we shall say that he has made a fundamental moral judgment. When and in so far as he can support a moral judgment with a reason, we shall refer to it as non-fundamental. Whether the statement offered as reason is true or false is immaterial—the moral judgment will be non-fundamental so long as it can be supported with such a statement, so long as it "does not stand on its own feet." In making this distinction I do not wish to rule out the possibility that some moral judgments may at the same time be both fundamental and non-fundamental. In such a case a man would be ready to support his moral judgment with reasons while insisting at the same time that he would hold to it even if he could not support it with any reasons.

Now, I wish to maintain that these fundamental moral judgments have "emotive meaning" only. They express a stand or an attitude on the part of their author. Usually they are also prescriptive—especially when the moral predicate is "right" or "wrong" or "ought" rather than "good" or "bad." On my view, however, fundamental moral judgments lack descriptive meaning. While naive subjectivism does not supply a fully adequate analysis even of fundamental moral judgments, in their case the subjective statements offered as translations would come a great deal closer to preserving the force of the original sentence.

It may at first sight appear very implausible to maintain that moral judgments do not all have the same *type* of meaning. "Your contention," a critic might say, "that moral terms are polyguous is not implausible in so far as you maintain that they tend to refer to different objective qualities on different occasions. But when you maintain that the same moral predicate has on one occasion objective descriptive meaning while on another it is used purely emotively, what you say sounds far-fetched. When you say about your friend, X.Y., that she is a good person and when you say (as I am sure you would) that happiness is intrinsically good, your meaning of "good" seems to be of the same kind. In both cases you wish to ascribe an objective quality or a set of such qualities to the subject you are judging to be good. In the first case a naturalistic translation is plausible while in the second case it is not. You are so prejudiced against the introduction of a non-natural quality that, when you come to fundamental moral judgments, you resort to the dodge of 'merely emotive meaning.' "

I am sure every opponent of intuitionism who has given prolonged attention to the whole subject has sooner or later felt the apparent force of this objection. It seems to me, however, that the objection derives its plausibility largely from a failure to note how different are the circumstances in which people make fundamental moral judgments from those which give rise to non-fundamental moral judgments. Once this difference is clearly pointed out it is no longer far-fetched to maintain that one class of moral judgments has objective descriptive meaning while another one lacks it. A detailed consideration of some examples will show what I mean.

I once knew a girl whom I shall here call Muriel and who was sharing an apartment with another girl by the name of Patricia. Both girls were well-educated and very intelligent. Muriel was out of work and consistently undernourished. Patricia had a badly-paid job as a waitress in a well-known restaurant. Unfortunately for her, the customers were as stingy as the owner and thus the tips did not at all make up for her low wages. As I got the story, the waitresses in conjunction with the cashier, who was also grossly underpaid, decided to "suppress" so-and-so many checks a day and keep the money for themselves. I do not remember exactly how the girls worked the scheme and eventually they were found out. But that side of the story does not concern us here. One day Patricia came home in high spirits, with a big shopping bag under her arm, and exclaimed: "We'll have a feast tonight. Here's three pounds of fillet mignon, two bottles of the finest sauternes and two big boxes of strawberries. Today I held back a check worth thirteen dollars." I then listened to the following exchange:

MURIEL: You can eat your fillet mignon alone. I don't feast on stolen money (She was later persuaded to eat the steak after all).

PATRICIA: You are mad. Schrödinger will never know the difference and even if he realized that he's been gypped thirteen bucks, he won't die, the poor man. He only owns fourteen hotels and makes only two and half million dollars a year. If he doesn't pay us decent wages I don't see why we shouldn't cheat him a little now and then.

MURIEL: I am not defending Schrödinger. I don't pity him for grieving over the loss of the thirteen dollars. I object to your being a thief

and not because it's against the law either; though you had better
watch out or you'll end up in jail. It's just that stealing is ugly and
wrong. It's wrong even if it doesn't hurt the man you are stealing
from and even if he is rich and exploits you.

PATRICIA: The way you are looking at me I can see the real reason for
your excitement. The old puritan in you is coming out again. What
you mean is that stealing will corrupt my soul. It will gradually
make me callous and hard.

MURIEL: Maybe that is part of what I mean, but it's certainly not the
whole of it. Even if stealing did not harden or corrupt the thief's
mind, it would still be wrong—just because it's stealing, because it's
the taking of money that was not earned and that belongs to someone else.

Now, I think that Muriel's judgment "It's just that stealing is
wrong" would qualify as a fundamental moral judgment by our
definition. Or maybe it would be more accurate to call it a "mixed"
moral judgment in the sense that it is partly fundamental and partly
non-fundamental. For it appears that she was willing to give a
reason for her view that stealing is wrong, namely that it tends to
make the thief harder and more callous. In any event, there was
at least a "fundamental element" in her judgment since she condemned stealing in part simply *qua* stealing.

It is worth adding that many people who condemn stealing would
not then be making a fundamental moral judgment. In justifying
their condemnation they would confine themselves to the conventional reason that stealing tends to weaken social bonds and thus to
produce general insecurity. Even if they added something about
the psychological effects on the thief they would very rarely say
anything equivalent to "It's just that stealing is wrong."

It should also be noted that the fundamental moral judgment or
the judgment containing the fundamental element is Muriel's *general* condemnation of stealing and not her original condemnation
of Patricia's action. Her opening speech may be regarded as equivalent to "*what you did* was wrong" and this was not a fundamental
moral judgment. If Patricia had asked "Why—what was wrong
about my action?" Muriel could have given a reason, namely, "It
was wrong because it was a theft, because you were taking money
you had not honestly earned."

Let us consider another case. In one of the most notorious exhibitions of religious bigotry, the Protestant Jean Calas was cruelly tortured and executed after a mock-trial before the Parlement of Tolouse in which he was found guilty of murdering one of his sons. There was overwhelming evidence that Calas' son had committed suicide. The only motives for the verdict were the political ambitions of certain aldermen and the general dislike of Protestants in the Tolouse area. Voltaire, who in his later years was often referred to as "l'homme aux Calas," succeeded in reopening the case and finally exonerating the whole Calas family. The surviving members of the family, on whom various lighter sentences had been imposed, were declared innocent and Calas' widow was awarded a substantial pension by the King.

Supposing a neighbor of Voltaire's who had heard something about this new case called on him and said: "I hear you are busy on a case about a man from Tolouse. I think his name is Calas. What's the story?" Voltaire might well have begun his answer by saying "The Calas case presents a terrible wrong, almost unequalled in the long history of religious intolerance. . . ." Or supposing that, on first hearing an account of what happened, Voltaire exclaimed "This is utterly dreadful!" Although there are important differences in the situations which gave rise to these two moral judgments, they are both clearly non-fundamental and thus possess objective descriptive meaning on my theory. If Voltaire had been asked "Why does the Calas case present a wrong? Why was this a dreadful sentence?," he would undoubtedly have given some such answer as this: "Because Jean Calas was plainly innocent. Because innocent or not, there was nothing but flimsy and forged evidence before the Parlement of Toulouse—not the kind of evidence that can ever be sufficient for a verdict of guilty. Because what inspired the verdict was not a desire to render justice but religious hate and unscrupulous political ambitions."

Many people tried to dissuade Voltaire from entering the case. There were some who admitted the innocence of the Calas family, but argued that in the long run the killing of an innocent man would do less harm to society than underming popular confidence in the magistracy. There were others who said that the question Voltaire should consider was not whether Calas was guilty, but whether, regardless of his guilt or innocence, the sentence tended to promote the social welfare. Similar views, by the way, were put forward 130 years later when Emile Zola was about to enter the even more celebrated Dreyfus case. One prominent defender of the conviction of Dreyfus proclaimed that no judge should hesitate to sentence an innocent man to death if it were to the advantage of the general public.

Let us suppose such a "utilitarian" defender of the conviction of innocent men had asked Voltaire the question "Why is it wrong to sentence an innocent man?" Very probably Voltaire would have answered partly in utilitarian terms. He could have pointed out that the innocence of the accused usually comes out in the long run, if it is not indeed widely known from the first, and thus leads to a widespread lack of confidence in the judicial system. But even if a particular conviction resulted in some social gain, Voltaire might have proceeded, such a gain would be insignificant compared to the suffering of the accused person, suffering which is all the more terrible because he knows himself to be innocent. From all we know about him, however, Voltaire would also have given an answer of a very different kind, somewhat along the following lines: "But regardless of the total happiness or unhappiness produced by such a conviction, it just is wrong. It is simply wrong to convict an innocent man. If everybody else became a hundred times happier as the result of the sentence, it would still be wrong. If the intention of the judges were solely to promote the social welfare and not at all to advance their personal fortunes by hook or crook, the sentence would still be wrong. If, finally, the accused man himself were mentally deranged and derived positive pleasure both from the accusation and from the sentence, his conviction would even then be wrong."

I believe that the sentence "It is simply wrong to convict an innocent man," as it occurred in the above context, qualifies as a fundamental moral judgment or rather as one with a fundamental moral element. But, as in the other example, it should be observed that what is the fundamental moral judgment is the *general* condemnation of convicting an innocent man and not the specific sentence of Jean Calas. As in the other example, too, I believe that with many people "It is wrong to convict an innocent man" would be entirely a non-fundamental moral judgment.

In both of these examples the fundamental moral judgments occur in a context and have a purpose significantly different from those of non-fundamental moral judgments. I believe that the same could be shown for any other case that is taken from a living context. When, in the main example of Chapter VII, I said "X.Y. is a good person" and when Voltaire said to his neighbor "The Calas case presents a terrible wrong," the primary purpose of these non-fundamental moral judgments was to give information about the subjects of the statements, X.Y. and the Calas affair, respectively. It was to give a rough summary characterization, to be followed, if necessary, by more detailed descriptions of the subjects. When Muriel, in her opening speech, said in effect "What you did was wrong" or when Voltaire on first hearing a description of the events in the Calas case exclaimed "This is dreadful!," their primary purpose was certainly not to give information about the subject of their statements. Patricia knew the "facts of the case" more intimately than Muriel and Voltaire may well have been alone when he exclaimed "This is dreadful!." Their primary purpose here was certainly "emotive"—to vent their feelings and possibly in Muriel's case also to produce a certain effect on the other party. But although the primary purpose of these judgments was emotive and not to give information, here too the features of the subjects of the statements were clearly involved. The context made it quite clear that Muriel was not *just* condemning Patricia's action. She was in no way asserting or indicating that the statement "stood on its own feet." On the contrary it was put forward in such a way that it would naturally be succeeded by one or more statements of the form "Because what you did was. . . ." Similarly, the context in which Voltaire exclaimed "This is dreadful!" made it evident that he was condemning the events *because* of certain characteristics they possessed.

In all these instances the objective features of the subject are somehow involved in the moral judgments, either directly or at least by implication. For this reason it would be grossly inadequate to substitute for the moral judgment an exclamation or a subjective statement, unaccompanied by any description of the features of what is disapproved or abhorred. It is interesting to note in passing that such a substitution seems less inadequate in those situations where the primary purpose of the moral judgment is emotive and the objective features are only implied. But it would lead too far to develop this point here.

In contrast to the instances considered so far, when Muriel said "It's just that stealing is wrong" and when Voltaire exclaimed "It is just wrong to convict an innocent man," they were primarily concerned to indicate their stand or attitude. Moreover, they were concerned to indicate that their judgment did stand on its own feet, that it did not require to be followed by a sentence beginning with "because." Here it seems to me extremely plausible to say that to the extent to which they were maintaining that stealing or the conviction of an innocent man were *just* wrong, their judgments had emotive meaning only. In saying this I do not believe I am adopting a dodge to escape the need for admitting a non-natural quality of wrongness. I believe that I am giving the intrinsically most plausible account of what a human being is doing in such a case. While subjective language might here too not entirely reproduce the force of the original sentence, it does seem very much less inadequate, especially if it is sufficiently picturesque and emphatic. In fact many people would in such situations more naturally use subjective language of some kind. Muriel, for instance, might easily have said "I just abhor stealing—*that's all*" and Voltaire frequently did say such things as "It *just* goes against my grain to see an innocent man convicted." Here, unlike in the case of nonfundamental moral judgments, what seems to be lost in the subjective translations is emotive meaning only, or that and certain mental associations. What seems lost are the prescriptive or "dynamic" associations of "wrong" as well as certain of the "objectivity" images or feelings which tend to be excited by any sentence which has the form "S is P"—i.e., the form characteristic of sentences which are objective statements.

What about "happiness is intrinsically good" or "unhappiness is intrinsically bad"? What about these old war-horses which have

often been regarded as the only fundamental moral judgments? The
first thing to note here is that nobody in any living context ever
says "happiness is good" or "unhappiness is bad." I can say nothing
about these judgments unless some concrete context is specified. But
when that is done, my answer is the same as before: in any concrete situation, when sentences more or less resembling "happiness
is good" or "unhappiness is bad" are used, they will usually be
found to be non-fundamental moral judgments with natural features
as their descriptive meaning. On the few occasions on which they
really are fundamental moral judgments, the background against
which they are made is very different indeed and there it is very
plausible to maintain that these judgments have no descriptive
meaning.

What I have been saying in this section may sound like a retraction of the objectivism which I have been advocating throughout this volume. Such an impression would only be very partially
correct. Of course, if by "objectivism" one understands a metaethic which maintains that all moral judgments without exception
have objective descriptive meaning, then I am not an objectivist.
To this observation it should be added, however, that, if I am not
mistaken, fundamental moral judgments are very rare in actual discourse. Especially when people engage in moral disputes, the conflicting moral judgments are practically always non-fundamental,
whether the disputes are capable of settlement in the "objective"
sense we called sense (3), or not. All the disputed moral judgments
in the examples we analysed in Sections 3-5 of this chapter—Hook's
and Howe's conflicting recommendations about Communist teachers, the moral conclusions of the defenders and the opponents of
euthanasia, my friend's judgment that we should remain at the
table and my own that we should move in the dispute about the
seating at Camp T.—every one of them was a non-fundamental
moral judgment.

It should also be noted in this connection that, as I am using the
term, non-fundamental moral judgments include not only all those
moral judgments that are usually referred to as "instrumental" but
also most of those which are concerned with "intrinsic" good or
right, which are about the qualities and not the effects of the sub-

ject judged to be good or right. When I said about X.Y. that she
was a good person and when Muriel in her opening speech made
statements amounting to "What you did was wrong," neither of
us made an instrumental moral judgment. I was referring to intrinsic qualities of X.Y. and Muriel was, at least in part, referring
to an intrinsic quality of Patricia's action. Yet, since we were willing and able to support our judgments with reasons, we too were
making non-fundamental moral judgments.

Finally, even those sentences which are fundamental moral judgments are usually only partly so, as we found in both of our examples. Most of them, moreover, are frequently used by other
people as non-fundamental moral judgments. For all these reasons
my view that fundamental moral judgments have no descriptive
meaning constitutes only a very partial retraction of the objectivism
of earlier discussions.

I believe that many of the points I have been making in this book
are in harmony with the general views of John Dewey and certain
of his followers. It must be apparent from the preceding pages that
I owe much to these writers, especially as regards my insistence on
taking moral judgments in their concrete contexts and my sus-
picion of such artifacts as "Happiness is an intrinsically good thing"
—myths concocted by philosophers who have temporarily lost all
contact with ordinary human discourse. It must also be evident,
however, that I cannot go along with their contention, if I understand them correctly, that fundamental moral judgments *never*
occur in an actual situation.[13] I have already given some examples
which would refute such an extreme claim. But I should also like
to explain in a general way why I recognize the existence of fundamental as well as of non-fundamental moral judgments. In doing
this I am simply trying to note the following facts: very frequently
human beings approve or disapprove or have some other moral

---

13. Cf. Sidney Hook's *Education for Modern Man*, pp. 132 ff and Charles
Frankel's review of *Essays in Political Theory* (ed. Konvitz and Murphy),
Journal of Philosophy, 1950 pp. 716-717. Mr. Hook's introduction to this
volume was written before I revised the section on "Fundamental Moral
Judgments." Some of my remarks were suggested by what he there says about
Dewey's position.

attitude towards a specific action or towards a class of actions *because of certain attributes* of the action or the class of actions. Sometimes, however, they have this attitude towards a class of actions "for its own sake" or *just* because it is that kind of action. In the latter case we might say "they *just* have that attitude." My point has been that moral predicates are used to express moral attitudes both in the former and in the latter kind of case.

8. A Note on the Emotive Theory

STEVENSON, even in his later writings, does not admit the possibility of reasons for moral judgments in any other sense than that of factors *causing* attitudes or changes in attitudes. Nor, as we also saw in Section 6 of this chapter, does he allow for the possibility that moral disputes can be settled in any sense other than our sense (2). On these matters my position does not coincide with his. However, as regards the "meaning" of moral judgments, what I have been urging does appear to coincide to a large extent with his view. For, in *Ethics and Language*, Stevenson seems to hold that moral judgments generally have both descriptive and emotive meaning. On this, which is perhaps the most basic of our three questions, my theory is therefore very close to the emotive theory as it is expressed by its foremost American exponent.

On the other hand, it may at first sight appear that, in so strongly stressing the objective meaning of most moral judgments, my theory is very far removed from the emotive theory as it has been stated by several of its British supporters, especially by Ayer and Hampshire. For these writers have usually expressed their position by saying that moral judgments, that is *all* moral judgments, have emotive meaning only. "A valuation," writes Ayer, "is not a description of something very peculiar; it is not a description at all."[14] "Moral judgments," in Hampshire's words, "are not properly classified as statements of any kind, autobiographical or otherwise . . .

---

14. "On the Analysis of Moral Judgments," *op. cit.* p. 179.

they are not normally taken to describe facts, but to prescribe or recommend policies of action."[15]

On further examination, however, it becomes clear that my theory is on this point very close to the emotive theory, even in the version of it just quoted. I am sure that in the case of most of the sentences for which I claimed descriptive meaning Ayer and Hampshire would endorse my claim. What they would refuse to do is call them "moral judgments." They would say that these sentences are not moral judgments because of their descriptive meaning. Ayer and Hampshire would not, in other words, deny that what I am calling the ethical predicates usually have referential or at least descriptive meaning. But they would add that, to that extent, these words were not used for their "distinctively ethical" purpose. Thus Ayer grants that "a great many ethical statements contain, as a factual element, some description of the action, or situation to which the ethical term in question is being applied,"[16] but "it is not *qua* descriptive that they are ethical. If, for example, the word 'wrong' is simply equated with 'not conducive to human happiness' some other term will be needed to carry the normative implication that conduct of this sort is to be avoided; and it is terms of this kind, which are not descriptive, that I am treating as distinctively ethical."[17] Similarly Hampshire concedes that it is "very easy to find multitudes of sentences which could, as normally used, be interpreted as partly descriptive and partly prescriptive."[18] But it is their prescriptive and not their descriptive aspect which makes them into moral judgments: "To distinguish in ordinary usage an utterance or part of an utterance as being a moral judgment is always therein to *contrast* it with a statement of fact. Consider a case in which it is doubtful whether a sentence is intended as a statement of fact or as a moral judgment—e.g., 'He is a very vicious man': in order to make it clear that I am using this sentence simply

---

15. "Fallacies in Moral Philosophy—A Reply to Mr. Baier," *Mind*, 1950, pp. 541-2.
16. *Language, Truth and Logic*, 2nd edit. introduction, p. 21.
17. "On the Analysis of Moral Judgments," p. 181.
18. *Mind*, 1950, p. 543.

to *describe* how he in fact behaves, I might add 'but I do not intend
a moral judgment by this' which would be the same as to say 'In
using the word 'vicious,' I am not prescribing how he ought not
to behave, but simply *stating* that he in fact behaves in the way
ordinarily called 'vicious.' I am here contrasting the statement with
the prescription, the declarative with the imperative."[19]

The difference on this topic is then largely verbal. It is nonetheless of some importance. There are advantages and disadvantages in
both formulations, but I believe that on the whole the language I
have been using is preferable. The Ayer-Hampshire language, as I
shall call it, certainly possesses the merit of drawing attention to the
fact that it is their expressive and prescriptive meaning which distinguishes the moral predicates from all purely descriptive terms.
It is also true, I think, that, especially among more educated people,
there is a tendency to regard the emotive meaning of terms with a
double function—not only of "good" and "right" but also of words
like "perverse," "smear," "indecency," "depraved" and many more
—as their "moralizing," their peculiarly moral aspect. To this extent the Ayer-Hampshire language is in accord with ordinary usage.

However, among those who speak of moral judgments and moral
predicates at all or who use expressions roughly equivalent to them,
the term "moral" is generally employed in a far less restricted sense.
When I say "X.Y. is a good person," for instance, my sentence
would count as a moral judgment and the word "good" in it as an
ethical predicate not only because of its expressive, but also because
of its referential meaning. The sentence would be considered
"moral" *both* because it expresses my approval and also because I
am referring to such qualities as her kindness, gentleness, and lack
of envy and not to her figure, income, or excellence in ping-pong.

This brings me to the reasons why the formulation which I have
chosen appears to me preferable. For one thing, the theory is then
less likely to be misunderstood by philosophers who habitually use
the word "moral" in the broader sense just mentioned. These
writers are apt to believe that the emotive theory implies the truly
staggering paradox that the goodness or badness of an event or an

---

19. *Ibid.*, pp. 542-543. Hampshire's italics.

action "depends for its existence" on the presence of a person who
feels approval or disapproval, just as idealism, in some of its varieties,
implies that the existence of physical objects depends on the presence of a perceiver. I shall show in detail in the section entitled
"Blanshard's Rabbit" (Chapter IX, Section 1) how the emotive
theory has been misinterpreted in this connection.

But, furthermore, and what is far more important, since moral
philosophers are of course primarily concerned with the "moral"
aspect of terms, the language to which I am objecting is very apt
to divert one's attention from an exploration of the descriptive
function of the moral predicates. Yet, unless I have been completely
mistaken in practically everything I said in previous chapters, such
as exploration is extremely clarifying, not least in the light it sheds
on the interrelations between the emotive and the descriptive aspects of the terms in question and the exact place of feelings or
attitudes in the total situation.

Among other things, I have tried to show in this section that, as
regards the answer to the first of our three questions, my theory
largely or wholly coincides with the emotive theory not only in
Stevenson's formulation but also in that of Ayer and Hampshire. As
regards the other two questions, my answers are I think in accord
with Hampshire's view and they are in fact largely derived from
his article. But my answers to these questions do differ substantially
from the emotive theory as it is stated both in Stevenson's and in
Ayer's writings. I shall therefore avoid confusion if for the re-
mainder of this book I distinguish "my theory" from "the emotive
theory," meaning by "my theory" the answers I have offered to
the three questions and by "the emotive theory" the three answers
offered by Stevenson and Ayer.

In the next chapter I shall try to show that my theory accounts
for or that it is at least compatible with various of the facts concerning moral discourse which we noted in earlier discussions. In
that connection and also in the final chapter I shall consider certain
well-known objections which have been brought up against the
emotive theory and in some cases against all theories that reject a
special moral faculty. I am sure that most of these objections would

also be advanced against my theory. I shall of course be primarily concerned to show that my theory is in no way shaken by these objections. However, since this is of considerable interest, I shall also try to show that most of these objections fail to refute the emotive theory, if it is not misunderstood. Hence even if I am wrong where I differ from the emotive theory, these discussions may not be without value.

CONTENTS

Chapter IX

The Logic of
Moral Discourse (III)

1. Blanshard's Rabbit

Brand Blanshard, the ablest and certainly the most lucid American champion of intuitionism, has attacked the emotive theory and also naive subjectivism on the ground that both theories have the following absurd implication: the goodness or badness of an event, according to these theories, depends for its existence on the approval or disapproval of a human being who happens to arrive upon the scene and pass a moral judgment about the event. I have little doubt Blanshard would maintain that his criticisms apply equally to my theory.

I shall try to show now that his arguments refute neither my theory nor the emotive theory if it is correctly understood. I shall first reproduce them in Blanshard's own words:

Let us work through an example, the simpler and commoner the better. There is perhaps no value statement on which people would more universally agree than the statement that intense pain is bad. Let us take a set of circumstances in which I happen to be interested on the legislative side and in which I think everyone of us might naturally make such a statement. We come upon a rabbit that has been caught in one of the brutal traps in common use. There are signs that it has struggled for days to escape and that in a frenzy of hunger, pain and

[199]

fear, it has all but eaten off its own leg. The attempt failed; the animal is now dead. As we think of the long and excruciating pain it must have suffered, we are very likely to say: "It was a bad thing that the little animal should suffer so." The positivist tells us that when we say this we are only expressing our present emotion. I hold, on the contrary, that we mean to assert something of pain itself, namely, that it was bad—bad when and as it occurred.[1]

The positivist or emotive view, now, has two absolutely incredible consequences:

(1) On that view, nothing good or bad happened in the case until I came on the scene and made my remark. For what I express in my remark is something going on in me at the time, and that of course did not exist until I did come on the scene. The pain of the rabbit was not itself bad; nothing evil was happening when that pain was being endured; badness in the only sense in which it is involved at all waited for its appearance till I came and looked and felt. Now that this is at odds with our meaning may be shown as follows. Let us put to ourselves the hypothesis that we had not come on the scene and that the rabbit never was discovered. Are we prepared to say that in that case nothing bad occurred in the sense in which we said it did? Clearly not. Indeed we should say, on the contrary, that the accident of our later discovery made no difference whatever to the badness of the animal's pain, that it would have been every whit as bad whether a chance passer-by happened later to discover the body and feel repugnance or not. If so, then it is clear that in saying the suffering was bad we are not expressing our feelings only. We are saying that the pain was bad when and as it occurred and before anyone took an attitude toward it. The first argument is thus an ideal experiment in which we use the method of difference. It removes our present expression and shows that the badness we meant would not be affected by this, whereas on positivist grounds it should be.

(2) The second argument applies the method in the reverse way. It ideally removes the past event, and shows that this would render false what we meant to say, whereas on positivist grounds it should not. Let us suppose that the animal did not in fact fall into the trap and did not suffer at all, but that we mistakenly think it did, and say as before that its suffering was an evil thing. On the positivist theory, everything I sought to express by calling it evil in the first case is still present in the second. In the only sense in which badness is involved at all, whatever was bad in the first case is still present in its entirety, since all that is

1. "The New Subjectivism in Ethics," *Philosophy and Phenomenological Research*, 1949, p. 505.

expressed in either case is a state of feeling, and that feeling is still there. And our question is, is such an implication consistent with what we meant? Clearly it is not. If anyone asked us, after we made the remark that the suffering was a bad thing, whether we should think it relevant to what we said to learn that the incident had never occurred and no pain had been suffered at all, we should say that it made all the difference in the world, that what we were asserting to be bad was precisely the suffering we thought had occurred back there, that if this had not occurred, there was nothing left to be bad, and that our assertion was in that case mistaken. The suggestion that in saying something evil had occurred we were after all making no mistake, because we had never meant anyhow to say anything about the past suffering, seems to me merely frivolous. If we did not mean to say this, why should we be so relieved on finding that the suffering had not occurred? On the theory before us, such relief would be groundless, for in that suffering itself there was nothing bad at all, and hence in its non-occurrence there would be nothing to be relieved about. The positivist theory would here distort our meaning beyond recognition.[2]

"The positivist," we are further told, "holds that goodness and badness *lie in* feelings of approval or disapproval."[3]

There are several serious confusions in these arguments. (i) Only a philosopher, writing in a vacuum, could ever suppose that anybody would really in this situation say "It is a bad thing that the little animal should suffer so." If a person finds a rabbit in one of the traps Blanshard describes and if he has some sympathy for the suffering of living things, he will say "This is terrible" or "Something dreadful happened here" or "The poor animal!" or maybe "What wicked traps these people put up!" All these sentences or exclamations may quite properly be regarded as moral condemnations. I am not in the least concerned to deny that in the circumstances people would pass a moral judgment. What I am challenging is that the subject of their condemnation would be the suffering or the pain. The subject would be "this" or "something" or "the traps." This may seem like a trivial point, but in fact it is all-important since, as I hope to show in a moment, the plausibility of both of Blanshard's arguments depends entirely on the confusion as to what it is that is condemned.

---

2. *Ibid.*, pp. 505-506.
3. *Ibid.*, p. 506. My italics.

To be sure, one can imagine circumstances in which a person might say *something* like "It is a bad thing that the little animal should suffer so." These circumstances, however, would be significantly different from Blanshard's example. Supposing a little frog has been used in a vivisection experiment and supposing A, who is very fond of animals, is horrified by the frog's suffering. After A has made a vigorous protest against what he deems to be the needless torture of the animal, B, the experimenter, defends himself by claiming that in the long run experiments like the one he just carried out will help to avoid a vast mass of human suffering. To this A might very conceivably retort: "No, I am unimpressed by what you say. I still maintain *it was wrong that the little animal should suffer so*. What you say about the long-term benefits derived by the human race from these experiments is highly speculative and far-fetched. But even if the experiments led to some real benefits, I remain to be convinced that the same results could not have been achieved by employing more humane methods."

It will be convenient to let the sentence *"Something* bad happened here" represent the sentences which human beings would actually utter upon finding the rabbit and seeing the evidences of its painful struggle. I shall from now on refer to it as "sentence (1)." To the sentence *"The intense pain* suffered by the little animal was a bad thing" or anything equivalent to the sentence mentioned by Blanshard, but used in a context like the vivisection-dispute, I shall refer hereafter as "sentence (2)."

Now, both sentences (1) and (2) clearly have referential meaning and it is easy to show that their referents are made up of natural features. The main element in the referent of sentence (1), as most of us would use "bad" in such a context, is precisely the excruciating pain suffered by the rabbit. The occurrence of this intense and prolonged suffering is what we primarily wish to assert by means of this sentence. To be quite accurate, it is not the complete referent. We also assert, I believe, that the pain suffered by the rabbit was pointless or unnecessary. By this I mean that either the killing of the rabbit did not have any useful results such as helping to rid the neighborhood farmers of a nuisance or that, if it did, the same results could easily have been achieved without sub-

jecting the little animal to such extreme agonies. These features—
the pointless suffering of intense pain by the rabbit—are the "bad-
making" features in this particular case. They are what the badness
consists in. If they really characterize the event, sentence (1) is
true. If they do not characterize the event, if for instance the rabbit,
contrary to our information, did not really die a painful death but
was at the time and place in question fed and fondled by a gentle
child, sentence (1) would be false. In the case of sentence (2) the
referent of "wrong" is simply the needlessness of the pain suffered
by the frog and the doubtfulness of any benefits that might accrue
from it.

On my theory, the word "bad" in sentence (1) has a double
function: it both refers to the features just mentioned and it also
expresses the speaker's unfavorable attitude towards events having
these features. While not endorsing all their formulations, it is I
think this which most defenders of the emotive theory have also
wished to maintain. That is to say: their position is *not*

A sentence like (1) has no referent and only expresses the speaker's attitude.

Their position rather is

A sentence like (1) does have a referent but the only thing
which the use of the word "bad" does and which is not done by
the use of non-ethical predicates is the expression of the speaker's
attitude,

Or, stated in a slightly different way: the position of the defenders
of the emotive theory is *not*

"bad" is only used to express the speaker's attitude—it does not
refer to any features of the event in question.

It is

"bad" does not refer to *any additional features* over and above
(in this case) "suffering intense pain to no useful purpose." Its
only *additional* function is the expression of the speaker's attitude.
As already noted at the end of the last chapter, Ayer and Hampshire would not at all deny that "bad" in such an instance has the
referent I mentioned. They just would not regard this as the peculiarly moral aspect of the term.

Since the rabbit's suffering of avoidable or useless pain, which would constitute the event's badness, is causally quite independent of the approval or disapproval of the person who comes along and makes the moral judgment, it follows that both of Blanshard's arguments are case of *ignoratio elenchi*. The emotive view, as now clarified, does not imply that the badness "came on the scene" with the disapproval of the person who made the moral judgment; and it equally does not imply that the badness vanishes if and when he ceases to disapprove.

I think we can see now why the example, as Blanshard presents it, seems to support the view that in this case we are attributing a non-natural quality of badness to the subject of our moral judgment. When we make a moral judgment in the kind of situation which Blanshard describes, our judgment is indeed an objective statement, but one with a natural referent; and the main element of this natural referent, as we saw, is the occurrence of the extreme pain. If we restate this analysis in the form of an equation we get for this case

bad $=$ the pointless suffering of extreme pain.

Blanshard, by the way in which he words the moral judgment, has transferred the pain into the subject, from the right hand side of the equation to the left hand side. Then, of course, when we look for the objective referent we find no natural feature, that is, we find no natural feature on the right hand side. Since we are rightly convinced that our judgment has an objective referent, we are now tempted to introduce a non-natural quality of badness.

The main point of the preceding discussion is in my opinion of the greatest importance and I shall therefore try to explain it once more by taking another illustration, and a very real one too. Senator Flanders of Vermont is probably best known to Americans as the man who has repeatedly spoken out on the Senate floor against the activities of Senator McCarthy and who finally introduced a motion of censure. In November 1954 Flanders made a Thanksgiving Day broadcast to Russia over the Voice of America in which he explained that Americans have nothing but feelings of friendship and sympathy for the Russian people as distinct from their autocratic rulers. In addressing the Russian people Flanders used the expression "my Soviet brothers." It was impossible for anybody who is not mentally deficient to misunderstand this reference. However, a month later, in the special Senate session dealing with the censure motion, one of McCarthy's most ardent supporters and a man who has frequently shown himself to be eaten up with hate, Senator Jenner of Indiana, angrily turned to Flanders and shouted: "By what course of twisted thinking did the Senator refer to these tyrants, these murderers as 'my friends, my Soviet brothers'?" Flanders repeatedly explained the real and plain meaning of his remarks but Jenner contemptuously brushed the explanations aside. Flanders is in his seventies and, according to the newspaper report from which I am quoting, "his face flushed and for a moment he appeared about to collapse. . . . (Eventually) Flanders sat down, his face still flushed, and Jenner, suddenly all smiles, walked over to Welker, McCarthy's self-appointed floor-manager, and shook hands heartily. Both looked at Flanders and chuckled."

I should like to consider the judgment which I, and I am sure very many other people, would make about this event—that Jenner's performance was evil through and through. I am assuming and I have no reason to doubt that the report from which I quoted was accurate. Supposing I were asked: "What makes Jenner's action so evil? What does its evil consist in?" I would give this answer: he deliberately misrepresented what Flanders had said in order to upset him as much as possible and then took great delight when this had been accomplished. Jenner's action, I would say, was the work of spite and a desire for revenge pure and simple.

Now, neither my theory nor the emotive theory deny that the sentence "Jenner's performance was evil" has referential meaning. We deny that the word "evil" in this context refers to any special additional features over and above those mentioned—Jenner's deliberate distortion, his spite and desire for revenge, etc. "Jenner's performance was evil" is a summary statement of these facts. The word "evil" adds a definite indication of the speaker's attitude, i.e., it adds expressively but not referentially. The evil of Jenner's action did not come into being as a result of my disapproval, but the objective features of the situation symbolized by the word "evil" can also be symbolized by non-ethical terms.

A word of caution has to be inserted before going any further.

Many philosophers, including Blanshard, conduct their discussions in the so-called material mode of speech. These philosophers are apt to report the theory I am advocating by saying that according to it the badness of an action *consists partly* in certain objective features of the action and *partly* in the attitude of disapproval on the part of the person who makes the moral judgment. This would be a misinterpretation of my theory and I shall now try to explain why.

Let us suppose we have a term, x, which has both referential and expressive or emotive meaning and that we have given an account of both. That is to say: we have produced an expression, say y, giving the referential equivalent of x and we have also described what kind of feeling or attitude in the speaker x expresses. Now, if we reformulate our result in the material mode by saying "x-ness is y-ness" or "the x-ness of a thing, A, consists in its y-ness," we are exclusively concerned with the referential meaning of the term. Such a reformulation does not and is not meant to take into account any expressive meaning the term may have. If y is really the full referential equivalent of x, then it will be perfectly correct to say "the x-ness of A consists *entirely* in its y-ness" even though we have left out all mention of x's expressive meaning. We shall be entitled to say "The x-ness of A consists partly in its y-ness and partly in something else" only if y is not the full *referential* equivalent of x, if for instance there is some other expression, z, which has to be added to y to give the complete referential equivalent of x.

To make this clearer let us once again consider the steak at Barney's. When I said "the steak at Barney's is nice," we found that "nice" in this context referred to the tenderness of the steak, the freshness of the meat, its being done to the degree of rareness desired, etc., and that at the same time it expressed a favorable feeling on my part. Now, it would be quite incorrect to reformulate this result by saying "the niceness of the steak consists partly in its tenderness, freshness, etc., and partly in the person's liking of steaks having such features." The niceness of the steak, if we wish to talk in this mode, consists *entirely* in the tenderness, the freshness, the degree of rareness and whatever else we found to be the referent of "nice." My liking of such features in a steak is *not* part of its niceness, though, as we saw, it is the cause of why I call a steak "nice" if it has the features in question.

Similarly, it would be quite incorrect to say that on my theory the badness of Jenner's action consists partly in his spite and vengefulness and partly in my disapproval of actions which possess such features. It would be equally incorrect to say that on my theory the badness of what happened to the rabbit consisted partly in the extreme pain suffered by the animal to no useful purpose and partly in the repugnance felt by the man who came upon the scene. The badness of Jenner's action consists *entirely* in the spite, the vengefulness and whatever else makes up the *referent* of "bad" in this instance just as the badness of what happened to the rabbit consists *entirely* in the pain suffered to no useful purpose.

To suppose that my disapproval of Jenner's action is, on my theory, part of its badness is to regard expressive or emotive meaning as a species of referential meaning, which is absurd. There are indeed *some* good reasons why, rather than speak of expressive or emotive "meaning," we should confine the term "meaning" to what we have been calling referential meaning and speak perhaps of the expressive or emotive "aspects" of a term.[3a] In any event, whether my theory is expressed by saying that "bad" has both referential and emotive *meaning* or by saying that "bad" has referential meaning and also certain characteristic emotive *aspects*, the badness of an action according to it will always consist *entirely* in certain features of the action.

(ii) But, it will be said, what about fundamental moral judgments which on my view have emotive meaning only? Is not Blanshard's argument valid so far as they are concerned? We found that on certain occasions people make such fundamental moral judgments as that stealing or convicting an innocent man is just wrong. Though we did not illustrate this, they also of course make fundamental moral judgments in which the ethical predicate is "good" or "right." Now, is it not preposterous to maintain that in such cases the goodness or badness, the rightness or wrongness depend on the existence of the approval or disapproval in a human

---

3a. Cf. Max Black: *Language and Philosophy*, pp. 255-257.

being? Is it not preposterous to maintain, keeping to our two illustrations, that stealing or convicting an innocent man would not be wrong, if people did not feel disapproval of such actions?

Here again the reply is, though for different reasons, that the position which Blanshard attacks does not have the alleged consequences. The two propositions which he now confuses are as follows:

P_1—when a person makes a fundamental moral judgment of the form "x is good" he feels approval toward x; and this approval (i) produces the quality of goodness in x, and (ii) is a necessary condition for its continued existence so that when the approval ceases the goodness disappears with it.

P_2—when a person makes a fundamental moral judgment of the form "x is good" he expresses his pro-attitude towards x.

The position here advocated and the position of the logical positivist is P_2 and not P_1. I do not know of anybody who has ever held P_1. It is a bad dream dreamt up by Blanshard. He so strongly believes, it seems, that "x is good" always asserts that x has a feature of some kind that he cannot, in stating the views he attacks, conceive that anybody else does not accept this.

Blanshard makes it appear that, according to the view he is attacking, what is approved miraculously acquires some *new quality*, as a result of being approved. This is indeed preposterous. But neither my theory nor the emotive theory asserts anything of the sort. It may well be that my theory does not do justice to fundamental moral judgments, though it should again be pointed out that sentences like "It is wrong to steal" or "It is wrong to convict an innocent man" are often not used as fundamental moral judgments at all, and that even when they are so used, they have non-fundamental elements and are thus on my theory to a certain extent objective statements. But, whether my theory about fundamental moral judgments is tenable or not, Blanshard's arguments at any rate fail to refute it.

(iii) Blanshard is guilty of yet another confusion. As quoted above, he says:

In the only sense in which badness is involved at all, *whatever was bad* in the first case—is still present in its entirety, since all that is expressed in either case is a state of feeling, and that feeling is still there.[4]

This suggests that according to the emotive theory, "The pain is bad" means "The feeling of disapproval of the person who says 'the pain is bad' is bad." This not only confuses the emotive theory with naive subjectivism. It also travesties naive subjectivism. For a naive subjectivist maintains that when a man, A, says "X is bad" he means "An attitude of disapproval *exists* in me." A naive subjectivist does not say that when A says "X is bad" he means "The attitude of disapproval towards X which exists in me *is bad*."

2. Concerning the "Naturalistic Fallacy"

IN THIS SECTION I wish to show how my theory can account for all the facts to which Moore drew attention in his famous argument against what he called the "Naturalistic Fallacy"—the facts to which brief reference was made in Chapter IV, Section 2, (vii). Moore's argument, stated in the formal mode, is roughly as follows: consider *any* suggested definiens of "good." Let x be the suggested definiens. Then construct questions of these two types:

(1) Is goodness good?
(2) Is x good?

If the definiens is really synonymous with "good" then (2), no less than (1), should be a senseless or self-answering question. It should be a senseless question in the sense that "x is not good" would be a *verbal* mistake. But in fact an investigation of any definiens that has ever been or could ever be suggested shows that (2) is not a senseless or self-answering question. "Is happiness good?," "Is obedience to the will of God good?," "Is aiding the struggle for survival good?"—none of these is a self-answering question. A negative answer to any of them, however mistaken, is never a *verbal* mistake.

To make Moore's point clearer, examples of admittedly correct and admittedly incorrect definitions may be produced. Thus suppose we consider the admittedly incorrect definition which asserts that "father" means "old man." Let us construct the two questions:

---

4. *Ibid.*, p. 506. My italics.

(a) A is a father, but is A a father?

(b) A is an old man, but is he a father?

(b) is here obviously not senseless or self-answering. Let us next consider the admittedly correct definition which says that "father" means "male parent." Constructing the two questions we get

(i) A is a father, but is he a father?

(ii) A is a male parent, but is he a father?

To anybody who is familiar with the usage of "father" and "male parent," (ii) instantly appears a senseless and self-answering question. A person who answer (ii) in the negative *is* clearly guilty of a *verbal* error.

Now, people are as familiar with the use of "good" and of most of the expressions offered as definitions of "good" as they are with the usage of "old man" and "father." Yet in the case of "good" the second question does not appear any more senseless than in the case of (b) above.

The reply has sometimes[5] been made that a utilitarian *would* regard the question, "Is happiness good?" as self-answering or senseless, and that certain theologians *would* regard the question, "Is it good to obey the will of God?" as senseless and self-answering. In view of the remarks of Chapter I, Section 7, it is easy to see what is wrong with this retort. The question of meta-ethics is the function or meaning of ethical predicates as they are *normally* used. Definitions of ethical terms are to the point only if they are *public* definitions. If people normally use "good" in such a way that "Is happiness good?" is not, in their usage, a self-answering question, and if utilitarians use it in such a way that in *their* usage the question is self-answering, this only shows that utilitarians use "good" differently from ordinary people. It does not make the statement, " 'good' means 'producing happiness' " into a true public definition. On top of that, observations show that utilitarians do not *use* ethical predicates differently from the rest of mankind, however different their moral *views* may be from those of some other people. As Moore also took great pains to point out, they very much want the statement, "Happiness is good" to be a synthetic and *not* an analytic statement.

---

5. Cf. Frankena, "The Naturalistic Fallacy," *Mind,* 1939.

So long as we confine ourselves to the question, "Is x good?" when asked in a vacuum, when asked in the abstract and not in the context of a concrete situation, Moore's point is unanswerable. Put in the abstract, the question will never appear self-answering, no matter what is substituted for x. But I shall try to show that this does not imply that "good" is indefinable in concrete contexts. I also hope to show that there is no more reason to suppose that "good" has a simple non-natural referent because it is, *in a certain sense,* indefinable, than to suppose that "nice" has a non-natural referent because it too is, in a certain sense, indefinable.

Once we turn to actual concrete situations in which "good" is used, it is not at all impossible to provide a definiens. Thus in the case of Example I of Chapter VII, Section 2, when I said, "X.Y. is a good person" I roughly meant, "X.Y. is truthful, loving, gentle, and free from envy and malice." Moore's second question is never self-answering when asked in the abstract not because "good" has no referent or because it has a non-natural referent but because, among other things, its referent tends to vary from group to group and even from person to person.

The question, "X.Y. is truthful, loving, gentle and free from envy and malice, but is she a good person?" is not self-answering because there are people like puritanical and Communist fanatics who use "good" to refer to other attributes. The case is entirely parallel to the case of niceness. When I said, "the steak at Barney's is rather nice," I meant (roughly), "It is tender, made of fresh meat, thick but rather small, and done pretty much to the degree of rareness desired." Yet the question, "The steak at Barney's is tender, made of fresh meat, thick but rather small, and done pretty much to the degree of rareness desired, but is it nice?" is not self-answering, when asked in the abstract because there are people like Mr. Ved who use "nice steak" to refer to quite different features. The fact that there is no *one* observable feature or no *one* set of observable features to which one can point and say, "This is *the* referent of 'good' " no more implies that the referent of "good" is a simple, non-natural quality than the corresponding fact implies this in the case of "nice."

There is another reason too why a question like, "X.Y. is truth-

ful, loving, gentle, and free from envy and malice, but is she good?"
may not appear self-answering. That reason is the vagueness of
"good" to which I drew attention in Chapter VII, page 151. That
is to say: even in any concrete case a definiens, no matter how
complicated it may be, will never be exactly equivalent to "good"
for the simple reason that "good" is hardly ever used with anything like a *precise* referent. But though this implies that *in a sense*
"good" is indefinable, it does not imply any more than a similar
fact implies this in the case of "bald" or "rich," that "good" has
no referent or that it has a non-natural referent. In the words of
Ernest Nagel: "If the adjective 'good' is vague, no other word or
phrase (in terms of which an analysis might be stated) will be
strictly equivalent to it, simply because of the unique area of vagueness associated with each expression in the language."[6]

I conclude that in any sense in which Moore's claim that "good"
is indefinable is true, it does not imply either, as some positivists
have maintained, that "good" has no referent or, as Moore himself
thought, that it had a non-natural referent. All the facts which
Moore's argument help us to perceive are compatible with the
theory advanced in this work.

I should like to add here two comments on the alleged indefina-
bility of "ought," on which Ewing[7] lays such stress. Firstly, "ought"
is indefinable in a sense in which "good" and "nice" are not indefinable. But this is as compatible with the view that it has no referent as it is with the view that it has a non-natural referent. Furthermore, to say that "ought" has no referent does not imply, as I have
pointed out several times, that it has no objective meaning. It usually has objective meaning in the sense that it *implies*—in what we
are calling sense (2) or sense (3)—observable features of one kind
or another. And these features, like the features *referred* to by
"good," tend to vary with the users of the term. The fact that there
is no one set of observable features which are the objective meaning of "ought" can therefore be easily explained without invoking
a non-natural relation. If I am right, Ewing is *doubly* wrong: he

6. "Some Reflections on the Use of Language in the Natural Sciences,"
Journal of Philosophy, 1945, p. 621.
7. *Op. cit.*, p. 178.

is wrong in thinking that "ought" *has* a referent; and he is also wrong in thinking that its objective meaning is constant and something simple.

3. Higher and Lower Moralities

IN CHAPTER II we concluded that frequently when people say that one morality is "higher than" another, they do not merely mean "it is my morality." Frequently (at least) they are making objective claims and sometimes these objective claims are true.

My theory is perfectly consistent with and accounts for these facts. The words "higher" and "lower," when applied to moral codes, function in a way which is fairly similar to that of "good" and "bad" when applied to actions or to the character of human beings. The sentences in which they are predicates usually have a referent while at the same time expressing an attitude entertained by the speaker. The referent moreover tends to vary from case to case.

To take an example: like many other people, I believe that internationalism, in the sense of the advocacy of equal rights and opportunities for happiness for all people, independently of what nation they belong to, is a higher morality than nationalism. What is primarily meant here, in the sense of referential meaning, is that an internationalist has wider sympathies than a nationalist. This is an objective claim and one which seems plainly true. Again, I believe that the morality, i.e., the moral recommendations contained in Reich's *Sexual Revolution* and Russell's *Marriage and Morals* is higher than the teachings of the Catholic Church or Lord Elton or Mr. Sokolsky on sexual questions. What I mean by calling the former morality higher is (roughly) that it is based, at least in the case of Reich though also to some extent in the case of Russell, on extensive clinical and sociological data of which the other side is totally unaware, and that, unlike the other morality, it is not the result of neurotic anxieties and resentments and of superstitious errors. This, too, is clearly an objective claim and, if the factual assertions of Reich and Russell are correct, one which is true.

In most disputes, too, when one party maintains that a certain

morality is higher than another and the other denies it, they do *at
least in part* refer to the same thing by the words "higher" and
"lower." To this extent their dispute is capable of settlement in
sense (1) and not only in sense (2) of the term.

This is perhaps the place to clear up Russell's dissatisfaction with
his own theory, which we noted in Chapter II, page 62, Russell
first maintains in general terms that moral judgments are nothing
but the expressions of a desire on the speaker's part. He then says
that he somehow feels that when he says, "the introduction of bull-
fighting in the United States would be a bad thing," he is doing
something more than expressing his desire or that his desire is
somehow objectively superior to that of a person who desires the
introduction of bull-fighting. My theory or Russell's own theory,
supplemented by a consideration of the *reasons* for moral judgments, easily clears up the source of this dissatisfaction without
any surrender to intuitionism. "The introduction of bull-fighting
in the United States would be a bad thing," in addition to expressing something concerning the speaker, makes some such objective
claim as, "The introduction of bull-fighting would lead to avoidable pain for innocent animals and to an increase in cruelty and
indirectly to the strengthening of illiberal forces and tendencies;
moreover, though it would produce a certain amount of pleasure
among the spectators, this very pleasure would reduce their capa-
city for other and deeper pleasures." Russell's desire *is* objectively
superior in the sense that its satisfaction would prevent the suffering of innocent animals, certain increases in cruelty and the strengthening of illiberal forces, etc. The satisfaction of his opponent's
desire would have altogether different consequences. This is, I
think, what Russell means by "superior," in the sense of referent.
It is certainly the sort of thing that I would mean. If the facts
concerning bull-fighting are as I described them a moment ago it
is clear that Russell is right. To the extent to which an advocate of
bull-fighting means the same by "superior" he would be mistaken.
If he means something different then he may or may not be mistaken, but Russell's claim remains objective and true.

If it is said that I am evading the real point because "the introduction of bull-fighting in the United States would be a bad thing"

is not a fundamental moral judgment, I have a two fold answer: if we could ever get a fundamental moral judgment in which one desire is claimed to be superior to another, I am quite sure the context there would be significantly different. In that context, I believe, it would not be at all implausible to maintain that the judgment only expresses the speaker's attitude. Secondly, it should be noted that the example is Russell's and not mine. It is in the case of a non-fundamental moral judgment that he finds his emotive theory unsatisfactory.

4. Moral Blindness

BY TERMS LIKE "moral blindness," "moral idiocy," or "moral insanity" we normally refer to two kinds of phenomena. We refer firstly to cases where a person acknowledges a certain general moral principle but then arbitrarily fails to apply it to a certain group or a certain person. We refer here to cases of what is sometimes called "special pleading." I do not see that situations of this kind require the assumption of some special faculty of moral intuition in which people whom we call morally blind or morally insane are defective. All we mean, in the sense of referential meaning, when we call a man like Harlow Shapley or Paul Robeson or Dean Inge or Father Coughlin morally blind is that on a certain topic their approval does not follow a consistent pattern.

The second type of situation in which we use the phrase "morally blind" concerns people who are devoid of sympathy. These cases may or may not overlap with the first type. To take the case of the teacher I mentioned in Chapter IV who took a delight in hurting defenseless girls and who gave people high grades if they were handsome or members of the Communist Party or both. I am told that he was quite capable of seriously maintaining in general terms that if A is academically inferior to B, but if he is more handsome than B, there is nothing wrong with giving him a higher grade. Of course we all know people who have seriously maintained that there is nothing wrong in giving an Aryan a higher grade than a Jew, although the Jew is academically superior or that there is nothing wrong in hurting a woman or a Jew or a German or an animal. In these cases when we say that a person is morally blind, we do not mean that he is engaged in special pleading. I have here deliberately taken some cases where people are not guilty of that. What we mean in these cases is I think, simply that the person is devoid of or *deficient in sympathy* for certain other living creatures. Now, if anybody wants to call "sympathy" a special faculty or even a moral faculty, I would not enter a protest. But sympathy is certainly not identical with the moral intuition whose existence the intuitionists assert. It is something which no sensible naturalist denies or needs to deny.

5. The Fact of Obligation

IN CHAPTER IV we noted that intuitionist placed a great deal of emphasis on the objectivity of judgments concerning obligation—judgments like, "Britain was obliged to come to Poland's aid" or "It is a parent's duty to see to it that his children do not starve."

From my remarks about "ought" in Chapters VII and VIII, it should be clear that, except for fundamental moral views, my theory fully accepts the objectivity of obligation-judgments. That is to say: obligation-judgments have descriptive meaning in the same sense in which ought-judgments have descriptive meaning. They imply, in the same senses, although they do not refer to, observable features of the action which is judged to be obligatory or a duty. Thus, "Britain was obliged to come to Poland's aid" implies "The British government had a mutual assistance pact with Poland" or something like that in the same sense in which "The bill legalizing euthanasia ought to be passed" implies "If euthanasia is legalized certain avoidable suffering will cease to occur without bringing about any other correspondingly intense suffering." "It is a parent's duty to see to it that his children do not starve" implies in the same sense, e.g., the factual statement, "the child came into existence not as a result of his own choice but a result of the parent's action." If we introduced the notion of "obligation-making feature" corresponding to "ought-making feature," we could say that obligation-judgments mean—in sense (4) of "meaning"—these obligation-making features. To account for the objectivity of obligation-statements we do not need to invoke a special realm of non-natural relations to which the obligation-statements refer. We only need to realize that a statement may have objective meaning without having a referent.

Many obligation-statements differ from other moral judgments in that they express not only the author's attitude toward something, but also his *feeling impelled* to perform a certain action. I doubt whether, as Strawson seems inclined to admit,[8] there is such a thing as a simple feeling, something *sui generis*, that is here expressed. In any case I hope to have shown that the existence of such a feeling *sui generis* is neither sufficient nor necessary to explain the objectivity of obligation-statements.

6. The Apparent Equivalence of Moral Judgments with Autobiographical Statements

IN EXPOUNDING one of the arguments for naive subjectivism (Chapter II, page 56), I pointed out that people are frequently willing to substitute a statement with an autobiographical referent for a moral judgment. E.g., a person who says, "Homer Lane was a profoundly good person" would, as a rule, be quite willing to put in the place of this, "I admired Lane very profoundly." How does this fact square with the objectivism advocated in the present work?

The answer to this question was, I think, given in Chapter V, when I pointed out that in a very plain sense, "I like the steak at Barney's," asserted in *certain* circumstances, is synonymous with "The steak at Barney's is nice." I there explained that what this shows is not that the latter statement is "merely subjective" but that the former is *not* merely subjective. "I like the steak at Barney's" implies, in sense (2), various factual statements about the steak at Barney's and is uttered for the sake of giving this non-autobiographical information.

The same applies to statements like, "I profoundly admired Homer Lane" or "I approve of inter-racial marriages" when people

---

8. Cf. his review of Raphael's *Moral Sense*, in *Philosophy*, 1948, p. 169.

are willing to substitute them for moral judgments. On these occasions they imply certain statements concerning the *object* of the attitude referred to and are *not* put forward for the sake of autobiographical information. That this is so is shown by the following facts: if somebody were to reply to the man who said e.g., "I approve of inter-racial marriages" with the statement, "You are wrong," he would certainly not mean, "You don't really approve of inter-racial marriages." He would mean in the sense of referent, "the factual statements or some of the factual statements concerning inter-racial marriages which you imply are mistaken."

7. Are Moral Emotions "Intellectual Emotions"?

IN CHAPTER IV we saw how intuitionists in some contexts insist on the "immediacy" of moral judgments, while in other contexts they insist that they are not immediate but based on deliberation. Ross, in particular, insisted that the moral emotions, i.e., the emotions which moral judgments express, "presuppose some insight" into the objects towards which they are directed.

If they are qualified in a certain way, all these claims are I think correct. But I shall try to show that in the sense in which they are mutually consistent and true, they can easily be accounted for by my theory. Many, though not all, moral judgments are "immediate." Thus let us suppose that the character whom I described in Chapter VII, page 153 and whom I there called Sekierer is sitting at a table with a very fat girl who obviously feels sensitive about her figure. Supposing, I hear him, as a certain look comes into his eyes, turn the conversation to the subject of the importance to men of a trim figure in a woman—"Yes, to all men, whatever they may say to be polite!" In a case like this I instantly judge, silently if not openly, that the man did something wrong. Does the immediacy here require the assumption of a non-natural faculty of "seeing wrong"? Hardly. It is quite plausibly accounted for by saying—roughly following Hume—that my attitude of disapproval towards sadistic remarks about people's looks or about their lack of ability in this or that comes instantly into play once such a remark is heard.

Again, we often deliberate before arriving at a moral conclusion. Thus to decide whether mercy-killing is or is not wrong in certain circumstances, people investigate its consequences on the person to be killed, on society at large, its relation to allegedly divine documents, etc. If by "insight into the nature of the object" what is meant is knowledge concerning the features of the object that is judged good or bad or right or wrong, then certainly many cases of approval and disapproval are based on insight into the nature of the object. But, in all the cases we examined, the features were observable, unmysterious features. There does not seem the least reason to suppose that in this respect our cases were to any extent unrepresentative.

8. The Origin of Ethical Terms

IN VARIOUS of his widely read books, C. E. M. Joad has maintained that naturalistic theories cannot account for "the origin and distinctive use of ethical terms." He has also maintained that naturalists cannot account for the fact that "ethics has come to be so sharply distinguished from esthetics." I shall now try to show that these objections are altogether invalid. I shall quote Joad's arguments as contained in his latest book, *A Critique of Logical Positivism*. His fire there is primarily directed at the emotive theory but, as will be clear from my quotations, he believes them to apply to all forms of naturalism.

According to the emotive theory of ethics, ethical judgments are ejaculations of the judger's feelings of approval or disapproval, so that the word "wrong" in the sentence, "stealing is wrong," adds nothing to the meaning of the sentence. If we ask how we come to feel emotions of approval for conduct X and disapproval for conduct Y, the answer falls, as we have seen, within the provinces of the psychologist, the sociologist and the anthropologist. Broadly, their answer is that we feel approval for actions which we think will benefit us or our social group, and disapproval for actions which we think will harm us or our social group—this, at least, is an example of the type of answer that psychology and sociology give. (There are many variants of the type, as, for example, that we are conditioned to feel approval of conduct which will benefit the governing class of our social group.) Now, either the word "right" carries some specific meaning not coterminous with "conducive to the advantage of self or group" or "felicific in respect of self or group," or it does not. If it does not, if its meaning is exhausted by the concepts of happiness and advantage, if, in other words, to say "X is right," is to make an ejaculation of emotional approval for what is thought to conduce to advantage or to promote happiness, why use the word "right" at all? Why not speak directly of happiness and advantage, as we do when we make judgments which express feelings of pleasure or adduce considerations of self-interest. I disapprove of toothache and, when the dentist hurts me, I make an ejaculation of pain; but it never occurs to me to say that toothache is wrong, or that the dentist is wicked. If on the other hand "right" does have a specific meaning, what can it be but an ethical meaning which is not wholly analysable into considerations of advantage and happiness? What I am here suggesting is that the logical positivist view fails to account both for the origin and for the distinctive use of ethical terms. Even if this apparently distinctive meaning is illusory and ethical concepts are figments which stand for nothing, why was it necessary to invent them? It is noticeable that we do not feel constraint to invent distinctive terms to express others of our feelings of approval and disapproval. I disapprove of cruelty, but I also disapprove of toothache and dislike spinach. But while I say "cruelty is wrong," I don't say "toothache is wrong." I say, "you did wrong to torture that child for your own pleasure," but I don't say "you did wrong to eat that spinach for your lunch." Why the difference, if the analysis of the propositions "cruelty is wrong" "toothache is painful" and 'spinach is beastly" are the same? If all three propositions merely express a feeling and do not, therefore, as Ayer puts it, "come under the category of truth and falsehood," why do I go out of my way to translate one of them and one only into what is prima facie quite a different proposition, namely, "cruelty is wrong"? According to Ayer, "cruelty to children is wrong," is equivalent to "hurting children!!" that is to say, it is an ejaculation of horror. Similarly, "toothache is painful," or "spinach is distasteful" is, I suppose, equivalent to "horrible toothache!!" "beastly spinach!!" But if this is so, *why do we moralize our disapproval of cruelty but not our disapproval of toothache and spinach?*[9]

Mr. Joad is a very remarkable man. Undoubtedly he is the first man in the history of the world who *disapproves* of toothache and spinach! Many years ago I knew a psychopathic girl who hated me with great intensity. Once, in her company, I had three orders of Zabaglioni, an Italian dish of which I am very fond. I shall never forget how, with fiery darts in her eyes, she said, "How disgusting!"

---

9. *A Critique of Logical Positivism,* pp. 127-129. My italics.

At the time I thought this was the most bizarre disapproval I would ever come across. But, compared with Joad's it was utterly commonplace. For after all she disapproved a voluntary human action.

To speak seriously: nobody, not even Joad *disapproves* of toothache and spinach. People are scared of toothache and try to avoid it; and they *dislike* spinach, as Joad in one place realizes. Thus, not even the most radical exponent of the emotive theory needs to be troubled by this objection. For no supporter of that theory has ever claimed that a sentence with an ethical term as its predicate expresses just *any* sort of feeling or attitude. These sentences on the emotive view express *certain* emotions or attitudes, such as approval and disapproval. Moreover, a defender of the emotive theory might go on to say that we do also use subject-predicate sentences to express our feelings concerning aches and foods. Thus we do say, "toothache is nasty (in a non-moral sense)" or "the steak at Barney's is nice." But because the feelings expressed by these sentences are not *moral* feelings like approval and disapproval, we do not use ethical terms as our predicates.

There is nothing very puzzling about the origin of ethical terms, if the metaethic of this book is true. In that case ethical terms are convenient ways of doing several things at once. They serve to refer to certain qualities or features, to express the speaker's moral attitude, and in several cases also to recommend a certain attitude or certain conduct to one's audience. The origin of ethical terms is no more puzzling than the origin of "nice" as applied to foods or of such "colored" terms as "Red," "Hun," "fellow-traveller," "pamper," "squeamish," or "new-fangled" which similarly do two or more things at once.

Joad's second point is as follows:

Again, I approve of Shakespeare's sonnets and Mozart's quartets. These feelings of approval I qualify by the epithet, "aesthetic." Aesthetic feelings are those commonly supposed to be aroused in us by what is beautiful, and I, accordingly, proceed to assert that Mozart's quartets and Shakespeare's sonnets are beautiful, attributing to them a certain quality or characteristic to which the emotions of approval aroused in me are a response. Upon this foundation a formidable structure of aesthetic criticism and evaluation has been raised.

On Ayer's view to say, "Mozart's quartets are beautiful," is not even to assert that one has a feeling, or to describe it; it is merely to express it. But if to say "generosity is noble" or "Honesty is a virtue and ought to be cultivated," is to ejaculate one's emotions of admiring approval for generosity and honesty, and to say "Mozart's G minor quintet is a work of exceptional beauty and ought to be valued," is to ejaculate one's emotion of admiring approval for Mozart, how is it that ethics has come to be so sharply distinguished from aesthetics? If, in short, ethical and aesthetic judgments are alike expressions of feeling, why do we distinguish what is good from what is beautiful and erect such different structures of judgment and criticism to accommodate and evaluate the experiences to which we give the name of ethical and aesthetic?[10]

Not satisfied with toothache and spinach, Joad also approves and disapproves of musical works. In this he is not alone since Stalin and Hitler and fanatics of various kinds do the same. However, most people in most circumstances simply like or dislike, admire or detest a composition without approving or disapproving of it. As before, even the most radical defender of the emotive theory could rightly reject Joad's argument on the ground that he does not claim that moral and aesthetic judgments express the same feelings or attitudes. Moral judgments, he would say, express moral feelings like approval and disapproval, while aesthetic judgments express certain forms of enjoyment and displeasure. Joad is in other words guilty of an enormous *ignoratio elenchi*.

As for my own theory, moral and aesthetic judgments are distinguished by the different attitudes they express and also by the different (natural) features to which they refer.

There is an underlying premise in both of Joad's arguments whose absurdity is seen as soon as it is explicitly stated. The premise is this: whenever there are two different terms or sets of terms there must also be different referents. The fact that there are synonyms and abbreviations is enough to show that this statement is false. But equally the existence of exclamations which express different states of mind but have no referential meaning shows Joad's premise to be untrue.

I should like to conclude this section with a brief comment on the view of Carritt and Ross, quoted in Chapter III, that "scepticism" is mistaken about moral but right about aesthetic judgments.

---

10. *Ibid.*, pp. 130-131.

Carritt and Ross, it will be remembered, maintain that in moral as well as aesthetic judgments the author is referring to a non-natural quality. They add that this quality is sometimes present in the former case but never in the latter. If my view is correct this bifurcation is totally unjustified. "Scepticism" is equally wrong in both domains. Aesthetic as well as moral judgments—with the reservations explained in Chapter VIII, Section 7—are objective claims and frequently true. But the referent neither of moral nor of aesthetic judgments is the same feature in different instances. Nor is it in most cases a single feature. Nor, finally, is it a feature or set of features disclosed only by some special faculty.

CONTENTS

Chapter X

Some Concluding Remarks

IN THIS CHAPTER I shall discuss two very general objections which have been levelled against other metaethical theories and which some writers would very probably advance against my theory also. Briefly, these charges are (1) that the theory is "nihilistic"[1] and (2) that, even if true, it is trivial since the questions which it answers are trivial questions. They are questions not suggested by any actual problems with which human beings are ever confronted.

1. Nihilism, Moral Chaos, Vishinsky!

THE CHARGES which I shall examine in this section are usually brought up against various forms of subjectivism and against the emotive theory, though sometimes they are brought up against naturalism as such. I shall try to show that they are unfounded both as regards my own theory and also as regards the emotive theory.

I shall take great pains not to misrepresent the writers who have voiced these charges, although the same cannot be said of them. I shall therefore quote at very considerable length both from serious philosophers like Blanshard, Mabbot, and Paton and from members

---

1. Cf., e.g., Urban, "Axiology," in *Twentieth Century Philosophy* (ed. Runes), p. 56; cf. also the same author's "Value Propositions and Verifiability," *Journal of Philosophy*, 1937, p. 591.

of the "underworld of philosophy"[2] like Joad. Thus Mabbott writes:

The basic difficulty of subjectivism is that it makes any person's approval as valid as that of anyone else. This reduces the moral world to a chaos of caprice and infinite variation. For it is not only each man who is the measure of all things moral but each moment in each man's life.[3]

Or, as Blanshard puts it:

According to the emotive theory, any attitude would be as fitting or unfitting as any other, which means that the notion of fitness has lost all point. Indeed we are forced to go much farther. If goodness and badness lie in attitudes only and hence are brought into being by them, those men who greeted death and misery with childishly merry laughter are taking the only sensible line. If there is nothing evil in these things, if they get their moral complexion only from our feeling about them, why shouldn't they be greeted with a cheer? To greet them with repulsion would turn what before was neutral into something bad; it would needlessly bring badness into the world; and even on subjectivist assumptions that does not seem very bright. On the other hand, to greet them with delight would convert what before was neutral into something good; it would bring goodness into the world. If I have murdered a man and wish to remove the stain the way is clear. It is to cry, "Hurrah for murder."[4]

The same author also writes:

The great problems of the day are international problems. Has the new subjectivism any bearing upon these problems? I think it has, and a somewhat sinister bearing. I would not suggest, of course, that those who hold the theory are one whit less public-spirited than others; surely there are few who could call themselves citizens of the world with more right (if "rights" have meaning any longer) than Mr. Russell. But Mr. Russell has confessed himself discontented with his ethical theory, and in view of his breadth of concern, one cannot wonder. For its general acceptance would, so far as one can see, be an international disaster. The assumptions behind the old League and the new United Nations was that there is such a thing as right and wrong in the conduct

2. I owe this term to Joad himself, used by him with reference to Christian Science in *Return to Philosophy*, Chapter I. Among other members of the underworld of philosophy I count Barrows Dunham, the author of *Man against Myth* and Churchman and Ackoff, the authors of "The Democratization of Philosophy," *Science and Society*, 1949.

3. *Op. cit.*, p. 145.

4. "The New Subjectivism in Ethics," *op. cit.*, p. 508.

of a nation, a right and wrong that do not depend on how it happens to feel at the time. It is implied, for example, that when Japan invaded Manchuria in 1931 she might be wrong, and that by discussion and argument she might be shown to be wrong. It was implied that when the Nazis invaded Poland they might be wrong, even though German public sentiment overwhelmingly approved it. On the theory before us, it would be meaningless to call these nations mistaken; if they felt approval for what they did, then it was right with as complete a justification as could be supplied for the disapproval felt by the rest of the world. In the present dispute between Russia and our own country over southeast Europe, it is nonsense to speak of the right or rational course for either of us to take: if with all the facts before the two parties, each feels approval for its own course, both attitudes are equally justified or unjustified; neither is mistaken; there is no common reason to which they can take an appeal; there are no principles by which an international court could pronounce on the matter; nor would there be any obligation to obey the pronouncement if it were made. This cuts the ground from under any attempt to establish one's case as right or anyone else's case as wrong. So if our friends the subjectivists still hold their theory after I have applied my little ruler to their knuckles, which of course they will, I have but one request to make of them: Do keep it from Mr. Molotov and Mr. Vishinsky.[5]

I shudder to think what Mr. Vishinsky would do if he knew about the emotive theory. I suppose his ignorance of it is the one thing that is stopping him from ordering an atomic attack on New York.

Paton is just as emphatic:

Mr. Robinson ought not to be surprised if some people display a shade of vehemence in their criticisms. It seems to them that if his doctrines are true, then life is merely trivial.[6]

The conclusions of the emotive theory

indicate that man's whole search for moral truth is a colossal blunder and that the effort ever to convince any one of his duty upon rational grounds is sheer folly.[7]

Now, for some Joadisms which are really little different from the other passages:

---

5. *Ibid.*, pp. 510-511.
6. "The Emotive Theory of Ethics," *Aristotelian Society*, Suppl. Vol. XXII, pp. 119-120.
7. Hill, *Contemporary Ethical Theories*, p. 26.

It follows from subjectivism, he says, that no one set of values possesses more validity than another. When we ascribe value to anything, saying for example, that one action, political system, poem or work of art is better than another, we are merely giving expression to our own preferences, preferences which on this view, are without authority or justification. For even if we say that one action or system is more liable to promote happiness than another, happiness which is itself, on this view merely something that some or most human beings happen to desire, has no authority to command men's actions. Happiness is not, that is to say, something that ought to be pursued, because it is desirable as well as desired.

There is, then, no ground for preferring kindness to cruelty—one's actual preference for the former is on a par with one's preference for asparagus over artichokes—and no *rational justification* for objecting to the Nazi theories of politics or the horrors of the concentration camps which were the instruments of their application. There are many objections to this view, but the most potent is that nobody really holds it.[8]

[On the emotive view] we have, therefore, nothing to say to the guard in the concentration camp who prefers cruelty; we can only make noises expressive of our feelings of repulsion.[9]

If there is no objective right and wrong, if moral judgments are, as logical positivists hold, merely ejaculations of emotions of approval and disapproval, then, as Mr. Dunham points out, one cannot demonstrate that fascist practices are evil; one can only express dislike of them. 'No philosophy,' he comments, 'would better please the fascists themselves, since moral questions could then be safely left in the hands of the police.'

If Logical Positivism is correct, you can say, 'one atom bomb can destroy 50,000 people' (statement of fact), but not, 'it is a bad thing to destroy 50,000 people' (statement of evaluation) or, rather, you can say it, but the word 'bad' adds nothing to the factual content of the statement.

Can anyone seriously maintain that the spread of such doctrines will have no consequences for ethics, politics and theology, or that their effect upon young and generous minds, protesting passionately against cruelty and injustice, and eager to set the world to rights will not be to sap effort, discourage initiative, destroy the hope of change and so to assist reaction and sanction inertia?[10]

Sap the foundations of rational belief in God, in truth, in goodness and in beauty, as Logical Positivism cannot help but do, confine meaningful assertions to matters of empirical fact and you' sow the seeds of

---

8. *Op. cit.*, pp. 110-111. My italics.
9. *Ibid.*, p. 119.
10. *Ibid.*, p. 148.

intolerance and dogmatism, as weeds spring up where a man cuts down
a healthy crop yet puts nothing in its place. Communism and Fascism
are the natural by-products of scepticism and nihilism. Most men need
a creed and there is nothing in the empirical world upon which a creed
can be based. For the empirical world contains nothing but the movements of matter and these, though they can be observed, cannot be
believed. It is thus no accident that Logical Positivism tends to undermine rational and to encourage irrational beliefs, and that, as Oxonian
remarked, the belief in Fascism should tend to spring up in the "vacuum
left by an abeyance of concern with fundamental human values."[11]

Shorn of their rhetoric, these passages seem to amount to the
following charges: (a) If the theory were true then neither party
in a moral dispute could ever prove his case, then nobody could
ever produce a reason or rational justification for a moral judgment, and (b) an *acceptance* of the theory is liable to have all sorts
of results which civilized people, whether or not they are intuitionists, would hardly desire—e.g., an increase in murder, cruelty, and
fascism.

I think it is important to realize that (a) and (b) are logically
distinct assertions. It is at least conceivable that (b) is false although (a) is true. I.e., it might be a fact that the parties in a
moral dispute cannot ever really prove their case and yet that the
adoption of this view and the more general theory from which it
follows would not have any of the practical consequences which
the critics mention.

It will be convenient from now on to refer to (a) as the "theoretical" and to (b) as the "practical" charge. I shall attempt to show
that the theoretical charge, while it has *some* measure of truth, is
largely false; and that insofar as it is true, it is hardly a "charge." I
shall also try to show that the practical charge is an utter absurdity.

I shall take the theoretical charge first. Why and in what sense,
to use Blanshard's example, was the Nazi invasion of Poland a bad
thing? It was bad because it led to an enormous amount of human
suffering, because it was an instance of breaking promises, etc.
These and similar *natural* features are the badness of the Nazi invasion in the sense in which most liberals would use "bad" in such
a context. Sincerely or insincerely—which of them is not to the

---

11. *Ibid.,* p. 152.

point here—the Nazis and their various apologists denied these empirical statements. They claimed that their invasion, in finally leading to the extermination of the Jews, would produce happiness for most men, that pacts were broken not by the Nazis but by the Poles, that the Nazis were acting in self-defense, etc., etc. To a very considerable extent, that is to say, the Nazis, in their official statements at least, used "bad" in the same sense as Western liberals, but denied that their actions had the features referred to by the word. It is in fact not at all difficult to show that their action had these features and therefore that it was bad. Thus my view does not imply that actions like the Nazi invasion of Poland cannot be shown to be bad.

Nor does this follow from the emotive theory. For the emotive theory does not say, as Blanshard suggests, that when a man says "x is good" he *means* that his group approves of x. It says that in that case, "x is good" *expresses* his approval of x. And this approval he would usually defend by statements concerning the features of x which we call his reasons for the moral judgment that x is good. Now, if and insofar as the Nazis offered as reasons the statement that their action, in exterminating the Jews, would lead to human happiness, and that the Poles and not they were breaking pacts, it is open to a defender of the emotive theory to say that they can be shown to be mistaken. It is open to him to say: when the Nazis invaded Poland and approved of their own action, their *use of language* in the judgment "the invasion is a good thing" was correct, but the approval which the judgment correctly expressed was based on demonstrably false claims. He may then go on to say: what we normally mean when we say that a person's moral judgment has been disproven is not that the facts it asserts do not exist (since it asserts none) but that the facts which are brought up to support it do not exist.

By the way, I do not remember that the Nuremberg Tribunal, when it condemned the Nazi leaders as war criminals, gave as its reason "because the defendants performed actions having the non-natural quality of badness." The reasons given were that the Nazi leaders had broken certain written or unwritten laws, that they caused enormous suffering, etc.

To all this, I am sure, it will be replied that I am evading the real issue. Supposing, it would be said, the Nazis admitted that they and not the Poles were breaking an agreement. Supposing they admitted that their acts were certain to lead to enormous unhappiness for most people all over the world. And supposing they had added "but we approve of things of this sort. These are the features to which we refer when we call an action 'good.' " How, on your view, could they *then* be proven wrong? How, on your view, could it *then* be shown that their action is evil?

If and to the extent to which there is no common, ultimate object of approval here, I must admit that in the sense in which the Nazis are here imagined to be using "good" and "bad," it is impossible on my view to prove that their invasion of Poland was bad. In *that* sense of course it was good, though in the sense in which liberals use the word, it was still bad and can be shown to be so in virtue of the very fact that the Nazis are here imagined to concede. To this admission, however, two very important supplementary remarks have to be added. Firstly, with cases like the one just imagined, no other metaethic fares any better. On my view, all one can say in such a case is that while in the liberal's sense the Nazi invasion was bad, in the Nazi sense it was good. But what can the intuitionist do once the *natural* features he points to are not accepted as good- or bad-making features? What if the Nazis said, "Yes—we admit that our invasion is going to lead to enormous suffering, etc., but our intuition tells us that this makes it good"? How could the intuitionist have *proven* them wrong? To be able to *prove* the Nazis wrong in a sense also accepted by them, the acceptance of intuitionism on their part is neither sufficient nor necessary. What is sufficient and necessary is their admission that certain types of action in virtue of being actions of that type are or tend to be wrong, whether this admission merely expresses a disapproval or refers to a non-natural quality.

Secondly, I wish to point out that the case we are now considering *is* an imaginary one. In actual fact, the Nazis *never* defended an action of theirs by saying it was going to produce enormous suffering. Nor do I know of anybody else who has ever done this. It is true that actual cases often have a *partial* resemblance to this imaginary case. But that is all. Insofar as they have this resemblance it is *a fact* that they cannot be settled in sense (1)—in the sense in which scientific disputes can be settled. Intuitionism implies the non-existence of this fact and is therefore an untenable theory. More plausible theories try to take this fact into account.

The seeming plausibility of the "theoretical" charge is due to no more than this: Blanshard and Joad suggest that the theories they are attacking imply with regard to all *actual* instances and *without any qualification* that neither side can be proven in the right. This is indeed an incredible consequence. But neither my nor the emotive theory implies it.

A word about Joad's charge that on the emotive theory—and I suppose on mine also—"no rational justification" is possible for "objecting to the horrors of the concentration camps." In the light of my analysis of the meanings of "reason" and "justification" and similar words in Chapter I, Section 6, and in Chapters V and VI, it should be clear that this is unsound. It *is* possible on the views in question to give a rational justification for saying, "there ought to be no concentration camps." The rational justification would be something like this: "Because they produce terrible suffering for the prisoners, because they brutalize the guards and those outsiders with whom they are in contact, and because they tend to produce an atmosphere of fear throughout the country." This, although not a justification in the sense of "deductive justification," is a justification in the only sense in which anybody ever in ordinary life uses the term "justification" with reference to ought-statements.

Joad might reply to this: "But what if the concentration camp guard presses you and asks: 'why ought the prisoners not to suffer, why ought there to be an atmosphere free from fear, why ought I not to be more brutal'?" I think I could give answers to some of these questions also, but admittedly there would come a point where I could give none. However, a statement does not cease to be a good reason or a rational justification just because this process cannot be continued *ad infinitum*. Moreover, Joad himself also comes to a stage when he can go no further. Supposing the Nazi guard admits that cruelty has the non-natural quality of badness but then says to Joad, "So what?"

In justifying the liberal judgment about concentration camps there is only one thing which Joad could say, consistently with his theory, and which I cannot say consistently with mine. After I have finished with my reasons, Joad can still add, "and these actions have the non-natural quality of badness." I have no doubt that hearing this would instantly convert the guard into an angel.

Joad in one place[13] complains that if Russell's metaethic were correct then the recommendations in his practical writings such as *Marriage and Morals* and the *Conquest of Happiness* would cease to be supported by any reasons. In this connection I should like to submit to Joad the following consideration: Russell wrote against the Churches and the militarists and authoritarian school-masters and Communists not because their actions had some non-natural characteristic which he for one claimed never to have perceived. He wrote against them because their actions were in his opinion calculated to produce misery, to undermine freedom, and in general to bring about character-qualities of which he (and many others) do not approve. Those were his reasons and not the further statement, "These acts have the non-natural character of badness."

I should also like to submit to Joad the following bold idea: The people who suffered in Nazi concentration camps complained not because the actions of their guards had the *non-natural* feature of badness. They complained because the actions of their guards caused them terrible suffering.

I do not suppose any of my readers has heard of the "fly-swat theory of history" propounded by an Australian historian whose name I am not allowed to reveal. The theory received its name from the following classical illustration: "One day, the French consul at Algiers was talking to the Bey. In the middle of the conversation a fly settled on the consul's bald head. The Bey thereupon seized a fly-swat which was near by and aimed it at the fly on the consul's

---

13. *Ibid.*, p. 123.

head. Unfortunately he missed. He missed the fly, that is, but not the head. France, as a result, declared war on Algiers. Such was the causation of the French Colonial Empire."

I am always reminded of this theory when I hear of the "sinister" consequences of the adoption of the emotive theory. I can just imagine the joy among the Joadians if one day a murderer were found who made the following statement to the police: "I always hated Gangle (the murdered man). But thoughts of killing Gangle never entered my head until recently. For I used to regard murder as something wrong. A few months ago, however, I took a philosophy course in which I was introduced to the metamoral theories of C. L. Stevenson and A. J. Ayer. These theories convinced me that if I murdered somebody this would be perfectly all right so long as I approved of my action. I then decided to murder Gangle. I do approve of what I did. Therefore I did not commit a wrong act and you ought to release me."

To speak seriously: the psychology underlying what I have called the "practical charge" of the Joadians is far more fantastic than the fly-swat theory. For they suppose that moral attitudes can be changed or removed simply by a change in a person's metamoral theory. Thus Joad writes:

If I consistently believe that the statement, "Stealing is wrong," does no more than express an emotion of horror at stealing, it will presently cease to express the emotion of horror. Not to put too fine a point on it, I shall cease to believe that stealing is wrong.[14]

This passage expresses very well what all proponents of the "practical charge" have been wanting to say. Incidentally, Joad's new method of eradicating horrors ought to be brought to the attention of psychotherapists. If true, it will certainly mean a revolution in psychiatry.

In the passage just quoted, Joad is asserting one or both of two things: (i) if I come to believe that a sentence of the form "x is wrong" does no more than express a certain emotion or attitude of mine, I shall soon cease to use this sentence to express my attitude. I will then start looking for some other phrase or sentence

14. *Ibid.*, p. 146.

to express my attitude. (ii) If I come to believe that a sentence of the form "x is wrong" does no more than express an attitude, I shall gradually cease to have that attitude. I may even develop the opposite attitude.

(i) is preposterous. If "x is wrong" allows others to infer that I disapprove of x and if I do not want to mislead them about my attitude, there would be no point in stopping to use "x is wrong" when I disapprove of x.

But I suppose (i) is not what Joad really wants to say. What he is really concerned with is (ii). Any observation of what makes and what does not make people change their attitudes shows that (ii) is also preposterous. People change their attitudes because they change their beliefs about the object of their attitude or because of some emotional upheaval. They never change their attitude simply because they abandon a theory concerning the meaning of the sentences by means of which they express the attitude.[15]

The absurdity of the practical charge is apparent as soon as we consider concrete examples. Supposing you are very fond of animals. You are not a very courageous person but you love animals so much that if you see a man maltreat an animal you instantly rush to its aid, even if the man looks like a professional boxer. To be specific: one day you walk along Riverside Drive and you see a child torturing a poodle. Unless you are a dried-out old prune, you *do not* say to yourself, "Ah, here is an instance of cruelty and anything which is an instance of cruelty tends to have the non-natural quality of badness. My disapproval is the appropriate attitude towards bad acts. Therefore I must disapprove of this boy's treatment of the poodle." Nor do you say to yourself, "Ah, an instance of cruelty. The non-natural relation of oughtness connects avoidable cruelty with its prevention on the part of the person in whose power this is. Therefore I ought to try and stop this boy from hurting the poodle." You will simply rush to the poodle's aid. If you love animals you will rush to the poodle's aid whether

---

15. As I shall point out in Section 2 of this Chapter, this does not imply that such a change in one's metamoral viewpoint need have *no* practical effect. But any practical effect will concern another, more general, attitude.

you believe that cruelty has the non-natural character of badness or not.

Supposing you are an intuitionist and a lover of animals. Supposing you one day become convinced that intuitionism is an untenable theory. Would this change in your philosophical position have the least effect on your love of animals? Everything we know about such attitudes and everything we know about people who have given up intuitionism show that it would have no effect whatsoever. If a person hates cruelty to animals, he could not get rid of this attitude even if he wanted to.

If a poodle bit your child or if you got badly bitten many times in succession by animals you have befriended or if you suddenly came to believe that animals are as hypocritical and cruel as human beings, this *might* affect your love. Abandonment of intuitionism quite certainly will not.

Much the same applies to attitudes like approval and disapproval. Even if you don't love animals you are likely to come to the poodle's assistance—provided you disapprove of cruelty. Supposing that in addition to disapproving of cruelty you are also an intuitionist, but supposing you one day become convinced that intuitionism is an untenable theory. Would this have any effect on your disapproval of cruelty? Everything we know about people who have given up intuitionism and everything we know about the causes behind changes in people's feelings of approval and disapproval point to a negative answer. If you changed your views about the effects of cruelty this might very well change your attitude. Again, a series of emotional disasters might turn you into a cynic or a sadist. You would then no longer care about cruelty. Or you would even come to admire cruel people. But a mere change in your metaethic could never have such an effect.

Let us briefly consider another case where intellectual considerations figure quite prominently. You very strongly disapprove of the code, still the official morality in our society, which forbids a sex-life to adolescents. You do so because you believe that this code makes people miserable, malicious, hypocritical, and full of envy and crazy ambitions. You disapprove of codes which have these consequences.

Now, you might abandon this attitude of disapproval if your own life became full of frustrations and if you underwent a long period of intense suffering. Or you might abandon it if you changed your belief about the consequences of the virginity code—e.g., if you came to believe that any other code would lead to the immediate destruction of the human race. But you most certainly would not change your attitude simply if you stopped believing that sentences of the form "x is evil" refer to non-natural qualities.

What is important in a practical problem like the prevention or reduction of cruelty is that people have a certain attitude. If they have such an attitude they will tend to act against cruelty whether they "see" it to be wrong or not. If they "see" cruelty to be wrong this still will not make them act against it unless they also disapprove of it.

"Whatever be the theory of it," writes Paton, "I am as certain that cruelty is wrong as I am that grass is green or that two and two makes four. If this certainty is merely contingent, then my whole universe is shaken."[16] To this I should like to add the following observation: if people started universally, without exception, to approve of and strive for cruelty, my universe too would be shaken. E.g., if they started torturing animals and gave each other prizes for the most extremely sadistic acts and if they furthered cruelty in other respects, I would find life unbearable. But if they became less cruel and approved of cruelty less than they do now, I would feel a great deal happier even though none of them believed that when he says "cruelty is bad" he is asserting the existence of a non-natural quality. I would then feel much happier even if nobody ever again said "cruelty is bad" or anything synonymous with it.

It is interesting to note that when the Joadians make their practical charge they arbitrarily confine their attention to moral beliefs like "stealing is wrong" which most of their readers consider desirable. But if Joad's point were correct, it would equally apply to the moral attitudes of sadists, Vishinsky, and the like. To stop Vishinsky from approving of cruelty against Trotzkyites and

---

16. *Op. cit.*, p. 125.

"saboteurs," all we would need to do is convince him of the emotive theory!

Bertrand Russell has stated essentially the same point which I have been trying to make when he says:

> We have wishes which are not purely personal, and, if we had not, no amount of ethical teaching would influence our conduct except through fear of disapproval. The sort of life that most of us admire is one which is guided by large impersonal desires; now such desires can, no doubt, be encouraged by example, education, and knowledge, but they can hardly be created by the mere abstract belief that they are good, nor discouraged by an analysis of what is meant by the word "good." . . .
> . . . When you meet a man with whom you have a fundamental ethical disagreement—for example, if you think that all men count equally, while he selects a class as alone important—you will find yourself no better able to cope with him if you believe in objective values than if you do not. In either case, you can only influence his conduct through influencing his desires: if you succeed in that, his ethic will change, and if not, not.[17]

In view of these statements, it is very surprising that, in a later book, Russell himself echoes some of the chaos-charges, without however abandoning his own theory:

> If ethical statements cannot be true in the sense in which scientific statements are true, we are driven in practice, whatever may be the philosophic truth, to a *contest by force or propaganda or both*, whenever an irreconcilable ethical difference exists between powerful groups. . . .
> Plato thinks he can prove that his ideal Republic is good; a democrat who accepts the objectivity of ethics may think that he can prove the Republic bad; but anyone who agrees with Thrasymachus will say: "There is no question of proving or disproving; the only question is whether you like the kind of State that Plato desires. If you do, it is good for you; if you do not, it is bad for you." If many do and many do not, the decision cannot be made by reason, *but only by force, actual or concealed.*[18]

Russell is here guilty of a false disjunction. Just because a given dispute cannot be resolved by an appeal to observations or "reason,"

---

17. *Religion and Science*, pp. 240-241, Cf. also his "Good and Bad," in *Polemic*, November 1946, pp. 6-7.

18. *History of Western Philosophy*, pp. 138-139. My italics. Cf. also Dewey, "Some Questions about Value," in *Value* (ed. Lepley) p. 10.

this does not imply that people have to resort to force. They often, as Professor Frankel has pointed out, resort, or are willing to resort, to compromise. Or, they may decide to resolve the issue by tossing a coin, preferring this to the use of force. Moreover, people frequently resort to force and propaganda even in the case of disputes where "the decision can be made by reason." The OGPU "settlements" of scientific disputes and the vicious slanders to which medical pioneers have often been subjected will illustrate my point.

2. The Charge of Triviality

IN THIS LAST SECTION of my book I wish to defend myself against the charge which is certain to be made that, even if I have succeeded in producing a plausible answer to my questions, what I have written is pretty much a waste of time. For, it will be said, instead of somehow contributing to the solution of the practical problems of human beings, I have engaged in "futile verbal investigations."[19]

I think there is *some* justice in this charge, but I think it is only partly just. I did often, while writing this book, feel that what I was doing was not very important. But insofar as this charge is just, it should, I think, be levelled against philosophy in general. For when I read the works of other philosophers, including those who make the charge, I find that, insofar as they are not simply dreaming or doing amateur science, they are doing very much the same sort of thing as I.

In any case, however, the charge is only partly just. In reply I should like firstly to make the very simple point that some people, including myself, have a strong craving for clarity. This craving, incidentally, is by no means confined to analytic philosophers. Stefan Zweig, in the *World of Yesterday*, records how Freud used to impress upon him that "clarity is the highest quality of thinking." The mere fact that there is a certain number of intelligent people in the world who wish to be clear about the way in which ethical predicates function in our discourse is, to my mind, a sufficient justification for concerning oneself with this topic.

---

19. Cf. K. R. Popper, "What Can Logic Do for Philosophy?" *Aristotelian Society*, Suppl. Vol. XXII, p. 143.

But secondly, I deny—and this is the reply on which I would wish to place the greater emphasis—that an inquiry like mine is necessarily devoid of practical consequences. Intuitionism and, more generally, all forms of non-naturalism in ethics from Plato to Ross,[20] have fundamentally had one and only one purpose: to help support the morality of self-denial and sin. I have already explained why I cannot plead guilty to the charge of promoting cruelty and fascism, but I do plead guilty to the charge of undermining morality in the sense of undermining the moralities of the fuddy-duddies and the sour-pusses.

Those who defend the morality of sin and self-denial usually have very little to offer in the way of an empirical justification for their moral judgments. In the last resort they fall back on God's alleged prohibitions and on conscience or what our moral sense is supposed to tell us. Now, once a person rejects non-naturalism, he will demand a factual justification for moral judgments—e.g., for the judgment "Birth control is wrong and sinful." At the very least, he will pay more attention to this than otherwise. If he accepts my theory he will say: "The words 'wrong' and 'sinful' are polyguous. I do not know what you mean by 'wrong' here, aside from expressing your own disapproval and anxiety. I do not know what you mean by 'sinful.'" If he investigates these matters further and has some intelligence, he will go on: "if by 'wrong' and 'sinful' you mean that the practice of birth control will lead to unhappiness for me or to unhappiness for the human race as a whole then all the evidence on the subject shows that you are completely mistaken. If you mean that there is a God who has forbidden birth control then what you say is false since there is no God. Or if there is one and he is kind, it seems incredible that he would wish to add to the unhappiness of any human life."

My remarks must not be misconstrued to amount to the immoderate claim that the rejection of non-naturalism or this together with the rejection of religious belief are *enough* to bring about a rejection of the morality of sin and self-denial. To suppose this would be tantamount to committing the same sort of error of which I

20. *Foundations of Ethics,* pp. 29-30.

accused the Joadians in the last section. A person who rejects non-naturalism and theology does not thereby get rid of deep-seated fears and guilt feelings. The latter may make him look for another justification of the ascetic morality which is very much in harmony with his fears. Or they may drive him into the arms of another equally irrational morality.

Maybe nothing can ever remove his fears. But unless he first rejects God in all his forms, whether in the form of Jehovah or in the form of "laws which are independent of my likings and dislikings" (Paton) or in the form of the non-natural quality called "good," he will not even begin to try.

Bibliography

Acton, H. W. B. "Moral Subjectivism," *Analysis*, October 1948.
Ayer, A. J. *Language, Truth and Logic* 2nd ed.; London: Victor Gollancz, 1946.
——. "On the Analysis of Moral Judgments," *Horizon*, September 1949.
Baier, K. "Decisions and Descriptions," *Mind*, 1951.
Baier, K. and Toulmin, S. E. "On Describing," *Mind*, 1952.
Barnes, W. F. H. "Ethics Without Propositions," *Aristotelian Society*, Suppl. Vol. XXII (1948).
Black, Max. *Language and Philosophy*. Ithaca: Cornell University Press, 1949.
Blanshard, Brand. "Personal Ethics," in *Preface to Philosophy*, ed. William P. Tolley. New York: Macmillan Co., 1946.
——. "The New Subjectivism in Ethics," *Philosophy and Phenomenological Research*, 1949.
Brandt, Richard. "The Emotive Theory of Ethics," *The Philosophical Review*, 1950.
——. "The Status of Empirical Assertion Theories in Ethics," *Mind*, 1952.
Broad, C. D. *Five Types of Ethical Theory*. London: Kegan Paul, 1930.
——. "Certain Features of Moore's Ethical Doctrines," in *The Philosophy of G. E. Moore*, ed. Paul Schilpp. Evanston and Chicago: Northwestern University, 1942.
Carritt, E. F. *Ethical and Political Thinking*. London: Oxford University Press, 1947.
Cavell, S. and Sesonske, A. "Moral Theory, Ethical Judgments and Empiricism," *Mind*, 1952.
Dewey, John. "Some Questions About Value," in *Value: A Cooperative Study*, ed. Lepley. New York: Columbia University Press, 1949.
Duncan-Jones, A. "Deadlock in Ethics," *Aristotelian Society*, Suppl. Vol. XXVI (1952).
——. "Assertions and Commands," *Proceedings of the Aristotelian Society*, N.S., LII (1951/52).

Duncker, K. "Ethical Relativity," *Mind*, 1939.

Ewing, A. C. *The Definition of Good*. New York: Macmillan Co., 1947.

——. "Moral Subjectivism—A Reply to Professor Acton," *Analysis*, December 1948.

Falk, W. D. "Goading and Guiding," *Mind*, 1953.

Feigl, Herbert. "De Principiis Non Disputandum . . . ?," in *Philosophical Analysis*, ed. Max Black. Ithaca: Cornell University Press, 1950.

Findlay, J. N. "Morality by Convention," *Mind*, 1944.

——. "The Justification of Attitudes," *ibid.*, 1954.

Frankel, Charles. Review of *Essays in Political Theory*, ed. Konvitz and Murphy, *The Journal of Philosophy*, 1950.

Frankena, W. K. "The Naturalistic Fallacy," *Mind*, 1939.

Gilman, E. "The Distinctive Purpose of Moral Judgments," *Mind*, 1952.

Haas, W. "Value-Judgments," *Mind*, 1953.

Hall, E. W. *What is Value?* New York: Humanities Press, 1952.

Hampshire, Stuart. "The Fallacies of Moral Philosophy," *Mind*, 1949.

——. "The Fallacies in Moral Philosophy—A Reply to Mr. Baier," *Mind*, 1950.

Hare, R. M. *The Language of Morals*. Oxford: The Clarendon Press, 1952.

Hill, T. E. *Contemporary Ethical Theories*. New York: Macmillan Co., 1952.

Hofstadter, A. and McKinsey, J. "On the Logic of Imperatives," *Philosophy of Science*, 1939.

Hook, Sidney. "The Desirable and Emotive in Dewey's Ethics," in *John Dewey: Philosopher of Science and Freedom*, ed. Sidney Hook. New York: Dial Press, 1950.

——. *Education for Modern Man*. New York: The Dial Press, 1946.

Hume, David. *An Enquiry Concerning the Principles of Morals*, ed. Selby-Bigge. Oxford: The Clarendon Press, 1894.

Joad, C. E. M. *A Critique of Logical Positivism*. Chicago: University of Chicago Press, 1950.

Kaplan, A. "Are Moral Judgments Assertions?," *The Philosophical Review*, 1942.

Laird, John. *The Idea of Value*. Cambridge: Cambridge University Press, 1929.

——. *A Study in Realism*. Cambridge: Cambridge University Press, 1920.

Ledden, J. E. "On the Logical Status of Value," *The Philosophical Review*, 1950.

Mabbott, J. B. "True and False in Morals," *Proceedings of the Aristotelian Society*, XLIX (1948/49).

Macdonald, Margaret. "Ethics and the Ceremonial Use of Language," in *Philosophic Analysis*, ed. Max Black. Ithaca: Cornell University Press, 1950.

Mackie, John. "The Refutation of Morals," *Australasian Journal of Psychology and Philosophy*, 1946.

Moore, A. "The Emotive Theory and Rational Methods in Moral Controversy," *Mind*, 1951.

Moore, G. E. *Principia Ethica*. Cambridge: Cambridge University Press, 1903.

———. *Ethics*. ("The Home University Library.") New York: Oxford University Press, 1912.

———. "The Conception of Intrinsic Value," in his *Philosophical Studies*. London: Kegan Paul, 1922.

———. "The Nature of Moral Philosophy," *ibid*.

———. "A Reply to My Critics," in *The Philosophy of G. E. Moore*, ed. Paul Schilpp. Evanston and Chicago: Northwestern University, 1942.

Paton, H. J. "The Emotive Theory of Ethics," *Aristotelian Society*, Suppl. Vol. XXII (1948).

Perry, Ralph Barton. *General Theory of Value*. New York: Longmans, Green and Co., 1926.

Prior, A. N. *Logic and the Basis of Ethics*. Oxford: The Clarendon Press, 1948.

Raphael, D. *The Moral Sense*. London: Oxford University Press, 1947.

Reid, Thomas. *Essays on the Active Power of the Human Mind*, ed. G. N. Wright. London, 1813.

Robinson, Richard. "The Emotive Theory of Ethics," *Aristotelian Society*, Suppl. Vol. XXII (1948).

Ross, David. *The Right and the Good*. London: Oxford University Press, 1931.

———. *The Foundations of Ethics*. Oxford: The Clarendon Press, 1939.

Russell, Bertrand. *Religion and Science*. ("The Home University Library.") London: Butterworth, 1935.

———. *What I Believe*. London: Kegan Paul, 1925.

———. *An Outline of Philosophy*. London: Allen and Unwin, 1927.

———. *A History of Western Philosophy*. London: Allen and Unwin, 1946.

———. "A Reply to My Critics," in *The Philosophy of Bertrand Russell*, ed. Paul Schilpp. Evanston and Chicago: Northwestern University, 1944.

———. "Good and Bad," *Polemic*, November 1946.

Schlick, Moritz. *Problems of Ethics*. New York: Prentice Hall, 1939.

Sidgwick, H. *The Methods of Ethics*. 7th ed.; London: Macmillan Co., 1907.

Smith, James Ward. "Senses of Subjectivism in Value Theory," *The Journal of Philosophy*, 1948.

Stevenson, C. L. *Ethics and Language*. New Haven: Yale University Press, 1943.

——. "The Nature of Ethical Disagreement," in *Readings in Philosophical Analysis*, ed. Feigl and Sellars. New York: Appleton-Century-Crofts, 1948.

——. "The Emotive Meaning of Ethical Terms," *Mind*, 1937.

Strawson, P.F. "Ethical Intuitionism," *Philosophy*, 1949.

——. Review of Ewing's *The Definition of Good*, *Mind*, 1949.

Thomas, V. "Ethical Disagreements and the Emotive Theory of Values," *Mind*, 1951.

Toulmin, S. E. *The Place of Reason in Ethics*. Cambridge: Cambridge University Press, 1950.

Urban, W. M. "Axiology," in *Twentieth Century Philosophy*, ed. D. Runes. New York: Philosophical Library, 1943.

——. "Value Propositions and Verifiability," *The Journal of Philosophy*, 1937.

Westermarck, Edward. *The Origin and Development of Moral Ideas*. 2nd ed.; London: Macmillan Co., 1912-17.

——. *Ethical Relativity*. New York: Harcourt, Brace and Co., 1932.

Index of Names